WITHDRAWN
UTSA LIBRARIES

CRYPTS OF POWER

By the same author:

Lowland Indians of Amazonia
Amazon and Andes
West Coast Republic of South America
Northern Republics of South America
Parables from South America
The Republic of Brazil
Religion in the Republic of Spain
From Pacific to Atlantic
Religion in the Republic of Mexico
Religion in South America
Christian Handbook of South Africa
World Christian Handbooks 1949, 1952, 1957, 1962
Co-existence and the Conditions of Peace
A Layman Looks at the Church

CRYPTS OF POWER

An Autobiography

by

Sir KENNETH GRUBB, K.C.M.G.

HODDER AND STOUGHTON
LONDON SYDNEY AUCKLAND TORONTO

Copyright © 1971 by Sir Kenneth Grubb. First printed 1971. ISBN 0 340 14963 9. All rights reserved. No part of this publication may be reproduced or transmitted in any form or by any means, electronic or mechanical, including photocopy, recording, or any information storage and retrieval system, without permission in writing from the publisher. Printed in Great Britain for Hodder and Stoughton Limited, St. Paul's House, Warwick Lane, London, E.C.4, by Ebenezer Baylis and Son Limited, The Trinity Press, Worcester, and London

TO MY WIFE NANCY

FOREWORD

Many have helped by reading and criticising parts of this book. They include Mr. David Bastin, the Rev. Alan Booth, the Hon. Alastair Buchan, Dr. Richard Fagley, the Rev. A. v.d. Heuvel, Dr. Michael Hooker, Sir John Lawrence, Sir Robert Marett, Mr. Bernard Nicholls, Dr. O. Frederick Nolde, the Rev. Canon David Paton, the Rev. Bruce Reed, Sir John Guillum Scott, the Rev. Canon J. V. Taylor, Mr. J. S. Tetley, the Rev. Canon M. A. C. Warren, the Archbishop of York (Dr. Donald Coggan), and the Church Commissioners. I thank them all, and not least Miss Muriel Fuller, my private secretary for many years.

I have not given references to many quotations because every schoolboy knows them.

I have been disgracefully inconsistent in the delicate matter of the proper use and citation of English titles and orders.

K.G.G.

DR. SAMUEL JOHNSON ON MEMOIRS

He [Johnson] observed, 'A man cannot with propriety speak of himself, except he relates simple facts; as, "I was at Richmond" or what depends on mensuration; as, "I am six feet high." He is sure he has been at Richmond; he is sure he is six feet high: but he cannot be sure he is wise, or that he has any other excellence. Then, all censure of a man's self is oblique praise. It is in order to shew how much he can spare. It has all the invidiousness of self-praise, and all the reproach of falsehood.'
BOSWELL. 'Sometimes it may proceed from a man's strong consciousness of his faults being observed. He knows that others would throw him down, and therefore he had better lie down softly of his own accord.'
The Life of Samuel Johnson LL.D., James Boswell. 25 April, 1778.

I regret that in spite of modest efforts here and there, I have not found it feasible to adhere to this stern but excellent advice.

K.G.G.

CONTENTS

Chapter		Page
1	'The Child is Father of the Man'	15
2	Amazon Years	26
3	A Tramp on Walkabout	52
4	A Continent on the Move	77
5	A Pause for Reflection	91
6	The Ministry of Information	103
7	The Church Missionary Society	136
8	Ecumania	163
9	A Man in Church	201
10	So What?	229
	Index	239

ILLUSTRATIONS

Frontispiece[1]
The author's parents   *Facing page* 24
The Rev. H. P. Grubb, 1877   24
The author aged seventeen   24
Three brothers   24
Jungle path   25
In Peru, 1928   80
The author with his sons   80
The author's family   80
With Sir Henry and Lady Holland[2]   81
An Anglo–Argentine Society Embassy reception   81
Investiture as Knight Bachelor, 1953[2]   96
C.M.S. reception   96
Civic reception in Sydney[3]   97
Luncheon in honour of the President of Peru[4]   97
The C.C.I.A. in Geneva   128
With Dr. O. F. Nolde   128
At a clinic in Malaya, 1955   129
In Athens, 1955   129
With H.M. the Queen Mother in Cheltenham   144
Laying the C.M.S. headquarters' foundation stone   144

Cardinal Archbishop of Bogotá, 1963	145
Party in honour of the Brazilian Ambassador	145
Lord Fisher unveiling a portrait[5]	192
With Billy Graham and Sir Cyril Black[6]	192
H.M. the Queen opening the C.M.S. headquarters	193
The Board of Hooker, Craigmyle Ltd.[7]	193
Presiding in the House of Laity	208
With Sir Kingsley Tubbs and the Archbishop of Canterbury	208
With Lady Grubb[7]	209
Outside the author's home[8]	209
After receiving the K.C.M.G.[9]	209

[1] Baron Studios.
[2] Universal Pictorial Press.
[3] Sydney Morning Herald.
[4] Crown Copyright.
[5] London Press Photos.
[6] Grosvenor House Photographic Service.
[7] Desmond O'Neill.
[8] Antony Miles Ltd.
[9] Monitor Press Features Ltd.

CHAPTER I

'The Child is Father to the Man'

I WAS a solitary even when young. A man must have some capacity for relationships if he is to build a career, but he need not have many friends; acquaintances, yes, but not friends. For this reason the writing of my memoirs is a dubious enterprise, because life and work with other people, the warmth of affection, the bitterness of parting and the joy of meeting, make such material live. It has always been my main defect that with a few exceptions, I have never wished to make or keep friends and have not succeeded in doing so.

I was once talking with Lord ('Clem') Attlee, and earlier that day I had received a letter from a publisher asking for my memoirs. I showed it to Attlee. He looked at it carefully and said, 'Grubb, don't do it. More quarrels have been caused in my Party because of what some of us leaders have written than the disputes over C.N.D. and Clause Four added together. Wait till your doctor says you have six months to live, and write and die!' Sound advice! But a reluctance to follow sound advice has always been one of my few strong points.

I was born on 9 September, 1900, in Queen Victoria's reign, in the tiny village of Oxton, in Nottinghamshire. My father, who had previously been an Assistant Secretary of the Church Missionary Society, was rector, and I was the youngest child, having two brothers and one sister. My brother, Norman, has written his own account[1] of our childhood days, and since he is five years my senior, his story is sure to be more accurate. My own recollections differ somewhat from his, although we went to the same preparatory and public schools. Five years' difference of age is not much in later life, but when one is ten, it is half a life-time, and when one is fifteen, it is a third.

Norman has described the origins of our family which appears to have derived from northern Europe. At the 1968 Assembly of the World Council of Churches in the historic University of Uppsala, Sweden, I

[1] Norman P. Grubb, *Once Caught, No Escape*, Lutterworth Press, 1969.

was in a committee and on the wall opposite was a stern portrait of one Grubbe. He was an academic potentate about 150 years ago and the Archbishop of Uppsala told me the name had been common in Scandinavia and Denmark.

Our ancestor fought in Cromwell's army, and moved from England (Northamptonshire) to Ireland in 1656 and settled in the south, taking up a grant of land. He became a Quaker and his descendants followed him, but in the mid-nineteenth century the 'Religious Society' of Clonmel expelled our grandfather and his wife for having music and dancing in their home. Some Grubbs were very proper Quakers and well known in the 'Society'. I have the second edition, of 1794, of a work entitled *Some Account of the Life and Religious Labours of Sarah Grubb*. Born a Tuke, she married a Robert Grubb of Clonmel. She travelled widely and indefatigably, not only in Britain but also on the Continent, being a vigorous evangelist and an early promoter of Christian education for girls. Our ancestors moved to Cahir, Co. Tipperary, where they lived at Cahir Abbey and built up a flourishing corn business.

My sister, Dr. Violet Grubb, has suggested that the mild anticlericalism which I cannot rid myself of is really a Quaker trait and this may well be so. It is equally possible that the same background has had something to do with my early liking for silence and solitariness when I was living in South America.

Shortly after the end of World War I, my cousin Henry and I visited some relations in Ulster. One 'First Day' (Sunday), after the morning meeting at least twenty of us, nearly all related or connected, forgathered for lunch in the house of the patriarch of that branch of the family, near Portadown. The lunch was entirely silent. Unfortunately I raised my eyes and caught Henry's answering twinkle as he was nearly opposite me. He burst out into a loud and unseemly guffaw. There was a moment of dreadful tenseness when our host looked like a late arrival on the Last Day and the butler froze in his livery. However, nothing was said and we resumed silence for the rest of the meal.

The forbears of Richard Nixon, President of the United States, came from Oxton. Robert Scothorn, aged twenty-five, emigrated to Pennsylvania in 1684 to join William Penn. Several others from Oxton followed. The Scothorn family descendants include Richard Nixon.[2]

[2] The connection is well-documented. I am indebted to the Rev. W. T. T. Wheeler of Peterborough, formerly Vicar of Oxton, and (on his introduction) to Mr. William H. Lane of Washington for details. Mr. Lane, like Mr. Nixon, is a direct descendant of one of Robert Scothorn's sons.

I recall the village, but imprecisely, 'as in a glass darkly', and have revisited it. The little church was charming even to a child. Our Rectory stood back from the road and there was a drive with a grassy bank which led up to it. For long I thought this was the bank where my parents kept their money. There were lovely fields behind the Rectory and we children rejoiced in the hay-making season and tumbled in the sweet mow. There were woods and banks where snowdrops, cowslips, oxlips, bluebells and anemones were a dream. We had a beloved pony, Tommy; what greater pleasure could there be than feeding it lumps of sugar? To get anywhere we took Tommy five miles to Lowdham where the railway drove, relentless, straight and steely, across the countryside.

By far the most vivid event of those years was when the hunt killed in our kitchen-garden. My sister, Violet, got the brush and we boys received pads.

We moved to Hurdsfield, on the outskirts of Macclesfield, in 1905. It, too, was a rural vicarage and beyond our low wall stretched fields and woods. There were lovely walks over the great hills of the Peak district and away up to the Cat and Fiddle Inn on the Buxton Road.

Nothing clouded my early years. It was a simple parson's household, and it was home. I have always been thankful for the life and memory of my parents. My father was not supposed to be a profound scholar, but he had gained the highest Hebrew distinction at Trinity College, Dublin, two years before the due time; he was a strong evangelical of Low-Church views and he knew his Bible well. At Cahir where he was born, he was said to have been the best horseman in the South of Ireland. He moved to England soon after completing his education. He was not an easy man with children, although he used to take me out for long walks alone. We would say in these days that he found it difficult to get on the wavelength of a child. He was a truly good man, gentle and tolerant, high-minded and devout. He was already fifty-one when I was born.

He married at the age of forty-three Margaret Adelaide Crichton-Stuart. Her mother who had married into the Crichton-Stuart family was a Labouchere, and a niece of the celebrated Henry Labouchere, the 'radical' politician of the last part of the nineteenth century, a sworn foe of Gladstone and a defender of 'free-thought' and Charles Bradlaugh. But mother, in her own right if the phrase can be so used, was a lady of convinced Victorian and also very practical Christian piety.

Various uncles and aunts loomed into sight over the horizon and then disappeared. The occasion was usually a family event such as a wedding, or perhaps one or another lived close to us. Father was one of eleven brothers and sisters. There had been a fat family fortune, but it was dissipated by an uncle who forged a cheque of his father's to meet his bets. Grandfather regarded this as a debt of honour and paid up £25,000 or (according to some) £50,000 on condition that he left the country and never returned. Thus Uncle Fred ruined the family but made good his exit to California.

We lived simply. There were a governess, two maids, a gardener and a boy to clean the boots. This was a very modest establishment before World War I. At Oxton we had oil lamps and candles at bed-time, but at Hurdsfield, then the centre of the silk mills, we sniffed gas and burned it. Even there, on the edge of Macclesfield, we relied upon pumped water. It took 170 strokes of the pump every morning to fill the cistern. I took my share and a wooden box was provided for me to stand on. In the evenings we played parlour games, read, arranged entertainments, or made scrap books. There was no radio; that came at the end of World War I when we acquired a crystal set and listened to 2LO. We had a 'phonograph' but not, as I once saw it spelt, a pornograph.

Hurdsfield is vivid in my memory. One of the delights was the penny readings in our church school: you paid a penny entrance and someone read famous passages of literature. There was local talent and some of the Dickens readings have remained with me to this day. There was Wakes Week, and there were organised rambles on Saturdays. If sufficient young people could get the whole Saturday off, we made the road to Buxton and back, around trip of twenty-four miles.

I was devoted to my mother. As the youngest I instinctively wanted her protection. To me she was a tender and infinitely loving being. On her lap I felt insulated from the world, and she was so cosy and inviting. When she drew our curtains in the morning she seemed so fresh and bright. Above all, I loved to hear her sing. Both at Oxton and Hurdsfield I would lie awake in bed of an evening and listen to her singing at the piano in the drawing-room. She sang the old songs and familiar hymns, some of which are still an abiding part of my heritage.

On Sunday, mother would read to us from a red-covered book. This contained a connected story about a virtuous boy and each week's ration was based upon the Collect for the day which we learned; it was a modernised *Eric, or Little by Little*. It was quite interesting and never impressed me as boring, but anything which mother read seemed at that time to be uttered in the tones of an angel.

I later learned and could readily perceive that mother was a very remarkable woman. Had she lived in the days of women's higher education, she could easily have gone to the top. Slight in stature and figure with well-defined chin and keen Crichton-Stuart features, she was full of energy without being in the least managing or domineering. She was a very true and loving wife to her husband and an admirable complement to his quieter and more reflective nature. In some of these traits she took after her own mother, and she shared something of her determination and purposefulness in whatever she undertook. In her later years she lived with us in our Highgate home and until she was ninety-four, went (latterly by air) every year to her favourite resorts in Switzerland, often with my wife. She died in 1958, at nearly ninety-seven years of age.

The second book of Homer's *Iliad* contains the delightful story of the dream which Zeus sent to King Agamemnon. It set forth on its errand and found the King asleep in his hut on the windy plains of Troy. It bade him plunge into the final struggle for Priam's famed citadel, and then, when it had done its work, it returned to high Olympus to present a report.

My dream first came to me at Hurdsfield and it has returned at intervals ever since, the last time being in 1968. I kept it a close secret. It is a dream of great waters, a dream of mighty falls, twice as high as Niagara, in the heart of an untrodden virgin forest. The scene is always the same, but I have never found the falls and never shall. I have seen many and wonderful waterfalls, such as Iguazú and Paulo Afonso, but none answers to the picture of my dream. So we are always pilgrims, always travellers, and, if we will, always worshippers.

My parents were generous to the point of self-sacrifice. For at least a decade they brought up two other children along with the rest of us, Cecil and Gladys (Joan) Lillingston Price. Their parents were C.M.S. missionaries in central India, and they had to leave their children at home for seven years at a stretch. Cecil and I were good friends.

Since my parents were so closely connected with missions, we had frequent visitors from overseas in our home, that is, frequent by the standards of those times. It can be fairly claimed that it was through the mission channel that at least a modest selection of families in England became first acquainted with men and women of another colour and race. This was a novelty then; it seems a commonplace even to mention it now. The visitor I best remember was Bishop James Johnson, a Nigerian who, at the time (1908) was assistant bishop in West Africa. Some fifty years later I came across his grave, still lovingly tended, near the cathedral at Bonny, once a focus of the slave-trade, now a transport centre for the oil of Port Harcourt. The cemetery is pathetic enough, for the old graves, dating from the early nineteenth century, are a vivid record of the brief lives of expatriates who came there as traders or missionaries, survived the fevers for two or three years with luck and succumbed to some dread infection, which today, if it ever took hold, would probably soon yield to a week in hospital and penicillin.

I was sent in 1909 to South Lodge, a preparatory school in Lowestoft. I took a train to Manchester and changed, crossing the city in a cab, with trunk and playbox, and then a train to Norwich and changed, and so to Lowestoft. The journey took all day, and the train went through a very long tunnel in the Pennines, the old Woodhead Tunnel, now closed. I used to celebrate the passage through this by singing to myself in the corridor 'Thy Kingdom come, O God, Thy rule, O Christ begin.' I do not know why.

South Lodge was run by the Rev. W. R. ('Dick') Phillips, a very virtuous clergyman. His wife had a red nose. I enjoyed myself in the five years I was there, although the homesickness on leaving home which seemed so far away was terrible. Mother wrote to me twice a week without fail and every Sunday and Thursday I eagerly awaited her letter. To receive *two* letters a week put me 'one up', literally, over other boys.

I already knew quite a bit of Latin, and a little Greek. There was another boy with whom I was friendly, George de Horne Vaizey. We were twins to the day, and are still in regular touch. We were both perfervid admirers of Bombardier Wells, the notable boxer of those years who met his Waterloo in his disastrous fight with Georges Carpentier.

At South Lodge I first caught something of the eternal warfare and wandering of the sea. The main school house was right on the sea-front, and the winter North Sea gales whined and howled around the building and rattled all the dormitory windows. The first night of term was made restless with the beating of the waves against the dunes and on the shore. There were rewards. The beaches were a treasure-store. When the herring fleets came home, and there were many smacks in service then, it was a glorious sight to touch even the heart of a Philistine schoolboy to watch the boats with their great tanned sails, catching the evening sun and beating up to and through the narrow entrance of the harbour in a long succession. It was a vision which has never left me. These were still the days of danger on the waters, and I used to hum quietly to myself the old song or dirge 'men must work and women must weep'.

I sailed through prep school without misgivings. The life was tough: we often broke the ice in the ewers in our dormitories. The teaching was good by the standards of those days: there was a young master, Sewell, who afterwards took over the school, who much impressed me. Scripture was taught every day, and we learned a chapter of the Bible, one verse per diem, recapping the lot at the end of term in a sort of all-school competition. I played soccer, hockey and cricket but did not shine.

One dramatic and tragic holiday incident has remained with me. I was at home when the great and famous liner *Titanic* sailed on her maiden and only voyage. We went off in a Bournemouth paddle-steamer and anchored in Southampton Water in line with scores of craft, to cheer her on her majestic course, slowly moving down the Water with the stately grandeur of a historic queen. There must be few alive who ever saw her at all.

In 1914 I mopped up the top Foundation Scholarship at Marlborough and was duly despatched to that academy in the autumn term. By then the family had moved to Poole, and later we settled in Parkstone. War had broken out and my two elder brothers disappeared into the Army soon afterwards and into different regiments. They both did very well and both received awards for bravery and all-round merit. My eldest brother, Harold, never really recovered from shock and gassing. He had a small pension and took light employment, but he never developed his full powers. He lived on till 1954, largely abroad, staying with my wife and myself in our London home when he was not on the Continent or in South Africa. I liked him because he was not conspicuously religious, and he had an endearing personality and a quaint and quiet sense of humour which was very refreshing. My next brother, Norman, became a missionary, and later Chief Secretary of the Worldwide Evangelisation Crusade, founded by his father-in-law, C. T. Studd. He settled in the U.S.A. and he has written his own story and written it excellently.[3]

Wynne Wilson, afterwards Bishop of Bath and Wells, was then Master of Marlborough. He was followed by a distinguished educationist, Sir Cyril Norwood who later went to Harrow. My housemaster was C. B. Canning who judiciously married one of Norwood's daughters and later became Headmaster of Canford; patronage is useful even in the highest-minded professions. We called him 'Foxy Ferdie'[4] because he went round

---
[3] See footnote, p. 15.
[4] Ferdinand, King of Bulgaria, was commonly regarded as excessively cunning. In October 1915 he entered the war on the side of the Central Powers.

the dormitories in carpet-slippers. All held that no master who professed to be an Englishman and a gentleman should so demean himself.

Marlborough was a hard school, but I did not notice this much. Others have written of it very critically. John Betjeman[5] in his *Summoned by Bells*[6] gives a lively but acutely unhappy picture of Marlborough; he was there shortly after I left. In my time I was one of those wicked Captains of Upper School whom he pillories. He says that these overlords could beat six strokes as a maximum; I do not recall that particular limitation. I do remember that a captain could draw two canes a term from Pantry (of all places!) and beer *ad lib*, although beating came naturally to me and did not require any alcoholic stimulus.

I had no great ambitions, was no dab hand at games and disliked heartiness. I was a good shot and this has proved very useful in later life. It was at Marlborough that I was first called 'the self-contained Flat' because I eschewed friendships and preferred my own company. There was an Astronomical Society but no one used the big telescope on a high flat roof, so I joined the Society, obtained the key to the skylight, and used it. Thus I had an excuse to get away on my own and I could lock the door in my rear. It was cold at night in the winter. When I became a prefect I was offered a small study to myself or a large one to share with another boy. But I rigged some ingenious and unchallengeable lies and secured the large study alone.

In my spare time, I learned the whole of Tennyson's *In Memoriam* by heart. Canning heard of this, did not believe it, and invited me to his room, where he picked different cantos at random, gave me the first line and asked me to carry on. He did not catch me out once, and I could not understand why he was such a fool. On another occasion, he heard that I had learned all *Hamlet* (which we were acting at the end of term) and he challenged me to repeat lines which were not mine on the stage, but I won. It has never done me any good! I founded the Shakespearian Society of those days.

Our parents instilled in all of us the love of good reading. At an early age, I had read most of Dickens, Scott, Thackeray, the eighteenth-century essayists, a deal of Shakespeare, and other classics such as *Pilgrim's Progress*. Before I left Marlborough, I had read Gibbon and large parts of Burke. But Wordsworth's longer poems to which father was devoted, got me well bogged down. These habits, early inculcated, have lasted a life-

[5] Now Sir John Betjeman.
[6] John Murray, 1960.

time, and the more buoyant pleasures of T.V. and radio have supplemented rather than supplanted them.

Father had a cultivated and disciplined literary taste, but his own library was in the main theological. Theology lacked appeal for boys, as no doubt it still does. His ideas of what might interest a lad of fifteen were, at times, mildly off-centre, for I remember him taking a volume off his shelves and recommending it to me. It bore the grave, even solemn, title of *Bates on Death*. Father's mind had a marked cast of melancholy. There is a story current in our family that shortly after he was engaged, he observed to his fiancée, 'My dearest, now we must decide where we shall be buried.' *Se non é vero, é ben trovato*.

Our home life at Poole, my father's last living, and Parkstone, where he retired, was punctuated by the excitements of war, with two brothers at the front. Cecil Price and I ranged far and wide on our bikes over the Dorset countryside. My father had several fishermen in his Poole church. They used to take me out and I sometimes got leave to go at night. Only the fishing-boats could go outside the Harbour during the war. It was a memorable experience to pass a calm night in Poole Bay, with the white cliffs of Old Harry faintly lit by the moonlight, and the surface of the Channel slowly heaving, as the ebb poured down against a westerly breeze.

In Parkstone we had a remarkable next-door neighbour, a patriarchal character. He was Captain Robinson, and had been the senior captain of the Union Castle fleet. He was spare, tall and dignified, courteous and restrained in manner, with a commanding presence, and, in his retirement, all the authority of white hair and old age. He was a man of simple piety and, as a widower, had settled with his two daughters near my parents, so that he could help them in good works. I stood in awe of him, but if he could be got to talk, which was like getting blood out of a stone, he was fascinating. He had known the days of sail; he could remember running north from the Cape in a strong following wind, and overtaking three steamships in succession.

During these years I respected the faith of my fathers but had no real grasp of it. There was a religious atmosphere in our home, but it was not oppressive. Our family was connected with the evangelical cause, and one of my uncles, George Grubb, was once a celebrated teacher of 'Scriptural Holiness' at the Keswick Convention. He was the first to travel abroad on behalf of 'Keswick', mainly in India and Ceylon, Australia, New Zealand, South Africa and Canada. Ultimately he was excluded from the Keswick platform for heresy; apparently he declined to believe in the eternal and conscious torment of the 'lost'. My mother, a woman who kept almost to the end her conspicuous natural ability and unmistakable vivacity, was an early pioneer with the Y.W.C.A. and other such movements.

At Marlborough several religions were in vogue in those war years. There was Christianity centred on chapel; there was the Public School Code; there was loyalty to King and Country; there was the Hang-the-Kaiser Cult. I regarded all with a certain detachment, secretly content with my dream and constantly pondering on its meaning.

Father was a good and faithful clergyman, but church had little influence on me. There was too much of it, although not oppressively too much. We children were so used to the Prayer Book services that, even if we were almost asleep we could note the slightest deviation. I have since found this habit useful. When I am almost asleep in the chair at an afternoon session of some assembly, I wake up by instinct if a speaker spouts manifest nonsense. In his latter years father sometimes stumbled over his words and on one occasion he mingled the sentences from two well-known prayers, and emitted the following formidable petition: 'Receive these our prayers which we offer unto Thy Divine Majesty, most justly provoking Thy wrath and indignation against us.'

No one else noticed so slight an aberration from the Prayer Book order, not to mention Christian charity, so all was well. From an early age I have been plagued by an eye for the ludicrous. Decades later it fell to me to unveil a brass plate on the main deck of a ship which had been given by a wealthy donor for mission work in the South Seas. When I pulled aside the little curtain, I read these words: 'This ship was presented for the work of God by Tom B. Smith' (the name is fictitious). And immediately underneath, 'The sea is his, and he made it.' This was just a shade presumptuous and lacked warrant in Holy Writ, but no one raised an eyebrow or batted an eyelid.

I was confirmed in Marlborough College chapel on 12 March, 1915. There was a phenomenal gale over the Wiltshire Downs the next day. For some time afterwards I did feel religious, presumably as a result of the Confirmation rather than the gale, but it wore off.

I slid into the end of World War I by getting away from Marlborough early, and I was sent to Keyham to train for the sea. After the war there was no future in this, so I left, and spent a year or two at home, with no inclination to go to a university (which I now much regret) but teaching in a prep school. About this time I began to experience severe nervous upsets and fits of depression. This subsequently led to a serious situation.

The author's parents, the Rev. and Mrs. H. P. Grubb

His father in 1877

Three brothers, (*left to right*) Kenneth, Harold, Norman, in 1915

The author aged seventeen

Jungle path cut and photographed by the author

Some little time after the end of the war I was converted. I cannot recall the exact circumstances, and must rely on the account of my elder brother, Norman. He had been praying for me, and one day, for no apparent reason, I suddenly announced that I would go to a church prayer-meeting at St. Luke's, Parkstone. This alarmed him, because it was a huddle of godly matrons, of slight interest to me. However, the next day I informed father that I had accepted Christ as my Saviour. I fully realise that today no one understands either such language or the experience which it imperfectly seeks to portray. Be this as it may, this was the beginning of a long, if modest, career in Christian and public service, to last some fifty years. I have modified my early views, but, as the years have slipped by, I have strengthened my early allegiance. To this day, I find it hard to enthuse over theological niceties, although such debate keeps clergymen from mischief, and is, therefore, not to be discouraged.

I might have got converted earlier had it not been for one of those silly trivialities which upset both older and younger people, especially if they are going through a restless and anxious time. Early in the yachting season of 1919, I was cruising single-handed in a borrowed half-decker and tacking about between Old Harry and Ballard Point. Suddenly I heard shouts and I saw a couple cut off by the tide on a tiny shingle beach at the foot of the beetling chalk cliff. There was a bit of an onshore breeze and a popple on the sea. However, I managed to bring them on board at a certain risk, and we put on some canvas and were soon home.

The man's name was Spencer Johnson. He was an evangelist in Bournemouth, of pale countenance, neat black beard and very dark eyes. Some weeks later he sent me a pamphlet describing his adventure, attributing his escape to the Lord, and merely mentioning that the latter had sent a young fellow (unnamed) to rescue him and his wife. This irritated me because the Lord had had nothing to do with it. I had managed the whole affair unaided.

CHAPTER II

Amazon Years

CONVERSION makes a great difference to outlook. I became a fervent student of the Bible, an affection which has remained across all the years. I already knew it pretty well, because we had been brought up that way. I set myself to try and win others to personal commitment to Jesus Christ. Never having been very intellectual, it just did not happen that I worried over the veracity of the scriptural record, or over science and the Bible and such questions, the tremendous significance of which did not then disturb me much.

Nor did I worry about the Church. The Church of England seemed a good holding-ground for a chap's anchor, but services in the Free Churches and in mission halls were just as good. To this day, although decent order and dignity of worship are impressive, I do not find elaborate architecture and decoration an assistance, or great plainness a deterrent, to spiritual worship.

I formed a new set of friends and acquaintances, and at an early stage I decided that God had called me to go overseas as a missionary or, to use the accepted phraseology, 'I felt called to go.' It did not seem presumptuous to take this line: such is the glittering and scornful pride of youth.

For many years I had been interested in South America. This interest was first aroused by a visit of W. Barbrooke Grubb, a namesake and no relation, to my prep school. He was a layman and had worked for many years as an Anglican missionary among the Indians of the Paraguayan Chaco. His life had been one of incredible hardship, danger and adventure, but he spoke that night in Lowestoft so quietly and unassumingly that you might have thought he was describing a holiday at Margate.

Shortly afterwards I secured and read his remarkable work *An Unknown People in an Unknown Land*.[1] This impressive book is much more than a story of missionary pioneering amidst astonishing risks, it is also a pioneer

[1] Seeley and Co., 1911.

anthropological and social study of a people, and was widely praised as such by many who had no interest in missionary endeavour.

Soon the interior of South America became in my mind the stage where my dream which constantly recurred to me, would find fulfilment. But I kept my hands close to my chest and said nothing about all that.

Then a difficulty arose. I was widely regarded, and not without justification, as a highly strung and unreliable person, and no mission would contemplate accepting me into their ranks. Moreover, my very first application to a mission came to grief for two reasons. First I would not consider getting ordained to the sacred ministry, since I did not have any call to do so. Barbrooke Grubb, one of my heroes, was a layman; and I knew that my cousin Henry Grubb was going to work among the Indians, today called Amerindians, as a layman, which he did for thirty-six years. My sister, Dr. Violet Grubb, later for two decades Headmistress of Westonbirt, worked similarly some years in the interior of China. Second, I would not affirm my unreserved belief in the various points of Christian doctrine which that mission required me to accept. I was, in fact, a damnable heretic.

Eventually a compromise was reached with another mission, the Worldwide Evangelisation Crusade. This curious and interesting body was founded by C. T. Studd, a celebrated cricketer of the last century, and his wife. At the time, he was in Central Africa where he died in 1930, and she was looking after things at home. My brother Norman P. Grubb had married one of the Studd's four beautiful daughters. He has given a lifetime of devoted service to the mission, spending many years as its boss, building it up and extending it. No tributes have yet done justice to Norman Grubb's great work, particularly his testimony at Cambridge and round the country just after World War I.

I had a lot to do with Mrs. Studd and could not stand her, but I concealed my feelings; even in those days I possessed something of that discretion which, along with boldness, is necessary for leadership. After all she was at least forty years older than I.

The mission would not put me on their roll of full missionaries, and they were right so to act. In the end, it was decided that I had a gift for languages and the mission wanted to start work among the Indians of the Amazon basin; I had already studied the source-material, such as it was, in the learned libraries of western Europe, and I was commissioned to travel in Amazonia and complete, as far as possible, a linguistic schedule of the lowland tribes. This I did and published in 1927 a provisional classification of 200–300 dialects. I made mistakes, but on the whole, time has proved this to be a surprisingly accurate work.

The job was suitable to me. I went out alone, and then and in subsequent years I was able to travel a good deal alone. I had to receive parties that came out and introduce them to the environment, but often I could work on my own. On my first sailing to Manaus (Manaos in those days), I went third class — i.e. steerage. I had the whole of the accommodation to myself between Liverpool and Leixões (Oporto). At this port some three hundred Portuguese emigrants came aboard. There were no cabins, even for a dozen people; there were just 'flats' in the stern and one crawled across others to get to one's own berth. One 'flat' was for men, the next for women and so on. We queued up on the deck for meals in calm or storm, at the cookhouse door. When we reached Belem (Pará) at the mouth of the river, I could speak Portuguese with complete ease.

In 1923 I started to write a journal or diary. Taking into account long travel letters, the record is fairly continuous up till 1968, except for the years of World War II. Thus it has been possible to check many details which had slipped from memory, or had become inaccurately lodged in the mind unintentionally. In later years the record is not daily but whenever a journey has had to be made abroad I have used the occasion for sketching in the previous months and then taking up the travel narrative.

I married Eileen Sylvia Knight on 20 May, 1926. She was the daughter of a family living in Oxton, Cheshire, and her father had founded a business in Liverpool which has flourished and expanded. She accompanied me on one long journey in the interior, and also on some of my travels in South Brazil. The climate seemed to suit her and she evidently enjoyed the experience.

In 1932 I was temporarily engaged on some research in Spain and Portugal, and she came out and joined me in Valladolid. A few weeks later, on 1 May, she died in the home of my friends Mr. and Mrs. E. R. Holden, of Almada, Portugal, after a brief and unexpected illness contracted in Seville. Her premature baby, a girl, only survived a few hours, and they are both buried in the cemetery of Almada at the edge of the cliff with its magnificent view over Lisbon, the whole estuary and bay of the Tagus, and the countryside as far as Sintra. She was thirty-one, and left me two sons.

I cannot say — who ever can? — how I came to fall in love with Eileen: it was not 'at first sight' but I had not met her very often. As a result of an evangelical conversion she had become much interested in mission work abroad. She was much influenced by her older sister Muriel who died shortly before her, after years of illness either in bed or in a bath chair; electric chairs were just coming in and she was an early possessor.

Eileen was a natural authoress with an easy and graceful style both in her descriptions of people and of nature. She had a deeply loving and spiritual disposition. Her writing has the touch of a miniature painter and she delighted in the hills and woodlands:

> Where no voice sounds and amid the shadowy green
> The little things of the woodland blush unseen.[2]

She left a small posthumous volume of her poems.[3]

Some of my early travels have been related in detail in my books of the 1930s. Briefly, in the 1920s I worked in the Amazon basin and mostly resided there. In the 1930s I ranged all over Latin America, including the interior, from the Rio Grande[4] to Argentina. This chapter is drawn from the records of early journeys in the Amazon basin, so first a glance should be taken at this region, in those years largely unknown except for the main rivers.

The Amazon is a considerable stream. In its upper course it bears the name Marañon. It rises in the central Peruvian Andes not far from Cerro de Pasco, and flows south for nearly 1,000 miles through the tremendous sierras and enters the forest near Jaen, in north Peru. It then plunges through a series of formidable gorges, known as *pongos*, of which the last and most feared is the Pongo de Manseriche, which is approximately where the river turns eastward for its long journey to the sea.

From the Manseriche to Iquitos is about 500 miles. Iquitos in the 1920s had about 10,000 people, today it has about 100,000. Nevertheless, it is relatively isolated except for air services. Heavy freight is moved by water, for large river steamers and ocean-going ships can ascend to Iquitos.

Below Iquitos the Amazon becomes the Solimões and enters Brazil. Nearly 1,300 miles downstream and a few miles up the River Negro is Manaus, the entrepôt of central Amazonia and capital of the State of Amazonas. Sixty years ago it sheltered over 80,000 people. With the collapse of the wild rubber boom, the population fell drastically in the

---

[2] Euripides, *Bacchae*, trans. Gilbert Murray.
[3] Eileen S. Grubb, *Ships of Desire*, Allenson, 1932.
[4] I.e. the river of that name which divides Mexico from the U.S.A.

early 1920s but is now about 180,000. When I revisited it a few years ago, it seemed to have changed but little in essentials. With its ups and downs of fortune, its incomparable position at the centre of a natural nexus of river and air services, its accessibility to ocean freighters, and its reasonable climate, although only 105 feet above sea-level, it has a definite air of its own. No one could mistake Manaus for Iquitos or Belém. But you cannot get into or out of it except by water, or air; forest and flood smother the land.

Belém stands on the Pará river, one of the mouths of the Amazon, and nearly a thousand miles from Manaus. It is a prosperous place and now has some 300,000 people. It presents a delightful combination of Portuguese colonial architecture and modern skyscrapers. But São Luis (Maranhão) is a better place in which to study colonial architecture.

If the Amazon is measured by the Ucayali which, under a different name, rises only about 100 miles from Lake Titicaca, the length is over 4,000 miles.

It has tremendous tributaries, many of which I have navigated. The Juruá, the Purús and the Madeira (measured from the sources of the Mamoré) are each over 2,000 miles long, and the Madeira has several tributaries of its own which are not far short of the thousand mile mark. The Madeira is undoubtedly a river. The Negro is wide and sluggish. I once fixed coordinates on its banks about 300 miles above Manaus; it was twenty-six miles broad. These rivers are either 'white' water, 'black', or clear. The Amazon and Orinoco are 'white', i.e. muddy, the Negro is 'black', with very dark but unmuddied water. The Xingú is clear.

To the north, in Venezuela, is the Orinoco, rising in the Sierra Parima, which is a confused jumble of distinct ranges on the frontier with Brazil. Even today this region is little known in spite of aerial surveys. It is hard for surface travel. The mountains are thickly forested; the escarpments are precipitous, and the going is very tough. In the south, the peaks of the Cerro de Neblina rise into rocky and open wastes of some 8,000–9,000 feet. I have never ascended this range, but I have seen it in the distance from the upper course of one of the northern tributaries of the Negro, which I was the first to ascend systematically (i.e. making a compass traverse). It rose in the haze over the forest, blue, passionless and vast.

This strange region has the eerie character of a lost world. Apparently it has not changed much and recent travellers on the Upper Negro and Orinoco have brought reports of depopulation rather than progress. It presents formidable obstacles to anyone who penetrates the forests, especially with heavy baggage, and it is the airplane or the hovercraft on the rivers that are shedding new light on it. No mules can be taken through that forest, and the foot-traveller only makes a few miles a day. Great outcrops of mountain, an extension, according to some, of the 'Guiana shield', rise, crenellated and castellated, closing in all horizons. They are the ramparts of the escarpments and standing at their foot the lone traveller almost seems to hear the bugle on the battlements. It is a setting where the mortal drama of Browning's Childe Roland could be played to a finish. 'There they stood, ranged along the hill-sides, met / To view the last of me ... And yet / Dauntless the slug-horn to my lips I set.'[5]

It is perfectly possible to pass from the Orinoco to the Amazon system via the River Negro, by water. We used to consider the portage between Yavita and Maroa both shorter and quicker, but the route was then well preserved and Indian labour fairly easily available. If you want to go by river, take the Casiquiare Canal which is said to be unique in the world. Start from the Upper Orinoco which pours about one third of its water into the Canal and so into the Negro. The Canal is 227 miles long. Geologically it is a development of an original drainage line which has persisted through long vicissitudes of change. It was first navigated throughout its length, not by Humboldt as is sometimes claimed, but by Father Roman in 1744 or possibly even earlier by Aguirre. If you still wish to amuse yourself with this kind of thing, you can also pass by water from the Amazon system to the Paraguay and come out at Buenos Aires.

Some forty years ago, I mentioned in print that this could be done, and I was taken to task by a reviewer in *The Times*. The journey, however, has since been effected.

I was similarly ticked off for saying that I was satisfied that on the Caroní, which flows into the lower Orinoco, there was a waterfall much higher than Kaieteur in Guyana. Since then, the Salto del Angel[6] has been discovered with its 3,200 feet of sheer fall; Kaieteur is under 1,000 feet. I obtained information from the Maquiritaré Indians and gradually formed an idea which I checked as far as I could. I should like to have visited the place, but it has not been possible: the sounding cataract still haunted me like a passion.

It is time to return to the Amazon basin proper. No description of it is complete without a reference to the Booth Line (Booth Steamship Co.). This company has served the area since 1889 and has been largely

---
[5] Robert Browning, *Childe Roland to the Dark Tower Came*.
[6] This name has no heavenly connotation. It was a Sr. Angel who first visited the Salto.

responsible for charting the navigation of the Amazon and building the remarkable harbour works at Manaus, a floating quay linked to the land by a flexible roadway, a very necessary provision for the Negro rises forty-five feet at Manaus between seasons. Booth still send their ships right up to Iquitos. In my early years Booth, through its officers, employees and local connections, was of indispensable assistance to me.

The navigable Amazon basin is bottlenecked. The lower tributaries, the Xingú and the Tapajos, as well as such rivers as the Tocantins and Araguaya, are interrupted by rapids not far from their confluence with the Amazon, and are only suitable for launches. Rivers like the Juruá and Purús, in the south-western segment of the great fluvial basin, can be navigated by river craft of several hundred tons for at least 1,750 miles, although it is always desirable in Amazonia to choose just the right season.

The current can be fierce, for in upper Amazonia the difference between high and low river can easily reach seventy feet. The lower Amazon is swept by tropical storms, and in the estuary the tides are tremendous. But it is dangerous to navigate anywhere after dark, since it is impossible to spot the trees which the floods have torn up and carried seawards. It has been said that the current sweeping eastwards can be detected in the flooded forest many miles from the banks. I do know that it is often impossible to find land on which to camp.

This once led to an amusing incident. A young man had begged to accompany me on a journey. One night we found no terra firme so I slung my hammock between the trees over the water. A wise man glances up the trees and makes sure that hosts of ants have not been forced up them by the floods. My companion was not wise but merely omniscient and therefore incapable of receiving advice. I had noted with interest that up the tree at the head end of his hammock there were ants, but it was hard to see in the twilight and I assumed that they were relatively harmless.

They were not; they were *saúbas*, or powerful leaf-cutting ants. They came down the tree in the darkness, and actually ate through the headrope of the young man's hammock. I woke up with the crash as did another fellow-traveller, the third of the party. I switched on a torch and laughed so much that we did not immediately realise that the situation was dangerous. We hauled the gentleman out of the water all tied up in his mosquito-curtain, just in time, deposited him on the bottom of the canoe and resumed our slumbers. Only in the morning did we discover that, to add insult to injury, under the water there was a thorn-bush, and he had spent most of the small hours extracting thorns from his person, and some of them were six inches long.

The seasons on the lower river should be carefully observed. I knew an elderly priest in Belém who used to publish a fortune-telling almanac foretelling weather and personal fortunes. Once, when I visited him he was dictating next year's edition, roughly as follows: 'February: violent gales, cold nights, torrential rains . . .' I presently interrupted and said, 'Father, this is too bad; next February I have to make a long journey.' He looked up and said, 'Ah, it is my little friend, Mr. Grubb! How can I oblige my little friend, Mr. Grubb?' I explained how, tactfully. He turned to the secretary and said, 'Cross that out, and write "Balmy nights, cool days, dry weather . . ."' And it was so. It is the only time I have changed the weather through personal influence. Good travelling weather makes a great difference. Often it is possible to make a journey for weeks without using a single blanket at night.

Temperatures are not excessive. At Manaus the average, day and night, is about 80°F. The damp, however, can be depressing, the sun scorching, and there may be little difference between midday shade temperatures and midnight.

The vagaries of the climate once led to a diverting incident. I was travelling with about a dozen Indians for a few days through the forest, at the fag-end of a dry spell. But one night it rained furiously, with brilliant lightning and explosive thunder. We made a shelter and slept on the ground. In a pause in the storm, through the dripping of the water from a thousand branches, I heard a suspicious sound near me and decided it was a snake. I took my Mauser rifle by the muzzle and hit out; at the same moment there was a terrifying crack of thunder, and an Indian leapt to his feet shouting 'The thunder's hit me; the thunder's hit me.'

Torches were brought, and the interpreter. It was awkward and a plain lie seemed undesirable. So I said 'The thunder's hit you, has it? I do not know, but if it be so, you are an honoured man; you have saved the rest of us; but the thunder would never hit anyone without leaving its mark.' We pulled his hand away from his forehead and there was a bad wound; you could see the bones of his skull bent inwards. They took him away and fêted him, and later he recovered, so no real harm was done. He had probably been creeping up to rob or murder, and I had first smack.

There is game in the forest, but it is patchy in its distribution. Anything like the great herds and flocks that roamed the African bush is unknown. There are said to be only seven species of deer, of which four are peculiar to the Andes, against some seventy in Africa. The life of deer in a forest is a dog's life and they prefer the more open country of Mato Grosso.

I owe a lasting debt of gratitude to one Manoel Gomes dos Santos who was a very good hunter and took me with him on some of his journeys. He was an evangelical pastor with the oversight of various groups of Christians on the Solimões and Negro, with his headquarters in Manaus. We had great times in the early 1920s, travelling often on his launch, sometimes in mine. He sang well and I played the guitar and the concertina. On one occasion, we taught a parrot to sing the first verse of 'Onward Christian Soldiers' in Portuguese, at a lonely *barraca* (primitive house) on the Jauapery. However, the local agent of the Indian Protection Service was a positivist of the school of Auguste Comte, and he objected that we were proselytising so we desisted.

On the same journey, on the small River Camaraí, we saw the largest and finest jaguar that either of us had ever glimpsed. It came out of the forest quite close to us, but unfortunately we had both run out of ammunition and were living on fish and by turning turtles, getting both the lady and her eggs. Another time, we shot a tapir as a joint operation; a few days later we were visited by that dangerous animal, the peccary, and, having first made sure that we could shin up a tree, we killed three. There were perhaps seven or eight in the band; the early travellers give accounts of great droves of seventy to eighty but these are not seen today.

Once I went down very early to wash in the river, and about 100 yards downstream I saw a beautiful jaguar fishing. He was stretched along the trunk of a fallen tree and swishing his tail over the water. This attracted the tucunaré fish, and every now and then he dipped his paw in and scooped one up. I moved very quietly to get my rifle, but he heard, looked round and was off in a flash.

Game otherwise consists of the capivara, a very large rodent and a great nuisance, the cutia, all kinds of monkeys from the guariba (howling monkey) down, the ant-eater, the sloth, the tortoise, the puma (black and tawny), the armadillo and sundry other animals and birds, not forgetting the valuable inhambú, a kind of pheasant, and the mutúm, a wild turkey. These creatures, including the monkeys, are eatable.

The rivers provide fish, from the great pirarucú which may reach 150 lb. to the infamous *piranha* (caribe) which eats and is eaten. Alligators do not appear much on the main rivers, but in the swamps and secondary streams they are plentiful. The River Mamoré, in lower Bolivia, used to be alive with them. One eats the tail, and the fat on the underside can be useful.

Freshwater turtles are shy, but when the water falls they can be caught on the sandy beaches in the remote rivers.

When I was lost for many weeks I camped alone on an island and lived largely on turtle, but they are very rich for regular diet. A turtle hunt is good sport, but they should not be wasted, and if not needed should be turned over again and chased into the river. The Amazonenses say that a large turtle will provide food for thirty people, and there are the eggs if she is a female. Amid the gnawing anxiety of unrelieved solitude, where no man is, it is something not to have to wrestle as well with the pangs of starvation.

There are, indeed, parts where the forest teems with game, but more often it is scarce, and food may run dangerously low, resulting in serious deficiency diseases or starvation. There is an entry in my journal from 1925, perhaps a little over-dramatic, when I was on the Marmellos, a sub-tributary of the Madeira: 'I took in the last hole in my belt a few days ago and now it is already too large.' But it is easy to slim in Amazonia. A few days afterwards I record a temperature of 106.4°F. with sub-tertian malaria. And a little later: 'One might be as rich as Croesus or shoot like William Tell, on the lower Marmellos, and starve, for there is nothing to shoot and no one has anything to sell.'

Don't worry about snakes: snake stories, like fishing ones, improve in the telling. Their distribution seems to be uneven, for some travellers encounter dozens, others very few. The rattlesnake is a denizen of the shrub and bush country rather than the forest. The jararáca is a deadly brute, a thin venomous snake about three feet long. The bushmaster is a larger and longer snake and is greatly feared. The anaconda is not poisonous; it has other compensations. It grows to a great length, reliable naturalists have reported specimens of over forty feet, and five to fifteen is common. It emits a stench and it can give a bad bite. Shoot it.

I was only once bitten by a poisonous snake, in the early 1930s, and I did not see what it was. In the early morning, I sat on the edge of my hammock fishing for my shoes with my toes. Herein lay grievous error for the shoes ought to have been tied up to the hammock. A small snake suddenly emerged from a shoe and bit me on the shin. Dawn was breaking but camp was not. The Indian *capatáz* (foreman) was up and smoking a cigarette. The proper remedies were down on the launch (they usually are!) and something had to be done. I called him, seized the cigarette out of his mouth and rubbed it into the bite. I was sick for several days and kept bleeding from various orifices of the body. The place on my leg remained till the middle of World War II, breaking out from time to time, as a healthy or unhealthy reminder.

For long afterwards the forest seemed full of snakes. I dislike them, but the mygale spider can also give a terrible bite, and the tucandera ant is not to be despised. It is said that half a dozen bites of a tucandera will end any career, however distinguished. Spruce relates that a woman in Barcellos on the Negro who was bitten on the heel by a mygale gave one sudden and terrible cry and fell insensible; she did, however, recover after some days. Spruce is always a cautious narrator, given to understatement. His own account of being bitten by a tucandera is graphic.[7]

Conditions were not easy in my early days. The whole area was going through a bad patch, and some useful settlements with nice little riverside villages were being abandoned. There was a lot of malaria, dysentery, beriberi, typhus and blackwater fever. On the Negro, village after village was depopulated and swallowed up by the devouring forest. The Casiquiare and Upper Orinoco were almost deserted. There were no plane services then and one travelled in river steamers, *gaiolas* (cages), or *chatas* (chato means flat), which were stern-wheelers like the famous old Mississippi craft. In those days stern-wheelers were also used extensively on the River Magdalena, furnishing an indispensable part of the link between Bogotá and the northern coast of Colombia at Barranquilla. When there was no public transport one travelled by launch or canoe with an outboard so long as the gasolene lasted. Through the forest, to go on foot was the only way: the day's journey would be between two and twelve miles.

Praga (plague) was very bad in those years. The word does not refer to bubonic at all, but is a general term covering the perpetual nuisance of mosquitoes, piums (*jejénes*), mutúcas, maruim *et hoc genus omne*. The Xingú was a terrible river for the pium, the highly irritating little fly which pullulates by day and leaves a tiny but nasty blood-blister which, when scratched, can easily degenerate into an ulcer. The common culex mosquito appeared in swarms at night, and anopheles, the malarial villain, stegomyia and other noxious varieties abounded, but, let's be fair to the mosquito, there were long stretches of forest and river which were 'clean', that is clear of mosquitoes. In other regions they ignored the Queensberry rules and were as common by day as by night. At times one had to wear a

[7] Richard Spruce, *Notes of a Botanist on the Amazon and Andes* (1908), Vol. I, ch. XI. Spruce found the Negro tough. One entry in his synopsis reads, 'Stung by tucandera ants— intense pain—poisonous snakes—boy killed by rattlesnake—man bitten by jararáca—insect plagues.'

head-curtain by day. On the Upper Orinoco I once visited a tiny village where there was a deathly silence, and not a soul gossiping or working. I passed my hand over my face and drew it away, bloody and covered with the bodies of just plain, greedy and unruly mosquitoes.

My companions on a journey, if any, resented my telling them to imitate the virtues of St. Makarios. This pious man is a recognised saint, at least in the calendar of the Eastern churches. He held advanced protectionist views about the killing of living creatures, and was one day visited by remorse for squashing a mosquito. In expiation he retired to a bog for six months, naked. On his return to civilisation, he was so covered with boils and ulcers that his friends could only recognise him by his voice. The moral was that mosquitoes served a useful purpose in education in the virtues, since they inculcated patience. The moral was even more unpopular than the story.

In such journeys food was Problem No. 1. It was usual to take as much *farinha* (i.e. the cooked and desiccated flour of mandioca, maniòc or cassava) as possible, and dried pirarucú, a really excellent fish. Then there was game for rifle or gun, and fishing, either by hook or line or by *tarráfa*. The latter is a circular net, as formerly used in the south of Spain and Portugal and in the Mediterranean generally. It is weighted round the circumference with pieces of lead, and a long stout line is attached to the centre. The fisherman loops the line over the wrist, pans the net out between his two hands and casts it in the form of its natural circle. The circumference sinks and, with luck, many good fish are caught. Fish are hard to catch when the floods are out. The Indians do it skilfully with bow and arrow. They make a small platform over the *igapó* (flooded forest), attach to the end of a long pole a false fish made from bark whitened in the ashes of the fire, hold the pole between their toes sloping down into the water, and thus attract and shoot their prey.

Bugs have their uses. One night among the Aguarunas (who at that time were Jivaro head-shrinkers) on the Marañon, I was trying to read by the light of the fire, and not succeeding. An Aguaruna noticed this, disappeared into the forest and returned with a long bug. You held this gently by the head and tickled the other end with a finger. It then glowed, either with pleasure or from a desire to be helpful. When held near writing or print, it made it quite possible to read. The vampire bat is common in some localities. It is a nuisance with its blood-sucking propensities. At night, it is well to keep a lantern burning. Cats can be trained to kill them.

In those years it was common in places like Manaus, Belém or Iquitos to speak of the 'decadence' of the region. By this was meant the story of the rubber and all that went on in that era. The subject merits a few words.

The sources and properties of rubber were known to the Amerindians, and games with rubber balls were fairly common among them from Mexico to Mato Grosso. In the middle of the nineteenth century its vast importance was realised. Spruce, James Collins and others wrote and reported on the *Hevea Braziliensis* and other latex trees. The first seeds carried from Brazil to India died. Sir James Hooker of Kew took up the matter with Henry A. Wickham, a planter and settler at Santarem. Wickham's first consignment of saplings was a failure, but shortly afterwards he was able to charter a steamship which had just arrived in the Amazon on behalf of the Government of India.

By then the Brazilian Government was aware of what, quite literally, was afloat. Wickham unashamedly hoodwinked Customs at Belém, and got his ship away in the same year that Dr. N. A. Otto of Cologne first demonstrated the possibilities of the internal combustion engine. By his own published account, Wickham was little more than an adventurer, but he did know about rubber and he did take his own risks. He was duly knighted, but not till 1920, and eight years later he died.

The authorities differ about the number of seeds and mainly of saplings in Wickham's consignment to Kew. It is commonly said to have been about 70,000. In the 1870s some 2,000 of them were sent to Ceylon and a few to Java and Singapore. From these modest beginnings, with some other very small consignments brought by Robert Cross, has grown the vast plantation industry of South-East Asia. For a long time success was in the balance, but at the turn of the century, precisely in 1900, four tons of Eastern plantation rubber were exported to the West.

Brazil never learned the lesson that systematic plantations were necessary to success. But for several decades, and right up to World War I, wild rubber was in tremendous demand, and prices were astronomical. In 1902, a peak year, the Amazon export was 44,000 tons, just over half the world total. Manaus became a fabled boom city; the fine floating wharf was lined with ships; the palaces of the rubber barons rivalled one another in splendours and the famous opera house, completed in 1896, dominated the higher part, as it still does. There were 80,000 to 100,000 people in Manaus, but by 1916 the market had collapsed. In the early 1920s there were 30,000–50,000 people there, and in 1932 six and a half thousand tons only of rubber were marketed and prices were low. Things have improved since then, but little plantation rubber has been developed, and the Ford enterprise on the lower Tapajos was abandoned in the 1940s.

The *Hevea Braziliensis* or rubber tree is pretty widespread, but of the twenty species only two are tapped. In certain regions *caucho* is also extracted, the tree being usually felled in the process.

Rubber men are known as *seringueiros* (*seringueira* means Hevea) and their life is hard. Thousands of Indians were rounded up in the great rubber years, enslaved and put to work, and thousands died, leaving a legacy of intense hostility among many of the surviving tribes against the *civilisados* or *gente decente* (decent folk). The best *seringueiros* are either *caboclos* or Cearenses. The former is the usual civilised inhabitant of the forests and rivers; the term is not racial and he may be either Indian, or Negro, or a mixture of white, brown and black. The Cearenses are natives of the state of Ceará, driven northwards by the remorseless droughts which are only today being tackled by modern engineering ventures on a vast scale.

The *caboclo* fundamentally does not like to be uprooted from his lazy and undemanding life, by the backwaters and hidden lakes where he prefers to dwell. Once I talked to some *caboclos* on one of the islands in the estuary of the Amazon, not far from Belém. I asked 'What do you chaps do to earn a living?' 'When it is day we watch the tide, when it is night we sleep.' 'So you do nothing?' 'Your honour must take it like that, if you wish.' 'All right, but don't you get tired of doing nothing?' 'Of course.' 'And what do you do then?' 'We take a rest, naturally.' The Portuguese has special point since it involves a play on words, *cansar* (meaning tire) and *descansar* (to 'untire', or rest). But why trouble? It is the old story. The *caboclo* likes his line, his gun and his little *roça* (plantation), all the rest is sound and fury, signifying skyscrapers.

In various volumes, written thirty to forty years ago, I have described the life of the *seringueiro*, and in my early years it was easy to know the great rubber barons and to check up on some of the more notorious abuses of justice and common humanity, but not always to restrain them. But there is no point in going over all this; it is a tale that is told; and no nation has clean hands before history and is qualified to throw the first stone.

The best literature of the life in the interior comes from Latin American pens and is little known in Europe. None has described its misery and strange magnetism better than José Eustasio Rivera, a Colombian author whose early death robbed South American letters of a writer of exceptional powers. In his remarkable, and partly historical, novel *La Vorágine*, he describes the rubber period with the vividness of poetry:

Well do the labourers in rubber know that the vegetable gold enriches no one. The minor potentates of the forest have no credits except those in their books against péons who never pay, unless with their lives, against Indians who waste away, against boatmen who rob what they transport. Slavery in these regions is lifelong for slave and owner; the one as much as the other must die here. A destiny of failure attaches to all who exploit the green mine. The forest annihilates them, the forest submerges them, the forest calls to them only to devour them. Those who escape, although they take refuge in the cities, carry the curse in body and soul. Worn out, old and deceived, they have only one desire: to return and return again, yet knowing that if they return they will perish. And those who tear themselves away, who refuse the call of the forest, decline in their misery, victims of unknown diseases, the malarial flesh of the hospital, handed over to the knife which cuts them to pieces, to expiate some sacrilege which they have committed against the Indians or against even the trees.

The bad old days lasted into my early years. There was much lawlessness in the interior, especially on the River Xingú. Some of this was due to the simple fact there were many real criminal types about. On the Araguarí (not the Araguaya), a river of the estuary region, north of Belém, there were violent men who had escaped from Cayenne, or, even, it was said from the Ile du Diable (Devil's Island) which fulfilled its notorious function as a convict settlement until 1949.

A nasty event occurred in the early 1920s. I did not witness it, but it was so often related in terms which agreed in all essentials that I regard it as established. A group of Indians came down a tributary to the main Juruá, and bargained with a Coronel (local magnate) who had an important rubber post at the confluence. They said they had found a dense stand of rubber trees up their tributary and they would guide the Coronel's men to these and help them. A large expedition was arranged. A valuable cargo of rubber was collected and rafts made to take it downstream. A few hours above the confluence there was a very dangerous rapid, but the Indians took charge saying that they knew the river well. And truly they did.

They put the whole flotilla deliberately on the rocks. Warriors of the tribe, hidden in the forest, then sallied out and shot down the Brazilians struggling in the water. Only a few escaped from an expedition of about fifty persons. I spoke later with several survivors.

They then crossed a neck of forested land and appeared on the main river at a point where the steamers called to pick up wood. They surprised the workers and killed them. They went aboard a steamer which arrived later, officers, hands and passengers being terrified to a man, and found out how to work the steam whistle. This is a sign that a ship is in difficulties on the mud and everyone in range comes round to help and earn some money. They thus attracted a number of civilised folk to the spot and killed them. They then disappeared.

My task in the 1920s (see p. 27) was to study and prepare a provisional classification of the dialects of the Amerindians, so that mission work could be established. Some of the vocabularies then compiled, by the latest phonetic techniques of that time, are preserved still among my papers, and they are beautifully written. But pacification comes before translation and I got involved in various operations; I mean, of course, pacification without the pacifiers using force or weapons against the attacker. You cannot present the Gospel to a vigorous fellow who is clobbering you on the head with a club. It doesn't work. Seize the club and then preach the Word.

These journeys have left an indelible impression to this day. Usually, in spite of my taste for solitude, I would have one or two companions with me, but sometimes, either through accident or design, I was alone for weeks together, and indeed was hard put to it to sustain life, to avoid being fatally lost, and to plan my own rescue.

I cannot recapture in cold print the spirit of the vast and cruel forest. After travelling in the scorching sun on the river, to plunge into the flooded undergrowth was like entering a towering cathedral to shelter from the noonday heat. It had the same subduing influence, it inculcated the same awe. Instinctively, one suddenly began to speak in whispers. Now and then there was a cry of a bird or beast, the crash of a rotten tree, or some unfamiliar sound. Once it was a clumsy tapir forging his way, careless and off his guard, down to the water to slake his thirst.

In the evening, a new and dissonant chorus of noises arose, the constant, high-song of the cicadas, and the shrill croak of the frogs, or the strange call of the howling-monkey (guariba) than which there is nothing eerier. To this is added the sense of impenetrable darkness, the knowledge that another day's journey, and yet another will yield no horizon.

When alone, it is advisable to take a firm grip of oneself. There are stories of men running amok in the forest, but I have never attempted to verify them. During the day the mere business of keeping alive and well, and travelling on, is sufficient to preoccupy all the strength and attention that can be summoned up. The nights are long near the Equator, the dusk quickly becomes dark and the dawn penetrates at first but fitfully. It is best not to think too much.

I never when alone experienced any specific mystical sense of the presence of God and any vision was of the vague, poetical kind, elevating, sustaining but of slight practical application. Equally, I never felt deprived of that access of which the Christian is assured when he offers his prayers in the name of Jesus Christ. The great forest was to me as much a temple of the Most High as the most solemn abbey, and ten thousand voices would cry 'Holy, holy, holy is the Lord God of Hosts.' I prayed for favourable material conditions since an answer to my prayer did not seem capable of harming anyone else. The point must be watched. I used to pray for a favourable wind for travelling on the lower Amazon, until I noticed that a fair wind for me was usually a foul one for the fishermen.

Only occasionally I allowed imagination to roam, or speculation to take control. Instinctively, in thinking of the existence of God and the mystery of the universe, I used to arrive at the position of Kant: 'We cannot bear, nor can we rid ourselves of the thought, that a being, which we regard as the greatest of all possible existences, should *say to himself*: I am from eternity to eternity; besides me there is nothing except that exists by my will; *but whence then am I?*'[8] I found it more profitable to stick to the Bible.

The Amerindian tribes of the lowlands have been often described, and this is not the place for a dissertation about their provenance and customs. They are distinguished by the colour of their skin and hair. The first is a warm yellowish brown, inclining either to red, or more often to bronze. The hair is long and straight, black and coarse. The face is not strongly expressive and the lips are not thickened. The eyes are brown or black, small and oblique; the height usually medium. In character the Indian is impassive and patient, cunning and silent, and capable of great endurance.

They usually live in small communities of a few score or a few hundred, building communal houses, called in Brazil *malocas*, where families live together, each in its own part, but with no walls between. The great majority of the tribes plant a few crops, but a different type is found, namely the entirely nomadic Indian, often enslaved by the more powerful sedentary groups. Such are the Muras of the Madeira, or the Macús of the Negro. In my time it was still possible, particularly on the Upper Orinoco and on some tributaries of the Negro, to find polished stone axes in use among them.

[8] *Critique of Pure Reason*, trans. J. M. D. Meiklejohn (Everyman's Library, 1934), p. 357.

Life among them has difficulties, and care must be exercised. I knew a traveller who lost his temper with a group of Indians who were conducting him through the forest of interior Peru. He threatened them with his revolver and they complied. Next morning they had all disappeared. When the man staggered into my camp, he was in a bad way.

The year 1925 was particularly difficult. A fellow-missionary, Harold Morris, and I went on an advance party to explore the situation among the Cauahib or Parentintin Indians. They live on certain tributaries of the Madeira, namely the Maicy, the Marmellos and the Ipixuna. We went up the Marmellos for about a fortnight by canoe. We then joined a party of these Indians who were going through the forest over to the Ipixuna. We travelled light, with what we could carry on our backs, a gun for hunting and some fishing-tackle.

We spent some weeks in a *maloca* near the Ipixuna. But presently the Indians turned against us for reasons which we never discovered. Nearly all our things were looted. We even had trouble to recover our clothes which were stolen when we were bathing.

Harold had injured his foot and a deep and agonisingly painful abscess had formed which made it impossible for him to move except on sticks, and then very slowly.

Suddenly, one morning, the Indians packed up and disappeared into the forest. They refused to take us and, anyhow, it would have been very difficult. Harold was in great pain and was getting weaker every day. But we could not stay where we were for we were some distance from the banks of the Ipixuna and therefore could not hail any passing boat.

I carried him on my back down to a more suitable point. There we made a little camp. I returned to the *maloca*, about half an hour's walk, collected some *farinha*, maize and such other edibles as I could find, and a tin containing matches which I had hidden. Thus we managed to live, on a near-starvation diet.

Some days later, a friendly Indian whom we had met on the Marmellos turned up. He offered to take us down the Ipixuna and, if we wished, right down to the Madeira. But he could not bring his canoe round to where we were because the water had fallen suddenly. So I took Harold on my back and we returned to the *maloca*. We rested there and the next day we started off in a different direction. It was hard going but after several hours we came on a small lake connecting with the Ipixuna. The Indian had a bark canoe there. He paddled in the bows and I in the stern while Harold lay on the bottom of the frail craft. But the worst was over, because a few days later we reached the first civilised house. Harold was in a bad way and it was still a long time before we could get him back to Manaus. It was a very difficult area to get stuck in. The current in the Madeira is is strong and dangerous and, as for the forest, mosquitoes seemed to be as numerous by day as by night. Although otherwise well, I had some very bad malaria.

A few of us were once among a tribe of some hundreds, and I knew that a launch was due from down-river with supplies. The Indians had been a great nuisance; they stole everything and even made hooks fixed to long rods which they pushed under the thatched walls of our temporary hut to pull out whatever they could. I heard that some officials were coming to visit us. So I summoned five of the leading men and said, 'You know that very important people are arriving shortly in a boat?' They at once asked if I would prepare a feast and invite them. 'Yes,' I said, 'but you know what the chief man will say. He will say, "Can I have a knife to eat with?" And I shall reply, "The Indians here have stolen all my knives." ' I then concocted a story which brought in most of our missing possessions, ending up ' "Can I have a hammock to sleep in?" And I shall say, "Sir, the Indians have stolen all my hammocks." '

I walked away. Next morning there was a nice little pile of our possessions outside our back door.

A little resourcefulness goes a long way. A journey in the early 1920s took Manoel and me up among the Jauaperý who lived in the remote and almost desolate forest lying between Manaus and the Guyana frontier. In those days they were a trifle unruly in their habits. At night they would not leave us in peace but insisted on coming aboard our boat to steal. I then remembered that Slocum, the first man to sail round the world singlehanded, had had similar trouble in the Strait of Magellan, and had dealt with it cunningly. So I sorted out from among our stores a heap of tintacks and drawing-pins. We put these on the foredeck with the business ends skywards. Presently we were awakened by screams and we beheld the edifying moonlight spectacle of the ring-leaders among the rascals diving overboard with pins and pains in their feet. We slept in peace.

Sometimes one gets the truth pretty crudely from the Indians. In the 1920s a score of Amerindians from a little-known tribe of the middle Negro area appeared in Manaus. They roamed about naked, men and women, seizing from the shops what took their fancy. The chief officer of the Indian Protection Service was away and his staff asked me if I could help.

They came from lands nominally the property of J. G. Araujo, who had founded one of the great trading houses of Amazonia. His son, feeling that the family had some social obligation, asked me to bring some of them to supper in his *palacete* (big house). I selected four and found them clothes for the occasion. It was a full-scale party with many guests.

We sat down at table. I put the Indians opposite me and told them to do exactly what I did. This worked well for a time, but presently I had a sneezing fit: they all promptly had the same.

After dinner, our hostess asked what the Indians would like and we decided on music. She had a fine contralto voice, and sang some familiar Brazilian songs. Our host, in his impulsive and attractive way, turned to me, and said, 'Did they like it? Ask them if they liked it.' I did so. The leading Indian, an elderly, slow man, at last said 'Yes.' 'Have they ever heard anything like it before?' asked our host and I translated. The old man thought again and then said, 'Yes. The big ship came in this morning (this was the Booth Company's *Hildebrand*) and when she came near the shore, she *sang*. That is where I have heard the noise before.' I translated as faithfully as I could and our hostess was very understanding. The 'song' was simply the blasts on the ship's siren.

The motto in many parts of the interior was 'The only good Indian is a dead Indian', a principle usually attributed to the early settlers of the Wild West. In Brazil it took a slightly different form. On the Xingú it used to be said, 'Here we do not observe the Constitution; we have one Constitution and one Article in it, the Article 44 of the Constitution Winchester.' The Winchester .44, although an unhandy weapon, was very popular in those days.

On the Tapajós, it was commoner to adopt the position that anyone who was known to have seen an Indian and not tried to shoot him, had sinned against public safety, and was fair game if some third party had a grudge against him.

One incident has always remained in my memory and is summarised in my journal. I was travelling with a sole companion, a *caboclo* whose great merit was his thorough acquaintance with life in the interior. Beyond this he had little culture and not much humanity.

One night we came to an empty *maloca*, and the next day we thought we could get home. The *maloca* was in full use, and there was a fine plantation of mandioca, maize, bananas, sugarcane and the like. But no one at all was about.

My friend slung his hammock at one end of the vast dark dwelling-house, and I at the other so as to get a little peace and space. Presently he called out to me in Portuguese, 'I have only a few bullets left so if I see a *bicho* (*bicho* means beast, used here for Indian) I will shoot him.' I replied, 'Same here, but I don't shoot Indians: if I see a *jacaré* (the local alligator) I'll have a shot.' Normally, if short of ammunition, one would not bother about an alligator.

The next morning my friend was dead. I had slept very heavily and had heard nothing. His head had been coshed in with some heavy blunt instrument. Not a soul was about and it was a trifle queer. I began to fear; the silence was deathly; and something had to be done. 'Fear, and be slain!' I said my prayers and read a little from the New Testament. I looked around again, but nothing was breaking the silence, except the usual sounds of the forest and the frequent harsh cry of a parrakeet.

I buried the body in the sand by the river which had fallen a few inches in the night. Nothing of the dead man's gear had been stolen, so I threw all our stuff into the canoe and pushed off downstream without starting the motor. About an hour later I was navigating some narrows caused by a high bluff of rock jutting into the river. Suddenly an Indian in full head-dress appeared on this bluff. He called out in fair Portuguese, 'You carry on, *compadre*, (*compadre* means popularly, 'my good friend') you are not the one to use your gun against us.' He must have been listening in the undergrowth the previous evening and was taking no chances. I carried on.

The Amerindian has a direct and simple logic of his own. Once from our launch, we saw a woman beating her child. She left the little one moaning. One of my companions took a doll from our stores, seized the canoe, and soon the crying ceased. Next morning the noise in the Indians' camp was agonising. All the women were beating their children.

It would be easy to multiply such stories. But the life, if exotic, was not dramatic. The stories told here are of experiences spread out over a decade. In Amazonia things do not happen often and monotony is the usual colour and framework of existence. Some people would not like it and others could not stand it. The Quakers with their taste for silence would perhaps enjoy it, but there were no Quaker missions.

The lone scout, or the small party, is at grave disadvantage in one respect, that is in coping with rapids. Some of the great tributaries are dangerously interrupted by falls. These are not gorges such as one has to wrestle with in the Andes, but true rapids caused by an outcrop or pier of crystalline rock jutting into or across the river. The Xingú and Tapajós in the south-east and the Japurá and Uaupes in the north-west are typical examples of such rivers. The sight is magnificent. The roar of the waters, the confusion and spray in the narrow channels between the greater rocks, the remoteness and fascination of the scene never failed to impress.

To work a small launch, or even a canoe, up a rapid is laborious. The crew are furnished with heavy poles, the freight is unloaded, the pilots struggle with the helm, but sometimes everyone is defeated. If so, and if it is an entirely pioneer trip, then a track must be cut through the forest and rollers used. Once on the Xingú, where today launch traffic is well-developed and the river accurately known, we got badly stuck. The owner of the launch, an elderly man, and several of us were standing on a small island and he asked me if I was a strong swimmer. I wasn't, but I wanted to help so I agreed to swim across a channel to assist the crew. I misjudged the distance, was carried down the flume and dislocated my left arm at the shoulder.

No one knew what to do till I suddenly remembered that, failing anything else, there was one painful exercise worth trying. I lay down and instructed a man to sit by me on the ground with his left leg outstretched and his heel in the arm joint, and then to pull strong and steady on the arm. It slipped back and has stayed there for some forty-five years.

Coming down-stream, it is best to make use of the height of the flood if there is a good pilot. On a tributary of the Negro we did get into trouble. All seemed well and we were happy and young when suddenly there was a crash and the launch swung slowly round with a horrible splintering and grinding noise. We tore up the floor boards. A needle-like point of rock was sticking up through the bottom in the bows and the water was pouring in. Half a sack of flour disappeared in that hole in no time.

I looked around desperately and suddenly saw one of our crew in a new light. He had a remarkably broad and well rounded bottom. We seized him and pushed him, doubled up, stern foremost and protesting into the hole. We listened to no arguments but promised him double pay. By that time we had swung off the point of rock, and the position was safely held until we could beach the boat. Repairs took several days, not of the man but of the launch.

The great gorges of the Andes where rivers such as the Urubamba, the Huallaga and the Marañon itself, burst through the mountain ranges are a different proposition, and one description must suffice, namely the passage through the Pongo de Manseriche, the famous gorge on the Marañon. No one would take a craft through it today, but at the relevant period there were no planes. I had been working in the area for some time alone, but in order to make the trip I recruited two Aguaruna Indians, Chavit and Puhúputa. Every civilised person thought it crazy to go through the Manseriche, but there were strong reasons for doing so. The journey over the mountains was almost as hazardous in a different way.

I had made a balsa raft, much the same as the *Kon-tiki* — itself based on the Peruvian pattern — but much smaller, and had already traversed some fifteen gorges safely in the course of several days. And then we had to face the Manseriche.

This formidable canyon is about five miles long and zig-zag, which does not contribute to smooth travelling. Immediately above it, at the mouth of the Santiago, then an Ecuadorean river, it is 2,000 feet broad. It narrows to 600 feet, and finally to about 180 feet. The walls of sandstone rise sheer on either side to 1,000 feet, and the depth is about 170 feet. From Borja at the lower end to the Atlantic there is uninterrupted navigation, over 2,600 miles.

Of the many whirlpools in the Pongo two are notorious and highly dangerous, particularly when there is the slightest pressure of water, which occurs whenever there has been rain in the Andes or the snow has melted. They are called in Quechua, cheerfully, Asua Huacangui ('Thou shalt weep bitterly'), and Atun Huacangui ('Thou shalt weep greatly'). Although I slipped through in January 1929, when the water was low and the pressure slight, we very nearly got sucked down in Asua Huacangui. The Marañon was exceptionally late in flooding that season.

Even so, such was the reputation of the Manseriche that it was very difficult to recruit labour, and I paid the two Indians highly, with machetes. We reached the Santiago, a black-water river, in the afternoon and tried to pull into the bank, but the current was too strong for us and we were swept into the gorge.

There was nothing to do except fend off the sides. Progress was strangely slow because of backwaters and the boiling upheaval of waters from the depths — 'the atom darkness of a slow turmoil'. If we began to be sucked under by one corner, we rushed to another.

It was all rather disconcerting. The walls of the canyon shut out the dying light. Mosses grew in abundance and strange tropical plants clung with despair and tenacity to the steepening cliffs. There were no tree-ferns, and no butterflies or flowers. However, we made it and had done well. Many have been drowned in the Manseriche, but by a little planning, careful choice of season, and good labour relations, we managed to get through. The giant of the turmoil was resting and did not even turn in his sleep.

This chapter had best be rounded off with an account of my death. The event occurred, according to some, in 1928, but I have never admitted the accuracy of the key fact. Like Mark Twain in similar circumstances, it was 'greatly exaggerated'. Of its desirability, I cannot take an impartial view.

In such a matter it is easy for the memory to err and it will be best to quote from a letter written at the time. But the main characters must be introduced, as in the prologue of a play. J. C. Field was the secretary of the Lima Y.M.C.A. and he was holding mail against my arrival there. Don Julio Navarro Monzó was the deputy editor of *La Nación*; at that time *La Nación* and *La Prensa* of Buenos Aires, and *El Mercurio* of Chile were the great newspapers of Latin America. Professor Erasmo Braga of Rio de Janeiro was a very distinguished Brazilian, and I was privileged some years later to be the joint author with him of a work on religion in Brazil. Dr. Webster Browning was a well-known North American educationist, resident formerly in Chile and at the time in Buenos Aires. All these are now, alas, dead.

Early in December 1928 I arrived in Lima from the remote interior and took a room in a hotel. As soon as I had secured it, I set out, bought a street plan, identified the Y.M.C.A., a few blocks off, and made for it. But a rather amusing thing happened when I got there. I will recite it as it is reported in my journal.

'On the stairs I saw Mr. Field, the Secretary, whom I had met at Piriapolis [Uruguay]. I went up to him and offered my hand. I don't think I've ever seen a man look so utterly taken aback in my life. Another American who was with him asked him if he was feeling ill. Finally, I said again, "You remember me, don't you?" or something of that sort. "But," he half stammered out, "I understand you are dead," or something very like that. I saw or guessed at once what had happened and I could not help replying, "Well, I'm exceedingly sorry not to be able to oblige you in any way and it's quite possible you have conclusive evidence of the fact that's unknown to me." He had more or less come round by then and told me the facts.

'The rumour has apparently got about in South Brazil and among all my friends of the River Plate region that I have been killed by a savage. Don Julio Navarro Monzó got hold of it and communicated it to Lima. I wrote to Navarro Monzó from La Paz, but of course I did not say I was alive and if he inferred the fact, he did not communicate it to La Paz where I am not known. His letter, here at the Y.M.C.A. in Lima, says "Your letter of 11th October caused me unspeakable joy. On arriving in Buenos Aires, after my journey in Bolivia and after passing about a month in the north of Argentina, the first news that they gave me was, in effect, that you had been assassinated by the Indians in Amazonas. It seems that Dr. Braga of Rio de Janeiro, wrote in this sense to Dr. Browning and thus the news began to spread. I myself, in two gatherings, one in Buenos Aires, and the other in Montevideo, made reference to this sad news, with detailed obituary references to you, my dear friend! Thank God we still have you here, serving the interests of His Kingdom . . ."

'The incident has caused considerable interest in the city [Lima] where it had got known. I have got an invitation to a reception tomorrow to meet President-elect Hoover when he arrives here.'

Things had to be done quickly. I found a cable office open and set the wires humming. Don Julio had published in *La Nación* a distressingly flattering account of my character and work on the principle of *de mortuis nil nisi bonum*, and I followed up my cable by a lengthy letter refuting his encomiums. President-elect Herbert Hoover insisted that I should go to the American embassy and spend a lot of time with him, the Ambassador and their staff. Hoover asked me whether I would like to do that particular journey again and having received my negative, remarked, 'Try politics; it's better for the health.' Augusto B. Leguía, then President/Dictator of Peru, asked me to see him and we had a pleasant chat.

On the very day on which I had arrived in Lima, J. C. Field, having previously made some enquiries of his own and having formed a pessimistic forecast, had gone to the British Consulate with all the letters to me unopened, and discussed the situation. The consul had agreed to take over the whole matter and to communicate in suitable terms with the Foreign Office and through them with my relatives. We just stopped him in time from taking what would at the best have been alarming action. No one had worried very much at home because I had not exceeded the time for that particular journey, during which I expected to be incommunicado.

In spite of many enquiries, the origin of the rumour was never cleared up. There was a lot of dirty work on the Madeira at that time and several Brazilians, including one of the best-known *patrões* on the river had been killed by Indians (a *patrão* is an employer/land-owner). So far as I know, no European was involved. Reprisals were launched and on some tributaries there was some very unpleasant fighting.

I have never shaken off the odd reputation which gathered around this incident. Years later, in the early 1960s, I was reminded of it by men of the younger generation in Buenos Aires who had heard of it from their fathers. Early in 1968, when I was in Geneva for the World Council of Churches, I overheard a Latin American acquaintance giving an account of the incident to a French friend, in terms that were 'greatly exaggerated'.

They say that death is the end of a chapter: I conclude this one.

CHAPTER III

A Tramp on Walkabout

AS the 1920s drew to a close my views began to change. I was particularly concerned over the feuding and in-fighting which went on in the Worldwide Evangelisation Crusade to which I was loosely attached. Correspondence with others, my contemporaries, revealed the same malaise. I had imagined that an organisation directed by pious people would be above all this. I had thought there would be no room for prejudice and favouritism in a group devoted to proclaiming the Gospel to the ends of the earth. It was a shock to learn that I was quite mistaken.

Since then I have learned that those who feel and believe deeply are often difficult to live with. Holy people on holy tasks are unholily quarrelsome. They are not more so than the rest of us; rows, usually due to personal antipathies, are common in business, professional and religious life. The mission inspired by the devotion of C. T. and Mrs. Studd had started in a blaze of enthusiasm, but 'tasks in hours of insight willed, must be through hours of gloom fulfilled'. So I have found it. As the poet puts it: 'Will and energy though rare, are yet far, far less rare than love.' It is all the harder to gauge the real situation when one has to emerge from a tropical forest to do so.

I did a lot of rethinking. I began to realise that I moved in very limited circles where people judged one another with uncompromising severity. I began to see that the Gospel had implications for society and not merely for individuals. Yet I strove to keep a balance and still prayed fervently that I might be a messenger of truth to any whose heart God had opened. This period just preceded the great economic depression of 1929–31, the effects of which were felt even in the far interior of South America. It was inevitable, therefore, that I should reflect in my solitude on the inequalities and inequities of the world. I began to perceive that in my free and self-reliant existence I knew little of the grim pressure of poverty and the impossibility of most people escaping from it. I took care of myself in a harsh and hostile environment, but I was beginning to realise that generally men cannot do this alone. I rarely felt the need of friends but in my heart I knew that I must love the brethren and that civilisation and progress were built on interdependence. I was not devoid of natural resourcefulness, and I had no right to live for myself: the Christian duty was for the strong to help the weak.

My first attempt to help my neighbour was a failure. I had crossed the interior border of Bolivia and was fooling around in the vast llanos and forests that lie between Trinidad and Santa Cruz de la Sierra, then the haunt of the Sirionó Indians whom I wished to identify. The whole area was terribly backward. The ox-cart with six to eight yoke in harness was the standard way of moving freight across the plains. In Santa Cruz there was not one paved street. There were broad alleys of mud with an open central 'drain', and high stepping-stones at the corners on which the ox-carts usually got stuck. There was much unrest at that time, over forty years ago, due to the revolt of the péons against the great absentee land-owners. The rebels seized and burned properties and the troops were called out. No one knew very clearly what it might lead to; in reality it was too much of a local affair to attract national attention. The rebel leaders invited me to join in the fight, because all men knew that I was an accurate shot.

I agreed to go with them but insisted that I would only shoot to wound and not to kill, because I was a foreigner: a logic which I have never been able to disentangle. I did shoot two majors and a colonel, but the rising soon collapsed and I found myself in prison.

I made myself comfortable there for ten days, sending out and hiring bedding and meals from the local hotel, as the custom then was. The Government took a lenient view and the British Legation were very helpful, so I was pardoned.

In prison I had met a young army officer who had got a few years for challenging and killing a senior colleague in a duel. Some months later I saw him in La Paz, and congratulated him on securing his freedom so soon. He explained that the authorities were satisfied so long as there was someone in prison, representing the crime, as one might say, and he had paid a poor relation to substitute for him. 'But,' I said, 'do you have a relation who is so poor, or who loves you so much, that he will spend several years "inside", whatever you pay?' 'Don't bother,' he replied, 'You think on Anglo-Saxon lines. Here things are different, why, the man has already sub-let the contract.'

There is much to be said for that kind of a society, but not quite enough. I began to see that the social regeneration of the public order was almost as difficult as the individual regeneration of a hardened sinner.

There was something to be said for doing a spell in prison. It afforded time for thought. I had, however, to cope with what is today called 'the problem of communication'. I solved it thus. When bored, I would catch a large cockroach from among the merry crowds on the floors and walls of the cell, write a message on a small piece of paper and insert the cockroach, with the message stuck to its back with a lick, into a large crack in the massive, old-fashioned wall. It would deliver its message to the officer who was next door, and thus we carried on an interesting if limited dialogue — at least that appears to be the modern term.

The crisis in the mission was severe. It broke up in South America, and ceased work in Brazil, its activities being taken over by another body, the Heart of Amazonia Mission. I left, looked elsewhere, and presently found myself on the research staff of the Survey Application Trust or, as it was usually called, the World Dominion Press. This was a small foundation, reasonably furnished with funds, which had various objectives. One of them was the collection of material about the progress of Gospel and Church in all the world, so that the areas of maximum need and the extent of the 'unfinished task' could be exposed. I was asked, as a start, to arrange for the production of a series of survey volumes covering the whole of Latin America from the Rio Grande to Cape Horn. I worked steadily at this for some eight years in the 1930s, travelling in all the republics of Mexico, Central and South America and the island states, looking for suitable writers, and, if I failed to find them, compiling the material myself. It was interesting work and I was later asked to apply my experience to countries outside the American continent.

On 3 December, 1935 I married Nancy Mary Arundel. She added a boy and a girl to the family. We acquired a home first in Enfield and then in Highgate. I was away for long periods and she brought up all my children with equal devotion. When World War II came we were again separated because of evacuation. Since 1945 we have travelled together, not only in Latin America but in other continents as well.

It is bad form for a man to praise his wife publicly. Be that as it may, my second marriage has been an unalloyed and deepening union. It was a true love-match and has so endured for thirty-five years. A man is supposed to mature when he grows old; in practice he either does this or his temper worsens. In my youth and middle career I was quite impossible, either very lonely and secretive, or dictatorial and domineering. My years in Amazonia or my nature, or both, had taught me to be uncommunicative, and to maintain a reticence, artificial in a home. I was not a martinet but I was efficient in small as much as in large affairs, and such people are apt to be inconsiderate, impatient and intolerant. Nancy understood all this instinctively, but *amor vincit omnia* and the years have deepened our mutual trust and love. A man could ask of God no lovelier gift, no better human source of strength and comfort. We had both been brought up to 'search the Scriptures'. With all my faults of character and excess of energy, I retain a wonder and an admiration for those who consistently practise the 'little nameless unrecorded acts of kindness and of love' which Wordsworth calls 'the best portion of a good man's life'. I have failed grievously here, but the words could have been written, without reservation, of my wife.

We did our best to cope with the children. They are all grown up now. My eldest son, Martyn, and my daughter, Margaret, alone are married. They produce children, thus keeping the race going and adding to the population problem. To take them in order: Martyn, formerly a worker-priest, is a Community Relations Officer in the borough of Ealing; Fred is a writer, a poet and a critic;[1] Richard quit banking for computerising; Margaret, my only daughter, is married to a clergyman in Lancashire, the Rev. R. Jackson.

In early days I travelled much alone; indeed I was nearly always alone in the sense that I had no travelling companion. Often I could only obtain necessary data by personal visits to remote parts. The post was very slow and uncertain. Moreover in those days anyone who went about 'numbering the people' was suspect. This was particularly true among those Protestant missions which worked in republics where there was persecution. But it was also true of the Roman Catholic authorities.

For this reason I never took notes in the presence of anyone whom I was questioning. I memorised all the headings on my schedules and framed a conversation which would introduce them all in such form as not to arouse suspicion but elicit a factual reply. All this was quite easy and simply required a modicum of ingenuity and a retentive memory. I spoke both Spanish and Portuguese fluently and I read as much of the literature as I could, until I had, for a foreigner, a pretty reasonable knowledge of the history, customs, economy, politics and culture of every republic.

[1] *Title Deeds and Other Poems*, Longman, 1961; *A Vision of Reality: A Study of Liberalism in Twentieth-Century Verse*, Chatto and Windus, 1965.

Every now and then my movements would be interrupted by some *pronunciamiento* or revolution. Normal communications were suspended, and a prudent man kept out of the line of fire between rival combatants occupying, say, the opposite sides of a plaza. People accepted violence more philosophically than they do today, although there is plenty of it in Latin America. Latin Americans have a verb, *desgraciarse*. It hardly means to disgrace oneself, but rather to have had bad luck. A man who has had to shoot his neighbour is said to have had bad luck—*se ha desgraciado*. The mortal fighting which occupied much of the 1950s in Colombia is commonly known as *La Violencia*. Young people in the universities today talk much of upsetting the old regimes by revolution, as though this were something new, a revolution to end revolutions: all revolutions nowadays are supposed to be that. But those who plan to seize the power through force had best not talk too much.

The rebels of the 1920s and 30s were frequently justified. Some of the dictatorships sacrified almost all freedom to an order which was almost a tyranny. Juan Vicente Gomez of Venezuela, one of the most famous dictators in all Latin America, although amiable to talk with, was a cruel man. Getulio Vargas of Brazil was quite a different type, but in the end he made himself unpopular and committed suicide. I knew both these, but much preferred Vargas. Simón Bolívar, the Liberator, considered Latin America ungovernable, and he died a disillusioned man having declared that he had ploughed the sea. Abraham Lincoln's words apply very much to Latin America: '... It has long been a grave question whether any government not too strong for the liberties of its people, can be strong enough to maintain its existence in great emergencies...'

A Uruguayan friend once described the position to me as follows. He said, roughly, 'You should explain to your friends that the key to Latin American politics lies in the fact that people are feminine, just the opposite of what you might think.' (He was, of course, exaggerating.) 'In politics our people act like women; they follow a man. They aren't interested in constitutions and laws: these simply provide the politicians with something to talk about. They are interested in a man. Since the time comes when a girl has to give up her boys in order to choose one man, so do the people, and he becomes the man they follow, the Jefe, the President, the Caudillo, or the Dictator.'

I knew a Brazilian whom we will call Pereira. He told me that he was going in for politics in a big way and was founding a new party. I asked him what his party stood for. 'Pereirism' he replied, What processes of law or administration did he intend to pursue in order to apply his policies? 'I don't know about processes of law, my method is Pereirisation.' What party name were his followers going to bear? 'Pereirists.'

Modern conflicts have been over more important questions of principle. The students of the universities, perpetual scenes of protest and revolt, have genuine grievances. The Aprista movement was founded by Haya de la Torre, over forty years ago, on a coherent and sincere basis of idealism, economic reform and democratic progress, but it never took root outside of Peru, its native heath. It is no longer correct to assume that the Church, the Army and the landowners are in perpetual league to keep things as they are. Castroism, Marxism and Mao-ism have many adepts and the revolutions of today have usually something of reforming depth and intent about them. Latin America is struggling to grasp and absorb the truth in one of Churchill's great wartime speeches in the Commons, 'Democracy is no harlot to be picked up in the street by a man with a tommy-gun.'[2]

The constant changes of the Presidency and Government used to lead to some quaint situations. I once hired a taxi in one of the small Central American republics. The driver was a regular Jehu and erratic as well. When paying him off I said to him, 'You ought to be a little more careful because you ply for hire.' He was a short man, about five feet four inches, but he drew himself up with great pride, 'Sir,' he said, 'I am a General-Commandant, but we lost the revolution.'

I began this phase of my work by travelling in the Andes all the way from Chile to Venezuela. Subsequently I returned to the east coast and trotted around first in Argentina, Uruguay and Paraguay, and then in north-east, central and southern Brazil. Later, I made my way through Mexico, Central America and the island republics.

There were but few roads and railways in the Andes and only irregular air-services. Wherever possible, I bought a seat on some lorry already overloaded, and clung on to the nearest sack or the Indian sitting next to me. No one could travel in those parts without being impressed by the tremendous feats of engineering which had opened up these republics, even to a limited extent. The Central Railway of Peru climbs to nearly 16,000 feet and, so the handbooks say, has sixty-six tunnels and fifty-nine bridges. It was the masterpiece of the railway engineer Henry Meiggs, and built between 1870 and 1893. Another line of metre gauge which reaches almost the same height is the branch-line of the Antofagasta and

[2] Hansard, 8 December, 1944.

Bolivia Railway to Potosí and Sucre. Lake Titicaca, 12,500 feet up, is traversed by steamer which joins Guaquí in Bolivia with Puno in Peru, a journey of about twelve hours. Such travelling is much more interesting than the air but it requires time.

Today no one goes the hard way, except to reach remote mountain villages which are off the beaten track. The ubiquitous camión, or the Land-Rover, climbs the heights or bores into the valleys. But only a few years ago it was not so.

Some trails were so difficult that no *arriero* (muleteer) would risk his animals. This was the case with the Via del Norte that led westwards out of the Amazon basin and over the mountains, eventually to reach the Pacific Coast. I encountered this little obstacle in trying to travel by this route from Yurimaguas on the Huallaga to Moyobamba in the foothills of the northern Andes of Peru. Yurimaguas is a centre for balsa traffic, but this only moves downstream and I was going into the sierra.

The journey had to be done on foot, and the usual cargo for an Indian was about 100 lb. carried on the back in a sling from the forehead. Passengers could also be carried and women usually were. In this case a small stool is placed within a light crate or box and the whole is slung from the Indian's forehead, the passenger facing the rear. One *carguero* (porter) will usually carry a woman all day, but a man must hire two, and there is a record of an American of such obesity that he had to take four. I preferred to walk, or rather to struggle on. There are over a hundred places between Yurimaguas and Moyobamba where streams or rivers with raging currents must be forded. One formidable and menacing ford is on a river called the Pomayacu. It forms a great pool dammed up by a horseshoe-shaped ledge of rock over which the current pours. The ledge is thirty to forty yards long, about two feet wide and very slippery. Below it a steep surface of smooth rock leads to a fatal sheer drop of about 150 feet.

There were several in our party. The leading *carguero* opened the proceedings by announcing that the post-carrier had been swept down only ten days ago and killed. Someone else then remembered that there was a safer portage several hours upstream. But a 'safer portage several hours upstream' did not interest me; the day was hot, the rain heavy and the river rising. I cut a stout staff, said a short prayer and put my best foot forward, looking onwards and not downwards. There were some narrow shaves but we all made it. Around there the Eucharis lily grew in lovely clusters, and its star-white flowers amid the monotonous green of the undergrowth seemed to beckon us on.

Elsewhere the trail is a real stinker. One has to haul oneself by creepers teeming with ants, almost vertically up the rocks in a tremendous climb for hour after hour, the only reward being the view of the far distant and boundless plain left behind in the east. However, we made Moyobamba in five days; ten are good going; it is said that some enthusiast once made it in three. The rain and mud made a quick passage for us impossible. A bath in the little hospital of the Scottish mission in the small town soon restored me to working order; I had acquired along the way a mixed assortment of bruises, cuts, bugs, dirt, fever, and fatigue.

The customary way to travel where there were no better facilities was by mule. The Indians sometimes use their llamas, but they are slow; they only carry sixty to seventy pounds and are not animals for the inexperienced. A good mule should make about six or seven leagues (eighteen or twenty-one miles) per day. You must hire an *arriero* whose duty it is to manage the expedition generally, to catch and saddle the animals in the morning; to load and unload the baggage; to find pasture for the beasts at night; and to cook for the party. In most places food can be bought, but not always, so it is well to have reserve rations.

If you cannot hire and have to purchase an animal, proceed carefully with local advice if obtainable. I once went into a market and announced that I wanted to buy a mule. Immediately the market hummed with men who had model mules to sell. One peasant said that he had an animal 'without defects'; he would bring it along that very afternoon. The mule turned out to be a sturdy enough beast, but a worm had eaten away a part of its lower lip, giving it a repulsive appearance. I reminded the man that he had promised a mule 'without defects'. He thought for a moment, smiled charmingly, and replied, 'I thought your honour wanted a beast to carry yourself or your cargo. Now I see you want a mule to whistle to you when you are lonely.' I bought the mule; a man who could improvise an answer like that deserved success.

A mule is sturdier than a horse although not so pleasant to ride. A good mule has great powers of endurance if well cared for, and this is important since a long journey may be a matter of weeks rather than days. But a horse has an advantage if there are many rivers to be crossed. Mules sometimes lose their nerve when swimming a river, turn suddenly downstream and come to grief. This happened to me once in Ecuador. A horse can be kept on a straight swim by throwing stones on its downstream side. Here and there in my journal I have noted down some of the amusing wise-cracks of the *arrieros*, e.g. when selecting a mule hang your hat on its haunch;

if it stays there, the beast is too thin. The best way to make a mule move is to fall off it. Do not suppose that a mule's ears are made for hearing; Balaam's ass only spoke. Do not let your baggage slip under a mule's belly unless the beast is reversible, and so on.

When I first visited the now celebrated ruins of Machu Picchu, the railway from Cuzco which today carries thousands of tourists was only in the early stages of building, and travel was by mule. The trail went as far as a spot known as La Maquina[3] and there one crossed the river. This was done by traversing a rope bridge: there was one rope to keep your feet on, two to hold on to, and the tearing torrent beneath. There was no proper bridge and no nice road up for the tourist buses, as there is today, but one scrambled up the steep sides of the mountain as best one could. At the top, by much searching I found an Indian, speaking only Quechua, one wife and one donkey. So I had the whole place virtually to myself.

The story of Machu Picchu has been often told. The conquering Spaniards sought it and could not find it, and small blame to them for armies could march up and down the gorge without suspecting its existence. According to Hiram Bingham who discovered it in 1911-12, it was built about A.D. 800. The Quechua tribes of the valley of Cuzco suffered some sudden disaster then, possibly an incursion of barbarian hordes. A remnant saved themselves by fleeing northwards, hiding among the almost inaccessible heights, and there building Machu Picchu. Manco Capac, the first of the conquering dynasty of the Incas, is supposed to have been born there and to have led his people out to reconquer Cuzco. By 1300 Cuzco had become so evidently the capital of the Inca Empire that Machu Picchu was abandoned. When the Spaniards came the priests and sacred virgins were sent for refuge to the already forgotten city, and they and it disappear from history.

This is not the place to describe the town and fortress which have been admirably restored. Much of the fascination lies in the incomparable site, for the ruins are on a great projection of rock, a kind of Gibraltar, thrusting out into the valley, so that the place is protected by the tremendous ravine on three sides. Far below, thousands of feet, the Urubamba pours down to join the Ucayali and the Amazon. On one side only, towards the south, the plateau or isthmus is connected with the mountain range of a slope carefully terraced in the Inca style.

On my first visit in 1928 I wrote as follows with the exuberance of youth: 'As I climbed the final few yards, toiling up the steep steps that give access

[3] Today one leaves the train at Puente Ruinas.

to the site, and sought a point of vantage, it was impossible to restrain an involuntary exclamation. In front stretched a line of peaks clothed with the spotless mantle of nature's perpetual and changeless ermine. I sat on the mighty stones, and behind me again the summits were white with undisturbed and virgin snow. Below and around, and on all the intervening slopes was the dank and struggling vegetation of tropical damp and heat. The whole climatic scale of nature was spread out as a panorama in a vision. The snow-caps sparkled and glowed with the imperial irridescence of the morning light . . .'

The highest peaks are very often hidden in clouds except at sunrise, so it is as well to spend a night in the little tourist hotel, run by the Peruvian Government, just outside the entrance to the ruins.

On my first visit I slept a night among the ruins, collecting dry ferns and bracken and dossing down in one of the old houses, for I had left my gear below. The next day I returned to La Maquina and found that I could not hire animals anywhere. So I walked all the way up the Urubamba valley, over forty miles, resting at Ollantaytambo where there is another Inca ruin. I started in the small hours and reached the village of Urubamba in the evening. Although tired, I would have gone farther because there was typhoid in the place, but no one could tell me of a good *posada* (inn). So I slept in the Urubamba inn.

Before the motor-road was built from Cali in Colombia to Bogotá, or air-services established, I once travelled out of the Cauca valley, over the Central Cordillera, down into the tremendous valley of the Magdalena and up the other side to Bogotá. We hired animals in Armenia and off we went over the Quindio Pass, getting magnificent views of the Nevada de Tolima, a superb extinct volcano of over 18,000 feet, glowing in the brief but fiery sunset. We slept at the top of the pass, posting guards because of bandits; even today it is said to be inadvisable to traverse the motor-road after dark.

These mule journeys were very agreeable, but today many of the old sites can be reached by more modern transport. The tourist must be attracted and his path smoothed. Mexico is famous for the great ruins of its former civilisations: some can be visited from Mexico City within the day. Oaxaca, some 330 miles from Mexico City, is an excellent centre for Monte Albán and Mitla, not to speak of numerous fascinating Zapotec villages. The Maya ruins are mostly in Yucatan, Campeche and Chiapas. Places such as Chichen Itzá and Uxmal, are visited by thousands, and Palenque and Bonompak by hundreds of travellers. When I first went to

Uxmal, I had the place to myself, and this was because a rather ripe skunk had wandered around during the night and I was the only person in the party who was prepared to ignore this olfactory inconvenience.

The Maya civilisation first arose in Guatemala and Honduras, but after four centuries and for reasons which are still conjectural, it collapsed. The towns were abandoned and the population, or at least a creative minority, migrated to Yucatan, and with prodigious skill and energy built the cities which fascinate the visitor today. There is much still to be discovered about the Mayas, but we know that, although they had neither llama nor horse, and, strangely, did not use the wheel, they produced a learned line of astronomers, mathematicians, priests, and artists. They were obsessed with time and worried incessantly over it. They used the zero long before it was common in Europe, and their calendar was much more accurate than the Julian or Gregorian systems. Experts say it was only 0.000069 of a day out of sidereal time in a year.

Copán in Honduras is considered their earliest city. I first visited it in the 1930s; since then the site has been cleared by the Carnegie Institute and is now maintained by the Government. I reached it by the mule trail from Chiquimula in Guatemala, and the Honduranean visa and special stamps took up five pages of my passport. I had a good look at the place and slept a night or two there. Then I went on to Santa Rosa, and from there got a plane to San Pedro Sula, and thence a bus to the capital, Tegucigalpa. This was emphatically a case of two sides of the triangle, but there was no plane or motor-road direct to Tegucigalpa.

The Indians of the high Andes are addicts of coca which is grown in the Yungas region of Bolivia. They mix the leaf with a little potash which can be bought in crude form in the local markets. It is claimed that by slightly numbing the senses, it enables a man to endure better the tough tests that the great altitudes impose. I have tried it often and like it. But the experts also say that the habit has a generally narcotic effect and accounts for a good deal of the apathy that characterises remote mountain communities in the Andes. People live at high altitudes in these republics, and it is said that in Peru there is a village which stands at over 17,000 feet. Today, many Quechua Indians are suffering a revulsion of feeling and are leaving their hard mountain refuges for the softer valleys or the coastal towns, particularly Lima itself. Thus arises the familiar problem of the urban dispossessed which can be vividly seen in the *barriadas* (slums) of the capital.

I crossed north Peru from Moyobamba to the Pacific coast, that is from east to west across the north of the country. Much of this can today be done by road and all by plane. The route traversed the great *quebrada* or gorge of the Marañon. The way from Moyobamba to Chachapoyas is wild and grand, the trail winding through the mountain passes. I hired fresh animals there and took the path to Cajamarca, about 9,000 feet, the old colonial town where Atahualpa, 'the last of the Incas', was betrayed by the signed consent of the priest Valverde into the hands of Francisco Pizarro, in spite of having carried out his promise to fill a room with gold for his ransom.

The trail passed not far from the little-known Inca fortress of Cuelap, one of many ruins which are only today being discovered. Beyond there, we slept at Leimebamba about 8,000 feet up in the central Cordillera. The night was clear and brilliant and the sky was studded with diamonds. I thought of Arnold's lines:

> The silent peaks but to the stars are known,
> But to the stars and the cold lunar beams,
> Alone the sun rises, and alone
> Spring the great streams.

We rose at about three a.m., the stars had gone, and rain was falling steadily, to turn to snow higher up. We had to cross by the pass of Calla Calla. This is not particularly high, somewhat over 12,000 feet, but it is notorious in the whole region for clouds and storms, mud, cold, wind and general discomfort. The trail was in a disreputable state, ponded with water, foul with slime, and furrowed laterally like deep corrugated iron by the regular tramp of scores of mules. The dawn found the *arriero* and myself still toiling up the mountainside, hemmed in by spurs of the main range with their frowning sentinel cliffs.

When we reached the summit the sun broke through for a few minutes and shone, stimulating and bright. A biting wind blew from the springs of the dawn, piercing, steady and keen. The country was *puna*, a rock-strewn moorland with patches of snow in the hollows, where not so much as a goat was nosing among the boulders, and only an inquisitive condor came soaring over our heads and having taken one disappointed look, disappeared into the south.

The divide is a well-defined ridge, and on crossing it the western mountainside presently falls away in one vast panorama. It is not broken up by spurs and valleys, but stretches almost in a single slope down to the Marañon running through its own gorge at about 3,000 feet. We could see it far below, but not for long, because the great valley became filled with whirling white clouds, unspotted in purity, the changing cirques and glaciers of the imagination, as though you were present at the mystery of things that escape analysis, the movement of primeval and eternal causes, the struggle of creative conflicts, the stir of the forces whence issued the world.

The *arriero* emerged from behind a rock where he had been brewing coffee. I came back to earth, and by evening we had crossed the Marañon at Balsas. We slept in that hot and airless village, to the gloating satisfaction of the hordes of starving mosquitoes and of that dangerous protozoan parasite, Leishmania.

During these years, communications were being steadily developed in the Andes by rail, motor-road and air. The early motor-roads through the *cordilleras* were one-way, that is you could go from A to B on Monday, Wednesday and Friday, and from B to A on Tuesday, Thursday and Saturday. Sometimes they were simply the enlargement of a mule-trail which wound its way through the wildest sierras, a wall of rock on one hand, a hungry precipice on the other. Some of us used to travel with a drill, sticks of dynamite, fuse and wire, so as to clear a way if rocks had fallen. I once profited from this practice when held up by a vast landslide across the Transandine Road in the Cordillera de Merida in Venezuela. There was a cavalcade of cars and I became explosively popular.

If you take a mule on a mountain trail, let it find its own way with a loose rein. Pack-horses and mules get accustomed to treading on the outside of a mountain track, because, if they do not, the cargo may bump against the wall of rock and below the *quebrada* (dry gorge or river-bed) awaits its prey. Therefore let the animal do its best while you think of a number, double it . . .

A railway runs north from Quito almost to the Colombian border. For some distance it is easy going, for it meanders over the plateau and the profane say that the politicians and the surveyors were paid by the kilometre, so curves were as profitable as they are with ladies who have something of their own to sell. I traversed it shortly after it was opened and the train would run off the line: it was put back by a crew carried for the purpose, and as speed was only eight m.p.h. or so, no harm was done.

The line passed above the beautiful Lake Imbabura. The volcano of that name rose majestic on the other side, while in the far north were the snowclad summits of Cotacachi: it was a splendid panorama but we did not stop there.

A few days later I returned to Quito. I went early to Otavalo station, found the engine-driver in a siding, and rustled some currency notes. I explained that I recognised that we had to run off the line because the wretched engineers had built it so badly, but there were some spots which were more interesting than others such as ... It was no doubt a coincidence but we did run off just at the best viewpoint overlooking the lake. To get the derailed coaches back took forty-five minutes and I took some nice pictures.

In Bolivia we once lost a large Buick in which I had hired a place as a passenger from Sucre to Cochabamba. The car belonged to a 'Turco', actually a Lebanese, called Seleme. It was the extreme end of the dry season and he had urgent need to get to Cochabamba. We left in the early evening, climbed up the *cordillera* and presently we could glimpse the *quebrada* of the Chaquimayo, down which we had to pick our way. We were making all haste because in Sucre it was said that rain had already fallen in the hills. About halfway down we stopped and, in the moonlight, we thought we could see an unusual gleam at the bottom of the gorge. We drove on a little and stopped again. Then, indeed, we stared at each other with a wild surmise, for we could detect far below the roar of waters pouring down in a mad, unbridled torrent. We were too late. Down the *quebrada* was rolling a chaos of stones and mud mingled with the floods which, from a thousand sources in the Andes, the Amazon is said to deposit in the Atlantic at 60,000 tons per second. It was a hard prospect for my friend the 'Turk' and his car.

By the early morning the flood had passed down the valley. We followed it, but the 'road' which is roughly cleared when the dry season begins, had been washed out, and we made slow progress. In the late afternoon we reached a more populated region and Indian huts were in evidence. And then, just as we were rejoicing in some signs of civilisation, the end came. We got stuck in a sea of mud and rocks. Nothing would budge the car and, tired and apprehensive, we decided that we had no option, but to take everything we could out of it, and wait for the dawn.

I lay down on my suitcase with a typewriter for a pillow, in one of the Indian huts whose roof leaked like a sieve. I had a bout of malaria, so I didn't bother about the rats which raced over my *poncho*. After midnight, through feverish dreams, I again heard that solemn and sinister roar of the waters triumphantly pouring down the valley, an awesome and memorable funeral progress. In the morning the waters abated but the car was a wreck. I was the only one of our party who could speak Quechua so I scoured around the village, and returned with thirty-five men and seven mules and we hauled the Buick out of the mud.

We were only a few hours from Puente Arce, where there is an old suspension bridge over the Rio Grande and a telegraph station. At last I got a message through to a friend of Seleme's in Cochabamba and he sent out a truck. We arranged terms, and I took the hat round for Seleme. I was too ill to help work on the car, so we said goodbye. It was a big loss for the man.

Indeed, the wine of life is sometimes sweet, but often bitter, in these remote parts. Philosophers may deride the mad pursuit of material progress and wish us all to be as content with tubs as Diogenes was with his. But mankind is made of frailer stuff. I prefer to rejoice with those who do rejoice, and weep with those who weep. It is recorded in my simple journal how one day I asked a widow in north-east Brazil whose husband had been killed by *cangaceiros* (bandits) how many children she had. She had eleven, she said. 'Seven are living in heaven, and four are dying on earth.' I welcome every sign of 'development', especially when it reaches right down to the homes of the people. Meanwhile, *sunt lacrimae rerum et mentem mortalia tangunt.*

In actual fact, wine is rarely, if ever, seen in the *cordillera*, except in the homes of the very rich. The popular drink is *chicha*, absorbed by the Indians and particularly agreeable to the palate of the *cholos*, or mestizos[4] in Bolivia.

Chicha is thus made in the *cholo* area around Cochabamba. A man sets out for the market with two or three days for the journey. He stops at certain houses and hands out maize for the old women to chew. He recovers the resulting product, pays for the labour with something edible, goes on to the next house and hands out some more. The masticated and desiccated product is brought into Cochabamba where a tax is levied on it and it is sold to other parties who by boiling, cooling and fermentation, possibly adding a dead fowl to the great clay jar, convert it into *chicha*. It is claimed that no other process can produce a final result of the requisite quality. Up and down the Andes there are hundreds of *chicha*

---

[4] Mestizo (Portuguese, *mestiço*) means a half-breed, Indian and European.

bars. No doubt the practice will die out with the spread of modern manners. *Chicha*, which I have often sampled, is not an unpleasant drink; it is certainly intoxicating. In other words, the savoury as well as the fermenting power of Granny's saliva is not to be despised.

On this note I take leave of these mountain scenes, for in the 1930s I travelled in all the republics, in the south (Argentina and Uruguay), in Brazil and Paraguay, in Mexico, Central America and in the island states, Cuba, Haiti and the Dominican Republic.

It was exciting to be in Mexico in the 1930s for it was then that the basic anticlericalism of the Mexican Revolution took an anti-religious turn. This did not last long but it was severe. In 1934–5 when I spent several months in the country, there had been no public religious services in the state of Tabasco for seven years, and conditions were not much better in Querétaro and some other states. About then the Cathedral of Villahermosa, the capital of Tabasco, was deliberately pulled down, but it was of no historical interest. The extreme rigour of the campaign against the clergy can be judged by the following figures which I compiled and published at the time, and which have not been questioned. Before 1926 there were 4,493 priests in Mexico licensed to practise their calling; in 1934 there were permits from the authorities for 307, but owing to local difficulties there were only 190 who were episcopally licensed. I called on the Archbishop of Mexico in hiding, every precaution having been taken.

This extreme state of affairs did not last long, and the situation later became pretty normal and has been so for many years. Mexico itself has become economically one of the strongest of the Latin American republics, but there is still a gulf between the rich and the poor, in spite of all that the Government has done for education and rural reconstruction. The Constitution of 1917 is the basic document and its regulations in regard to religion, the rights and status of foreigners, the nationalisation of oil and of certain kinds of property remain unchanged. In practice the many difficult situations in regard to land, the practice of Christian worship, and the kinds of business which non-Mexicans could pursue, were solved by compromise and adjustment. But the Mexican Revolution was a turning-point for the nation which in the 1940s began to enter a new era of economic development and prosperity, although the problem of the haves and have-nots is far from solved. It is often asked why other republics with a large Indian population do not follow Mexico's example. Guatemala, Ecuador, Peru and Bolivia are such countries, but in none of these did conditions exist comparable to those in Mexico at the end of the 'Porfirian'[5] era.

The anti-religious phase of the Revolution produced its crop of ridiculous incidents. Religious services in the open were forbidden. I record in my journal a summary of a newspaper report about an affair in the state of Querétaro. A fervent 'revolutionary' couple had a baby. They assembled their friends in the main plaza of the little town where they lived, and summoned the local secretary of the National Revolutionary Party. This official was a kind of nature-worshipper, and he 'baptised' the infant by focussing a ray of the sun on its forehead with a magnifying glass and announcing, 'I baptise you in the name of Zapata, Madero and Carranza, Amen.' (These three were among the early heroes of the militant phase of the Revolution.) Some of the local Catholics observed these proceedings from afar and sued the parents for causing a religious ceremony to be performed in public. My record does not show if they won the case.

Not long after that I had an interesting example of spontaneous religiosity. In the town of Aguascalientes, then a small place, the hotel manager indicated to me a gentleman standing in the street, and he used a phrase which meant that he had delusions of grandeur. He urged me to talk to him saying that he knew a lot about religion and liked a religious discussion. I accosted the man and presently turned the conversation on to religious beliefs. The man at once said that he could speak with authority because he was, in truth, God on earth, or at least in Aguascalientes. 'But,' I said, 'if that is so, if I may be so rude, how is it that you are so poorly dressed?' 'Ah,' he replied, 'that is easy to answer. Do you not see that there are three of us to feed?'

During this decade (1930–9) I revisited Brazil several times, because the collection of sociological and religious data in that vast republic is not easily done in one fell swoop. To comment on these journeys, particularly in Rio de Janeiro, the state of São Paulo and adjacent areas, would be tiresome since they are well-known, but a few experiences in the north-east and in the south may help to show the astonishing amalgam of races and customs which is Brazil. There was no Brasilia then; but years later I was present at its official inauguration.

The north-east, the 'Bulge' of Brazil was in an unhappy state in the 1920s and 1930s. About a quarter of the country's population live here, but in spite of the revolution in communications, there is still much

---

[5] José Porfirio Diaz was President and dictator of Mexico from 1876 to 1910.

social misery. Illiteracy is about fifty per cent and reaches over ninety per cent in the backward parts. The average income is distressingly low. Sugar has long lost out to the more southern states. Cotton is grown, but the opportunity has been seized elsewhere and São Paulo now produces about half the Brazilian crop. Cacao still comes from southern Bahia. The whole north-east area is today the concern of a vast federal development scheme.

The region, especially all that great zone which stretches south from Piauí to Bahia, is remorselessly scourged by periodical droughts. The most terrible of the last hundred years was that of 1877–9 when about 180,000 persons died. There have been years of *secca* (drought) at intervals throughout this century, the worst being those of 1915 and 1919. There is no clear agreement on the causes of these devastating visitations. The Federal Government has given special attention to the region through the Sudene corporation, and schemes of irrigation have been carried through on a massive scale. In the old days when a *secca* hit the north-east the *flagelados* (persecuted ones) fled to the Amazon basin. Since the phenomenal development of São Paulo in the last forty years they have gone south. But if they can return they do so, in spite of the local saying that in Ceará no fortune ever reaches the grand-children.

On one journey I went out of my way with a friend to see the falls of Paulo Afonso. The setting of these furious cataracts is truly surprising. There are no tremendous mountain gorges such as the Marañon flows through. There is little or no humid tropical vegetation such as adds so much beauty to Iguazú. There are 1,600 miles of the São Francisco above the falls, and 200 below. When I was there, no one was about although there did exist, even then, a tiny power-house which collected a few thousand kilowatts for a small cotton mill in near-by Pedra. There was just a haze of spray seen from afar above the uninviting waste of the *caatinga* (scrub and dry bush), and then the sound of many waters, and then the hard rocky edge of the Mãe da Cachoeira, the greatest of the four main falls. There was a sheer drop of nearly 270 feet into the vast gorge below. But it was not the fall of my dream.

We gazed at this in silence for some fifteen minutes. We then stepped back to look for another viewpoint. 'A wonderful sight!' I remarked tritely to my companion, shouting above the roar of the waters. 'Yes', he shouted back, after a pause, 'but what's to stop it?' Enough had been said and we resumed silence.

Today nearly a million kilowatts are generated and a small township, Paulo Afonso, has grown up in this remote spot.

On another occasion I travelled in the north-east in a drought year, but it was not all that bad as drought years go. Such green as there is soon withers. Pools dry up and streams fail. Stagnant, slime-covered water is of more value than gold. The scorching rocks and barren soil reflect the pitiless heat. I met a family on the road. The eldest daughter had already gone to the city and the eldest son had left to seek his own work, probably at the price of freedom. The mother held a dying infant to her breast, other children were naked or in rags, crying for the cup of cold water. Only the shining lizards, with thoughtless swiftness, slipped over the stones.

In those years the region was notorious firstly for the *cangaça* (banditry) and secondly for the religious dictatorship of Padre Cicero. Both were in some degree a reaction against the domination of the *coroneis* (colonels, or self-styled powerful landowners).

Several of the best-known *cangaceiros* (bandits) took to the life because of quarrels growing out of the feuds between the landowning families who kept armed bands engaged in assaults and reprisals. Others maintained themselves for years by supporting in power corrupt local bosses and petty politicians, at a price. A whole literature has grown up in Brazil about these men. The most celebrated was Lampeão, that is, to give him his full name, Virgolino Ferreira da Silva who ranged over the *sertões*[6] from the early twenties to 1940 with varying numbers of followers, until he was finally despatched in a minor clash with Government troops. Legend surrounds such adventurers with an aura of drama and romance. It was only necessary to travel through north-east Brazil in those years to learn the reality. I have myself talked with too many who have lost property, wife, sons, limbs, and all faith in good order and government, to be deceived in this matter.

Father Cicero, Padre Cicero Romão Baptista, came to interior Ceará shortly after his ordination and died in 1934 at ninety years of age. He is commonly considered typical of Brazilian 'Messianism'. At different times and places prophets have arisen who have wielded immense influence over the common people, sometimes performing miracles, sometimes defending them against the landlords, pleading with the authorities for them to secure peace and protection from bandits. Father

---

[6] The *sertão* (plural, *sertões*) is semi-desert country sustaining, at best, a thorny, xerophytic vegetation.

Cicero did most of these things. At one time he afforded hospitality and shelter to Lampeão, in order, it is said, to secure a respite for the countryside and to defend his own position.

He was appointed as Vicar of Juàzeiro (Joaseiro) in 1872. This was a wretched hamlet of no importance, but today it is a respectable township of some 50,000 people, with some small but active business. His career was typical. The director of the theological college where he studied was opposed to his ordination, since he was regarded as an eccentric, but the bishop decided to admit him to the priesthood. He spent his early years in an individual crusade against the crying public evils of that most backward part of Brazil. He lived simply, he was chaste at a time when the clergy normally had 'families', he intervened in feuds, often with success, he refused payments for baptisms, marriages and funerals. In the terrible *secca* of 1877 he bought fertile land, establishing starving families on it, and constantly pressed the authorities for relief.

He soon became known far and wide. When I first met him, he was old, worn and tired, and it was hard to reconstruct his story from his own lips. Indeed, his latter career was very different from his early years. In 1889 there commenced a series of miracles which were held to be the special reward of his charitable and godly life. It was difficult to persuade him in his old age to speak of these.

All this led to extensive pilgrimages to Juàzeiro and valuable presents of land and money. Father Cicero suddenly became not merely a spiritual but a political force in the north-east. The Church authorities intervened and he was officially suspended from most of his priestly functions, but he refused to leave Juàzeiro. Troubles came to a head in 1913 when a government force was sent to bring him to heel. His people, led by *beatos* and *beatas* (pious fanatics, men and women) dug a trench around the town, and, armed with their inefficient weapons, and some help from *cangaceiros*, won a pitched battle and captured a field-gun. The dead on Father Cicero's side rose to life after three days; at least so it was subsequently said, but I never verified this interesting claim.

For years afterwards, his political power, let alone his spiritual authority, was undisputed. No one could hold a post of authority up country in Ceará unless he was known to have Father Cicero's support. He wielded more power than any combination of *coroneis* against him. In the middle 1920s his powers began to decline and his influence to fail. He was proud of his achievement, and he had accomplished much.

His own idea of his real importance was somewhat inflated. He told me that he had sent a telegram to Lloyd George to congratulate him, on Armistice Day 1918. This is understandable because at the height of his fame the people identified him with God the Father, the Son, or the Holy Spirit. Others were more inclined to simply add him to the list, and the *violeiro* (travelling poet and musician), João Mendes de Oliveira, thus summed up the matter:

> Only a simple poet am I,
> But I know that in this I do not lie—
> Padre Cicero, a Person is he
> Of the most holy Trinity.

But Father Cicero himself never accepted these startling theological attributions and rebuked those who expressed them. His legend continued for long years but is now dying out. As late as 1959 it was reported that 'Our Lord had appeared accompanied by Father Cicero' and people rushed off by train or road to Juàzeiro to witness so interesting a theophany. My correspondence and press clippings do not reveal the result.

In a small interior town of Brazil I witnessed another strange scene in which the clergy played a leading part. There had been much robbery in the place. A journalist owned, wrote, printed and published singlehanded a little local fortnightly, and he remarked that the Church ought to be more concerned for the state of society than it was.

The journalist and the local priest were enemies. The *cura* announced that he would preach on the evils of robbery, so next Sunday I went to hear him. After Mass, he mounted the pulpit and read a good sermon on the eighth commandment, 'Thou shalt not steal.' Before starting he produced a feather saying he would blow it out over the congregation and, doubtless guided by the Holy Spirit who was the very breath of God, it would fall on the head of the guilty.

The feather drifted to the west end where several of us were standing. I did not want trouble, so I opened a door and this created a draught which carried it back to the front of the nave. Here it began to circle down just over the head of the journalist who was seated on one of the church's few pews. At the crucial moment he tilted his head and puffed. What I would not stand for at the west end, he would not sit for at the east. Others copied and the feather fell to the ground in the aisle.

The scene was interesting but hardly improving in a church. However, life is dull in these little interior towns and some diversions are necessary. Moreover, either because of the publicity or for some other reason, the thieves disappeared from the neighbourhood, or at least ceased thieving.

The Church today, let it be clearly said, would not stand for such goings-on.

I take leave of Brazil with a few remarks on the south, which I have approached both from the neighbouring republics, Uruguay, Argentina and Paraguay and from within Brazil itself. The extreme south of the state of Rio Grande do Sul is a great grassland stretching away into Uruguay and Argentina. It is a land of the *gaucho*, the cowboy or plainsman with his *bombachas* (baggy trousers), poncho and his constant appetite for maté.

Rio Grande do Sul is important to Brazil for other reasons. The German immigration is over a century old, and, as in other states of the south, there is a large German-speaking population and many Italians. In some towns and villages it used to be hard to make oneself easily understood except in German or Italian. In World War II this led to difficulties, for some of the ministers of the German Lutheran Churches had been summoned back to Nazi Germany 'for further studies'. It was rightly felt that these German colonies could easily provide the nucleus of a Nazi penetration in South America, and special steps were taken to keep the situation under control. Schools, and even churches, were used as centres of subtle or even open Nazi propaganda. I knew the situation pretty well, because shortly before the outbreak of World War II, I had wandered quietly through the area, talking innocently in Portuguese, Italian or German with community leaders, and sizing up the political and religious position.

No one who happens to be in those parts, should fail to visit Iguazú (Iguaçú in Brazil). This is easy because there are excellent air-services from such capitals as Rio de Janeiro, Buenos Aires or Asunción. I got there first time by train from Buenos Aires to Posadas on the Rio Paraguay, second time by train from Asunción to Encarnación opposite Posadas, and third by air from S. Paulo on a plane which went on to Buenos Aires. From Posadas you can go to the falls either by road, or, which is pleasant, by a two-hundred mile trip upstream on the river.

The Iguazú Falls are the most beautiful of those I have seen, not excluding Niagara, the Victoria Falls, or even Paulo Afonso or La Guaira. Even so, they were not the falls of my dream. The river Iguaçú joins the Paraguay about twelve miles below the falls. Above them the Iguaçú is about two and a half miles wide, being broken up by wooded islets. Some of the falls plunge sheer over the 200-foot precipices; others, perhaps the more charming, are broken up by rocky ledges. They are grouped around a sharp, almost horseshoe bend in the river, and are easily and closely approached either from the Argentine or the Brazilian side. They are set in a forest of dense semi-tropical vegetation where begonias, orchids, tree-ferns and palms abound, and even today, in spite of the tourist invasion, myriads of brilliant butterflies flash among the trees. On the whole it is better to make a visit in the dry season, that is from August to November. When I first passed that way I was the only stranger and the only guest in the one little hotel which then existed.

The falls are one of those vast and magnificent scenes which reward the traveller in South America, and among such scenes it is a prince. This is due not only to the scale on which this masterpiece of nature's moods is cast, but to the constant variety, the unique setting, the roar of the waters and the stillness of the forest, the peace and the tumult, the order and disorder which form that tremendous scenario. The most striking of the falls is the San Martín which is an amphitheatre of the waters. It falls into a furious cauldron from which the spray rises in driven clouds, whirlpool and whirlwind striving in mortal embrace.

The historically minded should visit one or more of the Jesuit ruins which, in terms of today's frontiers, are in Argentina (Misiones) and Brazil. There were thirty of these 'reductions' on both sides of the River Paraguay, some eight being in that republic, some fifteen in Argentina and seven, the Sete Missões, in Brazil. The Jesuits originally settled farther to the north but were driven south in the seventeenth century through the depredations of the *bandeirantes* (roving adventurers) of São Paulo. Only a few remain in a reasonable state of preservation, the most impressive being San Ignacio, which is easily reached from Posadas. It has been declared a national monument. Although well-acquainted with their history, I was astonished by the extent and sophistication of the ruins of San Ignacio.

Much has been written of these Jesuit missions. They triumphed because they expressed a civilisation immeasurably superior to that of the primitive Guaraní Indians and they presented it as the immediate consequences of a fiat of Almighty God. The splendour of ritual worship dazzled the minds and attracted the devotion of the Indians, and the semi-communal organisation of labour introduced them to the elements of collective discipline. They attracted the enthusiastic commendation of Voltaire, of all people, and Protestant historians such as Southey and Robertson were eager in their praise.

The order for the expulsion of the Jesuits from the Spanish dominions was received in Buenos Aires in 1767. There were then well over 100,000 Indians gathered around the missions. Bereft of their spiritual guides, within a few years they drifted away from the 'reductions'. The land was overwhelmed by secondary growth and rank vegetation, and the cattle roamed at large through the wilderness. I have traced their ruins not only in these parts but, far away, in lower Bolivia, in that illimitable stretch of llano and forest which lies between Corumbá on the upper Paraguay and Santa Cruz de la Sierra. Everywhere the 'reductions' collapsed when their European priests left. No longer did the morning song of praise echo in the great sanctuaries or the evening Angelus summon the faithful to their prayers. The temples erected as a tabernacle for the Most High crumbled into ruins. On the deserted altars where the Very God of Very God had once been adored in the canon of the Mass, the forest birds rested awhile, or made their nests.

In the great church of São Miguel, of the Sete Missões in Rio Grande do Sul, I quite literally stirred up a hornet's nest. The roof of the church had entirely collapsed, and trees, ferns and shrubs were growing out of the crevices of the red sandstone of the walls. I climbed to the top of one of these and made my way along it gingerly. Before I was aware of being an intruder I had stirred up the nest and was badly stung on the back of the neck. I dropped my camera like a ball of lead and had the greatest difficulty in keeping my balance. There was eighteen inches breadth of wall under my feet and a drop of forty feet on either side. I perceived the importance of preserving my position, without analysing the situation from every possible angle. With a spurt of desperate energy I fought the brutes off; there was no option, because another sting would probably have knocked me out—and down. I then worked my way a few yards back to where I could slip down a crevice to the ground. The day was hot, for around that particular ruin there was no shade, and my car five miles away since it could not get any nearer. We then had about half an hour to the village where I staggered into my modest headquarters in the inn. Luckily they had plenty of *cachaça*[7] and a generous tot was produced.

'But bring,' I begged, 'the bottle.'

---

[7] A local and lively spirit distilled direct from sugarcane.

CHAPTER IV

A Continent on the Move

THESE experiences add up to a tale that is told, a chapter that is closed. My interest in Latin America has remained, and I have revisited the area repeatedly. Otherwise I could hardly have believed the astonishing changes that have taken place, the progress achieved, the obstacles overcome. If this narrative is not to appear outdated, or even painful, to my Latin American friends, some very brief observations on how things go now must find a place.

To take some simple illustrations. How many of the thousands who visit Rio or study the glossy magazines think of Corcovado without the great statue of Christ the Redeemer on its summit? But Rio de Janeiro, forty or more years ago, was totally different from the modern city of nearly three and a half millions. There was no statue on Corcovado. The Santos Dumont airport on the Guanabara Bay was a *morro*, or steep hill. The Parque (park) de Flamengo was not heard of. The hill of Santo Antonio was demolished and 250 acres of land reclaimed from the Bay in order to accommodate it. Other capitals and great cities have witnessed similar development. Belo Horizonte, when I first knew it, had under 100,000 people; today it has one million. Brasilia simply did not exist until 1960. Caracas in the late 1920s had 160,000 people; today it has a million and a half. The first commercial airplane flight I made in South America was from Santa Cruz to Cochabamba, and the plane carried a notice requesting passengers not to open the door while in flight. Today there are 400 flights a week between Rio de Janeiro and São Paulo.

What has happened to the population? The population of all Latin America is about 220 millions, and some consider that it might be double that by the end of the century. Population projections cannot be made very reliably over so great an area where social conditions are rapidly changing. At the beginning of the nineteenth century, just before the Independence,[1] the total population was well under twenty millions. The annual growth is 2.7 per cent and is highest in the northern part of South America. It is a continent of the young, over half being under twenty.

As in other countries, the magnetism of the cities, particularly the capitals, is irresistible. Over a third of the Argentine people live in Buenos Aires, and another third in the adjoining pampa provinces. The causes of this invasion of the cities are well-known but hard to mitigate. Governments have given all too little attention to the amenities of the small provincial town, and to public health and educational and social institutions in the countryside. Agricultural wages have been low and the price of manufactured goods high. Housing in villages is poor and antiquated, local communications bad. Outmoded systems of land tenure have proved extraordinarily persistent, and too much land is owned by too few landlords.

The original inhabitants, or Amerindians as they are called today, were distributed over the area, all the way from Mexico to Patagonia. They were never numerous in the vast interior, in Mato Grosso, Amazonas or the Orinoco basin. They did not develop high civilisations in these areas, or on the coast of Brazil, or even in Paraguay, the homeland of the Guaranís. They did create monumental civilisations and sophisticated culture-patterns in the Andes and in Central America and Mexico. The ruined cities abandoned by the Mayas in Central America, before their migration northwards to Yucatan, are striking tributes to their mathematical and astronomical skill and solidity of construction. The Aztecs of Mexico City and the surrounding regions built up their empire by absorbing or dominating neighbouring peoples. They have remarkable cultural achievements to their credit, but the wholesale slaughter which accompanied their ritual occasions must have depleted their human resources terribly. The Incas developed their empire from the inspiration provided by the neighbouring peoples whom they conquered. They stand out for their humane administration of a vast territory stretching from northern Chile to southern Colombia, and embracing many peoples who came to owe their allegiance to the supreme Inca, the Son of the Sun, in Cuzco, his capital. The Chibchas of Colombia showed evidence of some advanced cultural development, but we know too little of their achievements. All these

[1] 'The Independence' is a phrase loosely used in Latin America to cover the several movements by which the republics broke away from Spain and Portugal.

peoples, except the Mayas, were of the plateau and the mountain, and in the tropical lowlands only the Mayas succeeded in conspicuously climbing the heights of administrative, constructional and artistic progress.

The Spanish and Portuguese conquistadores encountered an infinite variety of conditions. The precious metals, gold and silver, were in the Andes and for long the western coasts and mountains were more important to Spain and Portugal than the pampas, the Atlantic coast, or the interior. Negroes were imported by the Portuguese because of the paucity and rapid mortality of the Indians. Today Negroes form about fifteen per cent of the eighty-two million people of Brazil and are numerous in the countries of the Caribbean. Haiti is often called 'The Black Republic'. By contrast, the population of Argentina and Uruguay is almost entirely of European origin. It is into these countries, unimportant in the days of 'the Colony',[2] that the newer European immigrants of the nineteenth and twentieth centuries have poured, as well as to Brazil and Chile. Germans and Italians and also modern Spaniards and Portuguese, Poles, Syrians and Lebanese and many other nationalities have sent their cohorts to this invasion. The old Indian stock of the land is mostly in Bolivia, Peru and Ecuador, in Paraguay, and in Guatemala and Mexico.

Throughout the sub-continent, excepting Argentina and Uruguay and certain parts of Costa Rica, there has been extensive miscegenation. The early invaders from the Peninsula brought few women, and they knew of the mingling of the races during the long Arab and Berber occupation of half a millenium in some parts, particularly around Seville and Granada. There was little social discipline and Christian marriage required the priest, and there was none. Indians and Negroes cohabited, as did Indians and Whites, and sometimes Whites and Blacks. It has been said that south of the Rio Grande, the mestizo is the true American man.

Some attribute the well-known difficulties that beset order and good government in the Latin American republics to the alleged vices of the mestizo. A different view is emerging today and none too soon. Instead of invariably branding the mestizo as lazy and violent by turns, it is reckoned that great leaders have come from mestizo stock, and populations of mixed blood have displayed unexpected energy and

---

[2] I.e. the centuries of colonial government of Mexico, Central and South America and the Caribbean republics.

ability at critical moments in the history of Latin American development. Mexico conspicuously illustrates this. The Mexican Revolution, a violent and complex transformation, was carried through by men of Indian and mestizo birth, and its record of social achievement, economic development and aesthetic flowering is remarkable. Generalisations based on racial backgrounds are very misleading, and race has only been one of numerous forces of success or failure in the building up of a modern state and community.

It is a distortion of the truth to say that there is no race problem in Latin America. Even in Brazil there is discrimination, social and economic, and it has increased of late. Nevertheless, racial prejudice is surprisingly low and racial tolerance correspondingly high. A Brazilian is a Brazilian; there is no second-class citizenship, in spite of the survival of slavery until 1888 when emancipation, without compensation, was one of the reasons for the fall of the Empire. But in other Latin American republics the assimilation of the mass of Indians into the nation is still a challenge to statesmanship and civic progress. This challenge must be met on the land and in the market. Numbers of Indians and others (outside of Mexico) are, in effect, péons. Land is largely in the hands of a few rural bosses, and the distribution of wealth is tragically uneven. The ideal to which lip-service is paid, is of Latin America as the vast stage of the 'cosmic race', La Raza Cósmica, a phrase first popularised by José Vasconcelos, one of the most famous *pro-hombres* (leaders) of the Mexican Revolution.

It is not easy to generalise about the economy. Many of the republics, particularly the larger ones, have massive mineral, agricultural and livestock resources. Thus some forty per cent of Argentina's exports are livestock products, and another fifty per cent agricultural produce. In Brazil coffee accounts for somewhat under half her exports by value and other crops for another twenty-five per cent. But in Venezuela oil accounts for ninety-four per cent of exports. In Bolivia, a very difficult country where labour is badly distributed and products subject to violent fluctuations in price, non-ferrous ores and oil account for about ninety-nine per cent of the total exports by value (tin being much the most important), but only four per cent of the labour force are miners and oil men. In Peru production is more diversified. Colombia is dangerously dependent on the price of coffee.

In general, there has been a determined attack on the dangers of mono-production. Experts and statesmen have long realised the risks of

With his three sons, (*left to right*) Frederick, Richard, Martyn, in 1938

In Peru, 1928

(*Left to right*) Dr. Violet Grubb, Mrs. Norman Grubb, Norman P. Grubb. Mrs. M. A. Grubb aged 90, K.G.G., Lady Grubb

The author with Sir Henry and Lady Holland

An Anglo-Argentine Society Embassy reception, with Lord and Lady Davidson

depending on one or perhaps two leading products, and this was the classical Latin American pattern. The increasing mobility of the population, no longer tied to the soil by feudal bands, assists this diversifying process. The assistance given by the great international or inter-American economic institutions, the World Bank, the much criticised Alliance for Progress, AID – the U.S. Agency for International Development, the Inter-American Bank and so on, is gradually enlarging production, facilitating development, and incidentally stimulating inter-Latin American trade which for years has been disappointingly sluggish.

The republics have made commendably strenuous efforts to industrialise, but progress has been uneven, because of shortage of capital, lack of technical skills, inadequate plant and transport and market analysis. Brazil is Latin America's most highly industrialised nation and is self-sufficient in most manufactured goods. There has been a phenomenal expansion of power supply and of transport. Mexico has vastly improved food production by irrigation in spite of very difficult terrain, and the tourist trade has prospered beyond belief. Heavy industries have been established in these countries as they have elsewhere, often with United States' capital. In spite of all this considerable progress, wealth is still tragically unevenly distributed, and instability of exchanges and a large marginal population, which contributes but little to the life of the nation, mean that vast human resources are untapped.

The political malaise which is endemic in some of the republics is directly connected with the economic maladjustment. Moreover, as education spreads, thousands of Indians or country folk generally, come to realise that they are little better than péons, or *'rotos'* – the terms vary from one country to another. The radio, the new literacy and the press exercise a wide popular influence. Many years ago I recall giving a car lift to a *matuto* (an ill-educated countryman) in north-east Brazil. I asked him how far it was to a certain town. 'The people,' said he, 'make it ten leagues, but at the pace of a swift beast like this, it isn't a league-and-a-half.' When we arrived I asked him what he thought of the automobile. 'Don't worry, sir,' he replied, 'it is without doubt the best of the *navigations*.' Today that same *matuto* would have a transistor radio and would grumble if the local air-service was only timed to some 500 kilometres an hour.

Education, progress and technical achievement are in the air, as in so many other countries. It is doubtful whether the ruling classes perceive the full significance of this explosive and menacing revolution. 'Heard ye not the sound of mighty workings? Listen awhile, ye nations, and be dumb.' The silence of the vast open spaces is yielding to the hum of the factory and refinery. But this welcome industrial advance does not solve political tensions or relieve grave inequities of distribution. '*Le bruit ne fait pas de bien; et le bien ne fait pas de bruit.*' Political maturity is not easy to win. Labour trouble is acute, and the great unions are by no means always wisely or well organised. Sometimes they are a long arm of the authorities; often they are the schools of Marxism or Castroism where the stage is set and the play directed by a few determined leaders. The constant effervescence of student politics, the penetration of Communism in the Universities, and the prevalent revolutionary discontent among the young people, all add to the turmoil and keep a highly unstable and fermenting situation on the boil. There has been an ominous and increasing note of despair among the advocates of revolution, a conviction that the fruits of progress will never be peacefully and equitably distributed, but must be seized by force.

If this were all, the picture would be of a dissolving society. But this would be unfair. There is much revolutionary thinking of a positive character, particularly among the young. The transformation of Mexico in the last forty years is a witness to the recuperative and creative powers of Latin American culture, when extreme monopolies, selfishness and brute power, gross inequalities of land and wealth, and frustrating gulfs of ignorance and education can be bridged. There is more chance of this breakthrough today than at any time since I have been acquainted with the region. This is partly because social change and progress are requiring new forms of economic expression and demand, and partly because they are the seed and the source of new classes, the working class organised in trade unions, the industrialist class, and, in the cities, the middle class. This is a new thing in Latin America.

The death of Ernesto ('Che') Guevara in 1967 was a severe shock to revolutionary movements and guerilla plans, as Fidel Castro admitted. It is hard to say just why this event aroused so much more interest overseas, particularly among students, than in Latin America itself. Guevara's doctrine was that 'Two, Three, Many Vietnams' must be created in Latin America, for thus alone could the forces of revolution make headway against 'the great enemy of the human race: the United States of North America'. This was enthusiastically endorsed by the engaging and vital Mgr. Helder Cámara, Archbishop of Recife, who has moved so far to the Left as to lose sight of the centre, at least of his own Church.

I suspect that there is at present less chance for the triumph of guerilla methods and a consequent 'Vietnam' in South America than for many years past, whether in Bolivia, Brazil or elsewhere. Governments are now well alerted. The movement failed in Venezuela after a bitter contest. There are possibilities in Argentina but little more than that. Castro's support of guerilla movements has declined and his endorsement of the Soviet invasion of Czechoslovakia has disgusted many of his admirers.

There is an unconquered guerila movement in Guatemala; it is very closely watched by the United States. But Guatemala is a small republic.

It seems an even chance that the most vigorous revolutionary thinking and possibly action must be sought elsewhere, perhaps in the Catholic Church. The Church, by its very nature, and owing to its historical reputation, is not fundamentally well-placed to initiate a violent reform or revolutionary stroke. In Colombia the Government, so it is alleged, killed the well-known guerilla ex-priest Camilo Torres. 'Rebel' priests, however, have large followings, not only in Brazil, but in Bolivia and Peru. The students, classically the first source of agitation in Latin America, were surprisingly quiescent until 1968, but are now infected with active discontent and they can count on sympathisers in the armed forces. A combination of students, soldiers and priests, or at least active Catholics, almost a new combination for Latin America, might in some countries win where the guerilleros have lost, but the forces of repression are strong. Even if such a revolution triumphed, it does not follow that it would everywhere be Communist-dictated.

Modern social ferment does owe much to the Church. It is a mistake to decry too acidly the Roman Catholic Church in its Latin American setting. Volumes have been written about the religious abuses that followed the Conquest, about the arrogant intolerance towards minorities which was so tragic a feature of life in Colombia recently, or about the manifest corruption of worship which has perverted popular religion. Much of this indictment cannot be denied: it is much harder to disentangle the religious, the sociological and the historical threads in the skein. I could readily quote many bitter allusions and cynical asperities about popular Christianity in Latin America from conversations with Presidents, professors and plain men of affairs in many republics. I will not throw the first stone. Those who have done so have, indeed, sometimes been moved by profound pity and a desire for reform. Equally often they underestimate the positive achievements of the Church, and judge the failure of the past by the more polished manners of the present.[3]

In the last two decades many things have been changed. This has been partly due to the Vatican Council, but even more to the devoted work of such orders as the Maryknoll Fathers, the Latin American Conference of Bishops (CELAM) with its headquarters at Bogotá, special attention given by the authorities at Rome to the state of the Church, and the *formación* (training) of priests.

The swift conquest of a continent, however superficial, is no mean achievement. Latin America was the scene of the life and labours of some of the great crusaders of the Church, pioneers such as Bartolomé de las Casas, San Pedro Claver, Nobrega and Anchieta in Brazil, the Jesuits in the Guaraní missions. Yet it is hard to trace in the Latin American Church an alliance of mind between mystic and missionary. The Spanish mystics, Luis of Granada, the Carmelites Santa Teresa de Jesus and San Juan de la Cruz, Luis de León, and others of the golden age of Spanish mysticism have no parallel in America. The late Professor Allison Peers has said[4] that mysticism is inborn in the Spanish people: it has not been much in evidence in the Latin American Church. Perhaps it has been too often concealed behind a display of formal and elaborate ritual or submerged beneath an arid dogmatism which has been more concerned to maintain an orthodox uniformity, in detail, rather than to admit individual flowerings of the religious spirit.

A change has been coming over the Church in Latin America, the full meaning and direction of which are still to some degree uncertain. In the 1920s a religious conformism was usual except among intellectuals and in such advanced republics as Argentina and Uruguay. It was an Argentine President of this period who is alleged to have said publicly, 'I have met sincere and devoted Christians in public life in France; I have yet to meet one in Argentina.'

Such a remark, albeit more graphic than precise, would be out of place today. It is not so much that there has been a religious transformation, but there are signs of a new growth of the religious spirit and purer forms of its manifestation. Nor is this an anti-Marxist reaction. It is due to a serious search for a deeper spirituality by many of the clergy and

---

[3] See *The Church and the Latin American Revolution* by the Rev. Emile Pin, S.J. and Abbé François Houtart, Sheed and Ward, 1965. This is a very frank and fair appraisal.
[4] *Spanish Mysticism* (Methuen, 1924), p. 3.

some of the laity. The Holy Scriptures are now available in modern form, in good translation, and at a cheap price in almost every town of consequence. A stream of popular literature, well-written, frank, self-critical, but also of devotional and pastoral content, is coming from the printing-presses all the way from Mexico to Buenos Aires. There are fresh experiments in worship and liturgical renewal in capitals like Bogotá and Santiago, and in towns large and small like Cuernavaca in Mexico and São Paulo in Brazil. There are priest-workers and student chaplains, radio schools and rural institutes. There is active Christian *formación* of the laity. The list could be enlarged; it need only be added that there is less fanaticism directed against minority groups, more prayer and search for understanding, joint study of the common heritage of the Christian faith, and even a conviction that all Christians must act together in combating the old, feudal social patterns.

The Evangelical Churches—they prefer this name to 'Protestant'—have made striking progress in recent decades.[5] In Latin America there are over twelve million Evangelicals, but such statistics are notoriously difficult to interpret. Nearly eight million are in Brazil, nearly 900,000 in Chile, over half a million in Argentina, and some 700,000 in Mexico. The early Evangelicals were of two separate sources. One was the German immigration into South America in the last century and this. In Brazil there are some two million Christians attached to churches of Lutheran origin. Up till some thirty years ago these communities were self-contained, limited to certain areas, often using only the German language, and little interested in the religious status of their neighbours or the population as a whole. This has changed lately, since it has been recognised that the population in the progressive areas of, say, Brazil and Argentina, is largely secularised.

The second current also dates back to the middle of the nineteenth century when Evangelical missionaries of British and United States origin began to proclaim the faith as it is understood by the reformed or Protestant tradition. In some republics this work began in the first half of the last century; in others in the early decades of this one. For long progress was slow, but today the large Evangelical churches of Latin America are self-supporting and manage their own affairs; the majority of Evangelical Christians in Brazil or Chile, apart from the Pentecostalists, are probably of the second or third generation of Evangelicalism.

[5] For statistics see Coxill and Grubb, *World Christian Handbook, 1968*, Lutterworth Press for the Survey Application Trust, 1968.

Accompanying the growth of these churches was a considerable contribution by way of schools, colleges, literacy campaigns, rural reconstruction, technical training and theological preparation. From the beginning the spread of the Bible on a very wide scale has been at the heart of this movement. In its early stages, and in some areas even today, biblical Evangelicalism was viewed as a menace to the traditions and influence of the Roman Catholic Church. The early missionaries were unavoidably dragged into controversy and violent clashes were frequent. This stage has for the most part passed, and in the face of the general religious indifference of much of the western world, all Christians are increasingly concerned to achieve and propagate a common understanding of the Gospel of Christ as the means for transfiguring man's common life and illuminating his personal destiny.

An accompanying phenomenon and an integral part of the Evangelical movement in the last half-century, has been the astonishing growth of Pentecostalism. In Chile where this first appeared, some ninety per cent of the Evangelicals belong to the Pentecostal Churches. Some forty-five years ago, I stated in print that I thought this growth would take place and that something similar would follow in Brazil, as it has done. I was severely rebuked by an Evangelical leader of that period for encouraging 'heresy' and supposing that a movement which was guilty of excesses in conduct and worship could avoid strangling itself through its own extravagances and improprieties. Being neither a prophet nor the son of a prophet, I held my peace and retired to the forests of the interior from which I had temporarily surfaced to enjoy a breather.

The large Pentecostalist congregations of South America are an unexpected spiritual and sociological phenomenon. In these central churches thousands gather for worship and fellowship. I have often been in their services, but I have never 'spoken in tongues'; indeed in those years I was a silent person. The life of these Churches is free, expressive and enthusiastic, and there are many of the Latin temperament who find this a release from the ordered formalism of the dominant Church. The larger Pentecostalist churches are guided, indeed directed, by pastors who are often self-taught, but wield immense authority over their flocks. A Pentecostal congregation in South America is not an exercise in democracy applied to religious practice; it is a town-meeting of the faithful, closely ordered and managed behind the scenes. Nor are the Pentecostal Churches any freer from divisiveness than other Evangelical denominations; indeed, they have carried the art of splitting to a high degree of expression. But the reputation of individual Pentecostals as moral livers, good citizens, and assiduous workers is very high, and employers not infrequently go out of their way to identify them and attract their labour.

To a European Christian much of the Evangelicalism of Latin America is a reflection of North American Protestantism and sometimes a reflection on it. It is individualistic, producing remarkable conversions evidenced by radical transformation of life. It is ambiguous in its social implications so that an observer is left guessing whether the members of the congregation constitute a Christian society, or whether the conception of an ideal Christian society fills the individuals with a glowing sense of moral attainment. It is a hard saying, but it seems difficult to create in the materialistic setting of Latin America the self-forgetting atmosphere of Christian worship. A satisfying Christian worship, not selfish but devout, not formal but sincere, not merely intellectual but also deeply spiritual, not simply concerned with love of the neighbour but consumed with love of God, seems to be a discipline of life and personality hardly to be achieved. Yet the ritual and manner of the dominant Roman Catholic Church are often arid, and, particularly in the smaller towns and villages, the Catholic churches lack character and depth in their teaching and preaching.

The international posture of the Latin American republics is best discussed by considering first their relation with the U.S.A., the Colossus of the North, as the common expression goes all the way from Mexico to Argentina. But although it seems natural and necessary to start here, it is mainly because memory is short. By air Washington is nearer to Moscow than to Buenos Aires. During the nineteenth century, the great waves of immigration from Europe, mainly Italy and Germany, helped to build up the population of the southernmost republics. British enterprise was in the van of development and was the main exporter of 'consumer goods', if that modern title can be applied to the despatch of warming-pans and skates to Rio de Janeiro and Montevideo. As early as 1825 more than £20 million had been invested by British subjects in Latin America. The leading bulk Latin American exports, with one or two exceptions, found their markets in Europe. But that period is a tale of far-off things.

The famous Monroe Doctrine of 1823 was designed primarily to prevent European powers from 'any attempt to extend their system to any portion of this hemisphere'. Ironically it only made sense because of

British control of the seas, and a British posture was thus profitably used to maintain a North American hegemony. President Theodore Roosevelt extended the Doctrine to justify the use of police power and employment of armed force to collect debts. It was held that the United States could not tolerate disorder on her borders. From this it was a short step to military intervention in such countries as Nicaragua and Haiti. United States marines were landed and this sounded better than U.S. soldiers. Latin Americans call this 'the unilateral interpretation of the Monroe Doctrine', or simply American imperialism, but the latter must be wrong because all men know that Americans are not to be called imperialists. The most conspicuous instance of this was the events leading to the creation of the Republic of Panama and the Canal Zone, and Latin Americans have never forgotten Roosevelt's famous boast 'I took the Isthmus' (i.e. Panama).

What one Roosevelt did, another tried to undo, and it was not too soon for in the 1920s and early 1930s, U.S.-Latin American relations reached a very low point.

President Franklin D. Roosevelt in his first inaugural in 1933 enunciated the 'good neighbour' policy. This marked the beginning of the decline of certain aspects of North American imperialism, and the rise of the doctrine of Non-intervention by which the United States forwent the right of unilateral military action in or against the Latin American republics. This policy was almost breached—some would say it was breached—in 1961 when the Cuban exiles trained in the U.S.A. invaded Cuba, or in 1965 in Santo Domingo. Others would strongly hold that it was indirect intervention by the U.S.A. that brought about the fall of the pro-Communist Arbenz regime in Guatemala in 1954 and thus saved a hemisphere, but direct military intervention was not employed. If there is one shark, let alone a whale, in the pool, the other little fish have limited freedom anyhow and had best keep to the shallows.

U.S.-Latin American relations have developed steadily, but not always adroitly. The old Panamericanism, embodied in the Panamerican Union, gave way to a general reorganisation of inter-American agencies and procedures at the Ninth International Conference of American States at Bogotá in 1948. The Organisation of American States was set up. Most inter-American conferences have made declarations about the importance of human rights and this was duly done at Bogotá, but it is easy to prevent the application of these in practice. In Latin America the importance of provisions about human rights is that it gives the regime something to suspend.

One of the more imaginative gestures of this period has been the Alliance for Progress. What then went wrong so that it is so much criticised? The Alliance, contrary to what is often believed, was not in origin a United States programme; the concept was at the beginning a Latin American, and mainly a Brazilian plan, put forward first in 1960. The proposals to be undertaken and financed by and through it must come voluntarily from the Latin American nations themselves. The social, technological and cultural progress designed to be achieved by the Alliance is to be Latin America's answer to the rosy horizons offered by Communism. Latin American capitalism benefits a few very wealthy investors, and many hold that businessmen and land-owners do not bear a fair share of taxation. The Alliance implies a fundamental transformation of the economic structure of the republics, but ruling classes rarely surrender wealth and power willingly or tamely. They exist to rule, not to serve or to pay. So it comes about that a great movement designed to forestall revolution is, through the frustration of its purposes, fanning a revolutionary flame, particularly among the young and the intellectuals. And the young commit the unpardonable crime of being young, and the intellectuals of being clever. Much of the blame for the difficulties of the Alliance is by well-established routine thrown on to the United States. But mistakes have been made by all and the Latin American republics cannot escape their share of responsibility.

As an observer I regret the occasions when the United States has chosen to support, or has been manoeuvred into supporting, reactionary regimes or semi-dictatorships. The responsibilities of international power are heavy, and at times it has seemed difficult for the United States to put a foot right. Too often Washington has an impressive gift for ending up on the losing side. To most of those who had followed Cuban affairs it was next to certain that Fidel Castro would eventually win; the alternative was to bolster up the intolerable Batista dictatorship with all its brutality and corruption. This was a special case, but Latin Americans generally resent the apparent support which the United States accords to the heavy-handed oligarchs, and such critics find sympathisers among some of the shrewdest observers in the North. 'Since 1958, Argentina, Peru, Colombia, Venezuela, and Cuba got rid of their dictatorships, while General Anastasio Somoza was assassinated in Nicaragua and Generalissimo Trujillo in the Dominican Republic. In each case the people had the knowledge that the United States not only did not act as if it preferred democracy, but showed favour to the dictators.'[6] Truly the way of the do-gooder is hard. 'Anti-Yankeeism' has almost become an occupational obsession among Latin Americans, and for the Americans to favour openly even a genuinely progressive and liberal politician is to administer to him a kiss of political death. The converse is almost equally true, and the open dislike of Ambassador Spruille Braden for Juan Perón of Argentina was a positive reason for his election.

There are no easy solutions for the United States. The Cuban revolution has called forth some hard thinking and new orientations. But there are twenty Latin American republics, and although they share much in common, each has its own political sensitivity, requirements and individualism. Talking to Latin Americans I have often felt real difficulty in achieving a true 'confrontation', just as one feels it in discussing international affairs with a Spaniard. In so vast a field there can be no general expert; but there can be a certain humility, patience and far, far more understanding.

---

[6] Herbert L. Matthews in *The United States and Latin America* (Prentice-Hall, 1963) 2nd ed., p. 162.

CHAPTER V

A Pause for Reflection

THE 1930s were a difficult decade. They opened with the world economic crisis. Then came the rise of Hitler, the Chaco War, the Spanish Civil War, the grim years of 'Appeasement', the Hoare-Laval pact, Mussolini in Ethiopia, Hitler in the Saar, Austria and Czechoslovakia. These startling and ominous events, culminating in World War II altered my career and opened up prospects and opportunities to which I had not previously given a passing thought. A brief explanation of how I was placed in the late 1930s belongs to the story. It was in these years, too, that I did some of my best work in Latin America, namely the series of research studies on the penetration and expansion of Christianity, done for the Survey Application Trust.

The Survey Application Trust, or World Dominion Press, was a small foundation which had been set up in 1918 in a different form. The fund was a part of the fortune of a business man, S. J. W. Clark, whose life had been a characteristic 'success story'. He started with virtually no education, as a pawnbroker's boy, sleeping on the counter at night. While still comparatively young, he retired from his own business and began to visit overseas missions, particularly in China. He had a vivacious mind for detail and nothing escaped his observation. He used often to say, not always quite fairly, that if he ran his business as missions did theirs he would soon be bankrupt.

In the course of these early journeys he met Dr. Thomas Cochrane and the Rev. Roland Allen. The former was a medical missionary in China and the founder of the Peking Union Medical College, the most remarkable institution of its day and kind in China. The latter was an Anglican ex-missionary in China, of unusually critical and penetrating insight. These three men had become convinced that the methods then followed by Protestant missions were incapable of accomplishing the establishment of indigenous local churches which, in their turn, would pass on the Gospel to others. Roland Allen was the prophet, the visionary, of the group, and as he also wielded a powerful pen he became the exponent of that view of the growing Church which emphasises that from the start it should be self-governing, self-supporting, and self-propagating. He insisted that any other approach would be regarded as a kind of spiritual imperialism or foreign domination, such as a citizen in Africa or the East might expect from the prosperous but interfering countries of the West.[1]

The Trust also attached importance to ascertaining by research the real facts about the distribution of churches, missions and Christians throughout the world. Unless one knew what had been done, how could one know what there was to do? This led to the establishment of a Survey Department of the Trust under the Rev. Alexander McLeish of the Church of Scotland, a man of great devotion and wide experience of India. In this department I worked in Latin America generally, and also elsewhere. Facts which are common knowledge today were quite unknown then and could only be ascertained by work on the spot. The Trust also made generous donations to many allied causes, in addition to issuing a long series of detailed survey volumes, its own review *World Dominion*[2] and a continuous stream of literature on missionary methods. It was also the founder, promoter and for many years publisher, of the well-known *World Christian Handbook*.

I owe much to the Survey Application Trust. I was left to conduct my own work in my own way, provided the results were such as would answer the questions and stand up to criticism. When World War II came I had to sever my connection, only to renew it years later (1954). I then rearranged its affairs and finally had the sad responsibility of paying off most of the remaining capital and liquidating the enterprise. A study of the early material and documents had shown clearly that the 'founding fathers' had not intended it to continue indefinitely. The end of the 1960s seemed the right time to bring the enterprise to a close. It is to be wished that the founders of other small Trusts, not so well-endowed, with which I have had to do, had similarly and voluntarily limited their own enterprises. With the passage of time and kaleidoscopic changes of situation, it may be hard to administer a fund so as truly to interpret the intentions of the founder.

---

[1] For an account of the Survey Application Trust, see David M. Paton, ed., *Reform of the Ministry* (Lutterworth Press for the Survey Application Trust, 1968), pp. 59–84.
[2] This was merged in 1954 with another publication to form the quarterly review, *Frontier*, edited from the start by Sir John Lawrence, Bt., O.B.E.

But the gap was soon felt, and a new enterprise, 'The World Church Studies Trust', has been formed to carry forward some of the old Trust's purposes in the modern world.

In the 1930s the free societies had to face squarely the critical questions of international order, peace and war, justice and freedom, democracy and dictatorship. I was much less well-equipped than most of my contemporaries to consider these great challenges and reach a firm position. My education, through my own stupidity, had never been completed. I had lived much of my adult life out of the main stream of human relationships and political and economic movements, particularly European affairs. I had seen much of limited aspects of life, but there was lacking a breadth and penetration of vision. I recognised quickly enough when people talked sense, and had little confidence in idealists whose Utopian positions were unsupported by access to power, people unable to mobilise decisive interest and support. I respected goodness in any company, even when it lacked influence. But then, I said to myself, What about the Crucifixion, which seemed to be an exhibition of weakness? At once I found myself in the middle of the debate, which I have never resolved with any satisfaction, between individual action and collective ethics, that is, the proper discharge of Christian witness to one's neighbour and social action with him.

This dilemma defeated logic. I also disliked pacifism, and consistently refused to sign the Peace Pledge. Christian pacifism was much discussed then, as it still is, but its appeal lacked cogency and realism. I had used force to obtain, defend and secure what seemed right, and to protect the weak from men who were slavers in all save the name, and I had no qualms about being ready to do it again. I had no criticism to make of my pacifist acquaintances; if I could help to defend them and thus assure their continual existence, so much the better. But the possession of power, and the willingness, if need be, to translate it into force were the only last resort of a firm and constructive foreign policy. The 'nuclear stalemate' has modified the simplicity of this position and has complicated it, but has not destroyed it.

I studied foreign policy, and in spite of travels kept a close eye on the politics of Europe and the U.S.A. I had met Salazar and Mussolini personally, and had listened to Hitler entrancing and arousing mass audiences with his magic and evil spell. I had also followed closely the Spanish Civil War which so vividly divided different camps in Europe. I knew many of the republican leaders, Azaña, Negrin, Largo Caballero,

Indalecio Prieto, Fernando de los Rios and others including Miguel de Unamuno. As the years wore on, the folly of appeasement became every day more apparent. I had read *Mein Kampf* early and re-read it in the English translation: I also knew my Machiavelli well. I would not have *The Times* in my Highgate home. We had exceptionally large basements and these were strengthened and fitted with berths, and very handy they were when the bombs began to fall. Neighbours who had no doubt thought me mad, now (with an effort) revised their view.

There were mental reservations, but they were not of a kind or intensity to unnerve one's fighting will. No one seemed to agree on what we were really preparing to defend, other than our skins, and that was not to be despised. The usual answer was 'The Balance of Power', or 'The British way of Life', or 'the rights of small nations', or simply 'freedom'. But freedom to be what, to do what? Freedom did not exist in its own right or as something gained once for all; we all know the tag about the price of freedom being eternal vigilance. Even more to the point was Goethe's 'He only earns his freedom and existence, who daily conquers them anew'.[3] However, by the late 1930s things had passed that point. Demosthenes in his Third Philippic put the case in a nutshell:

> If another, having arms in his hands and a large force around him, amuses you with the name of peace, while he carries on the operations of war, what is left but to defend yourselves? You may profess to be at peace, if you like, as he does; I quarrel not with that. But if any man supposes this to be a peace, which will enable Philip to master all else and attack you last, he is a madman, or he talks of a peace observed towards him by you, not towards you by him. This it is that Philip purchases by all his expenditure, the privilege of assailing you without being assailed in turn.[4]

So as I moved to and fro, mainly between Britain and Latin America, I began to take a lively interest in international affairs, joining Chatham House (The Royal Institute of International Affairs) and attempting to make a modest contribution by writing papers and working on study groups. But natural shyness was a drawback, and I would frequently let pass, without contradiction, assessments of a situation which actual and recent experience had shown to be miles off-beam. I was equally slow in

---

[3] *Faust*, Part II, Act V, Scene VI, trans. Bayard Taylor, World's Classics.
[4] Translation by C. R. Kennedy. Everyman's Library.

grappling with the meaning of what I was trying to do, in any deeper sense than the mere collection of facts and figures. Nor with rare exceptions did anyone encourage me to think that I had any capacity for leadership. Thirty years later, I came across a letter written by a secretary of a missionary society to my chief, Dr. Thomas Cochrane. The letter suggested that I might be of use to the society on its committee. The reply was 'I don't think we shall ever get much more out of young Grubb than we do now.' Yet I was convinced that I ought to be less self-centred and must enlarge my vision. I knew that I could not be saved alone, could not conquer and come alone to my final goal.

Thinking back over early years in the far interior of South America I have wondered how anyone fairly quick in the uptake and sensitive, but not in any way exceptionally endowed either with insight or determination, could work in a strange environment for weeks, even months at a time, in complete loneliness. The question forced itself forward because in my first youth I was in almost every way nervously vulnerable. There did not seem to be an answer to this question except in the faith that our little lives were held by and could hold to the strength, power and love of God in Christ Jesus. I did not reflect on this in any depth. I was merely conscious of being, like all of us, a 'traveller from the cradle to the grave through the dim light of this immortal day'. I merely knew that I was borne forward on the ceaseless waves of an unpastured ocean of desire, hungering to find fulfilment. If I had learned better, if I had believed more truly, I could no doubt have been sustained by such words as Jesus spoke to his disciples, wafted as it were through the forest night from a presence for ever calm. That was not to be. I only dimly realised, in spite of much talk, that the triumphs of Christ were spiritual and his noblest work wrought *first* in the secret of the soul. All else, the conquest of environment and of prejudice, followed from that.

What did move me from time to time and spur me on was a sense of profound pity, not in the least of a paternalistic or patronising kind, but a conviction of identification with the sorrows and troubles of my fellow-men. I saw the ignorant and unlettered, capable of being cheated by the merest mountebank. I saw the landless and the *flagelados*, the outcasts from a selfish social order, or the strangers who had never been within it, such as the Indians of the great Andean *cordilleras*. Yet I could never come round to believe that the political solutions of the Left, least of all Marxism, could solve their fate. I knew that every human solution carried human failings, and that the best endeavours sometimes achieved bad results. But I had largely failed myself, and now I had to move on into other spheres and leave to others unfinished legacies of deed and thought.

My own belief in the essential truths of the Christian faith did not waver. I believed in prayer, and I have been a lover and reader of the Bible throughout life. It always has a word for the ordinary man as an individual, for the world of affairs, of education, science and culture, and for the conduct of societies and nations. It holds up a mirror to man in which he sees his sins—that unpopular word—and his failures, aspirations and misgivings, his greatness as well as his misery.

The Bible has a word for all. Through it the mystic can seek union with the divine Spirit as the author of all creation. To the Bible the most exacting theological mind must turn for fresh light to break forth on the full meaning of Christ's redemptive work. Those who yearn for the unity of mankind, not to say a closer union of Christians, will find their prayer taken up in the language and vision of the Bible. The prophetic souls, the great reformers, will read here the conditions of happiness, peace and justice among the nations. The contemplative will dwell on the quiet pastures and the beauty and perfection of the life of the Good Shepherd. It supplies those simple and profound truths, those flashes of insight from the Holy Spirit of God, which can help us order our lives as Christians in business and profession, in leisure and home life. It calls upon both the thoughtful and the thoughtless to consider their ways and the ways of God with men. In hours of trial and loneliness it strengthens hope and faith and opens to us the vision of eternal life. For these reasons I have been a reader of the Bible for well over sixty years, for it speaks of the mighty acts of God in history, and of the life, death and risen life of our Lord and Saviour Jesus Christ.

Therefore, in every radical development of thought and life, I sought to consider what the Bible had to say.

All Christians may not view the Bible thus. A year or two after the great earthquake of 1928 in north Peru, I sat one morning amid the ruins of Jaen, the capital of a department in the valley of the upper Marañon. I was reading my Bible when I was accosted by two or three of the locals. They explained that the earthquake had destroyed the church and broken in pieces the images. But, they added, these were capable of repair, or at least the fragments of several could be joined to make the figure of one. For this purpose they wished to know what the Holy Bible had to say about the lives of these apostolic figures. I asked whom they had par-

Investiture as Knight Bachelor in 1953: (*left to to right*) Mrs. Jackson (daughter), K.G.G., Lady Grubb

With Canon Max Warren at C.M.S. reception for author on becoming a Knight Bachelor

At a lunch given by Viscount Davidson in honour of Dr. Don Manuel Prado, formerly President of Peru

At a civic reception in Sydney in his honour, K.G.G., the Lord Mayor (*centre*) and Rear-Admiral H. J. Buchanan

ticularly in mind and received the answer, St. Francis and St. Dominic, St. Bernard, St. Antony and St. Christopher. But is this worse than a case related to me in Jerusalem by a canon of St. George's? An American lady whom he was showing round remarked, 'Oh, I didn't realise that Gethsemane was mentioned in the Bible. I have one at home. If I had known that I would have brought it with me.'

During these years I learned how little I had retained of whatever I had learned. The adventures of the hard way had crowded other things out of the mind. It is easy to suppose that weeks of loneliness afford occasion to call back into the mind the treasures of literature and the thought of the ages. In one sense it was so and whole passages of Shakespeare would come fresh to me and then dissolve. Anxiety, pre-occupation and foreboding would rush in to fill the void. More than ever I would feel that men were but 'such stuff as dreams are made on'.

As soon as chance and a more settled life offered, I set myself to do some serious reading and re-reading, particularly in the languages in which I could read easily, Spanish and Portuguese, French and Italian— and, of course, English!—for like most people I preferred to read originals whenever I could. I read again the whole of Gibbon and Von Ranke, the *Divina Commedia*, the *Lusiadas*, several of the Spanish mystics, and, of course, Hooker, Locke, Goethe, and even Hobbes; Marx, Arnold and Bertrand Russell, already well known to me, were studied afresh. I suddenly realised that I was classically and artistically illiterate although I had already been several times in Italy and Greece. I dug out Homer, Plato, Herodotus and Thucydides, and took fresh delight in Virgil and Horace. I studied Vasari and Berenson and a score of others. I read badly because I lacked guidance and system, but I made friends all the way from St. Augustine to Karl Barth, not omitting Calvin's *Institutes*. It was a jumble but it was fun, and my memory became retentive. If I was bored with John Wesley I could always turn to Boswell. If Aquinas was too grave, there was always Boccaccio. I took the dull with the humorous, and enjoyed Aristophanes and Cervantes as much as that irritating work *The Social Contract*. 'Seneca cannot be too heavy, nor Plautus too light.' In the course of all this, and with my background of solitary experience, I found myself 'moving about in worlds not realised', and so far from being shocked by 'obstinate questionings' I grasped again those foundation truths of the New Testament which for me, 'are yet the fountain light of all our day, are yet a master light of all our seeing'.

Perhaps in an unsuspected way I was beginning to find a different fulfilment of my dream, the Dream of Many Waters.

I rethought some attitudes and assumptions which had coloured my religious beliefs. For the first time I took the Church seriously, in my case the Church of England. It became clear again that selfish and even melancholy individualism, albeit tinged, like that of Jaques, with a touch of humour, was no attitude for a Christian. I knew from the Bible that St. Paul taught that the Church was the body of Christ. I knew from sheer experience that there were many in the Churches who were not in the Church of Christ; and others who were not in the Churches but who were in the Church of Christ.

I first thought seriously about the corporate life and meaning of the Church not because of any theological treatise, but by virtue of re-reading Carlyle, and in particular the well-known passage in the opening part of *The French Revolution*. 'The Church: what a word was there; richer than Golconda and the treasures of the world . . . Strong was he that had a Church—What we can call a Church . . . The vague shoreless universe had become a firm city for him, a dwelling which he knew.' It was all good, turgid Carlyle. After living in Latin America, some resolution was needed to take the Church seriously. At first it had no great influence upon my conduct and outlook, but gradually it came to have a lot. Membership of the visible Church was necessary for the discipline as well as the development of the spiritual life, and indeed for the evangelisation of the world. It was unnecessary to idealise the Church to the extent that Carlyle did. It is a fellowship of the strong and of the weak, of the successful and the failing, of the quarrelsome and of the reasonable, of the emotional and the impassive, and of white, black and brown. It had to be studied and understood, not only because of the teaching of the New Testament, but also because to undervalue the institutional was to forget that Christianity is a religion rooted in history.

But then the question came, what Church? It seemed wrong to unchurch in one's thinking any denomination. No Church was perfect; nevertheless in the New Testament the Church was the household built upon the foundation of the apostles and prophets, Christ Jesus Himself being the chief cornerstone. It was not the central principles and beliefs which offered difficulty; Roman Catholics, Anglicans and Plymouth Brethren could alike say the Apostles' Creed; rather, it was what lay at the circumference, Church order or government. In particular, there was the belief entertained by many Churches that there was some form of Church order which alone was primitive and enjoyed apostolic authority. I have never swallowed this whole and digested it. It was at least arguable that the early Christians achieved what they did because they were inspired by a spirit which favoured experiments.

The argument that unity was essential, or at least vitally desirable, in witnessing to divine and revealed truth was impressive. It was almost a condition for the fulfilment of Christ's message to mankind. 'Every kingdom divided against itself is brought to desolation, every city or house divided against itself shall not stand.' Increasingly, in the large world, internationally, sociologically, scientifically, men were striving for unity. Division was a fatal weakness to mission, and no one has expressed this more strongly than the leaders of the Churches of Asia and Africa. How could the people be expected to accept that religion as divine whose ministers seemed unable to agree on their own unity in Christ?

So much has been written about this that it would be otiose to develop the subject, but it was at this stage and through this simple reckoning that I began to be interested in the ecumenical movement. This interest afterwards bore modest fruit in a long association with the work, and with aspects of the leadership, of the World Council of Churches. But before all that could be a World War had to be won.

From an early stage mission and unity were interdependent in my mind. I had been concerned with the former, and now I saw that the latter must be taken seriously. I had begun to take the Church seriously, and now I took church unity seriously, and I began to study both intercommunion and ultimate reunion. All this not only deepened concern for mission, but also sharpened the difficulty of it. Yet considerations, attitudes and facets of belief which seemed to me petty as one faced the need of the world figured as matters of life and death with some of my friends. This was disturbing but the writings of men such as John R. Mott, William Paton and Roland Allen, and the contacts which I early made with them, were an immense strength to my modest convictions.

At the same time, it was clear that mission could only be successfully pursued with passion. In an age when all views, like all men, were held to be equal, and for many the safest thing was to believe nothing in particular, this posed a difficulty. Every attitude had a psychological or sociological explanation and as with Disraeli, there was a religion of all sensible men, but sensible men never told what it was. This was not good enough. It was Disraeli who also remarked that man is only truly great when he acts from the passions. (I must have been reading *Coningsby* at the time.)

This seemed true. Pity in the sense described in this chapter was not enough, passion in action was the highest expression of love for one's neighbour. The great reforming causes, religious and political, had been launched by men and women of passionate conviction. Such were Carey, William Wilberforce, Shaftesbury, General Booth, the early pioneers of the Labour movement, the early suffragettes. In spite of the indifference of our times, this is still true, as witness movements such as the struggle for peace, for racial equity, or to clear up domestic ills. This was not easy to swallow. It was of the essence of the Faith—Woe is me if I preach not the Gospel! But it was inconvenient. The Church of England seemed to be pretty easygoing, and enthusiasm was not welcome. Nor did passionate convictions appeal to me; living in the interior of South America, I had more need of resourcefulness than passion. But reflection presently showed that great things were only done by those who greatly believed. Passion, conviction, love, sacrifice—these were the abiding lessons of the life and death of Christ. It was hard in the comfortable western world to see just what it all meant. Yet, to accumulate truth which one could not or would not translate into life, was to make a bog and sink into it. Helena, the mother of Constantine, is depicted in Veronese's moving picture, dreaming on her balcony, and 'through the still morning air the angels bring her the symbol of God's pain', (Oscar Wilde). But the true Invention of the Cross is not on the balcony but in the street.

About 1935-6, I first began to be concerned over health. Around then I began to have curious 'attacks' or 'turns', which were sometimes painful, more often merely disconcerting. They had a decisive effect upon my affairs; since, had it not been for them, I might well have sought to go into politics after World War II. Indeed, I was urged to do this by Dr. J. H. Oldham and also by other friends, but it was clear that to make a success of it, starting in middle life, one needed a more robust constitution.

These 'turns' have continued to this day, and are, I am advised, properly described as an epileptic condition. They come in a series lasting a week or ten days. There may be five or six during the day, and, perhaps, several sufficiently strong to wake one up somewhat painfully at night. They are always preceded by a prior sentiment or conviction that one is 'for it', but it takes an excessive effort of the will to repress them. Unless a seizure of this kind is very bad, one can postpone or else conceal it, but not always. *Naturam expellas furca, tamen usque recurret* (Horace. Epis. I. x). A bad one, or the first of a series, which is usually bad, is preceded by a vivid mental vision, or 'aura'.

I cannot usually recover this vision or aura: the 'turn' obliterates it from the mind. Occasionally this is not so, and I have been able to call it back. Invariably, it is of a scene of acute social embarrassment which is entirely fictitious. I call it 'treading on the Countess's dress', because the one I can most vividly recall was just that. I was present at a brilliant reception of the pre-war society in a Mayfair mansion, men in orders and decorations, ladies in diamonds. On going up to dinner, I trod on the Countess's dress—and then the 'turn' came on violently and vividly.

The interval between a series used to be about three to four months, but it has narrowed in recent years to about six weeks, which makes the thing a great nuisance. It is assisted but not so far cured by the powerful modern drugs. The 'turns' themselves are not really a cause for anxiety; it is more a matter of one's own worries about them and the peculiar, almost uncanny regularity of their onset. I have had expert advice for many years and owe a great debt of gratitude to University College Hospital and the consultants and specialists there.

Late in 1938 I attended my first world conference. It was called by the International Missionary Council—the World Council of Churches did not then exist—at Tambaram, near Madras, and was in the succession of similar gatherings at Edinburgh in 1910 and Jerusalem in 1928. I had not previously been at such a widely representative gathering, so I watched carefully and tried to make myself unobtrusively useful. At night I sat up late writing up not so much the events of the day as the characters and weaknesses of those whom I had met during it. The Conference was the last such meeting at which Dr. John R. Mott played a considerable part, although the Chair was often taken by Bishop Azariah of Dornakal. It was also the last before World War II at which the Germans appeared in strength. They did not mix to any extent and always sat in a separate block at meals. It was generally felt (such are the ironies of history) that the delegates from the Chinese Churches made the best impression, and the prospects of Christianity in that vast country seemed promising at that time.

I spoke little and learned much. I returned home in easy stages and early in 1939 found myself staying with the late S. A. Morrison in Cairo. While there I received a message asking me to call at the British Embassy to receive a telegram and to discuss certain matters. From that day a new chapter opened and another story unfolded.

CHAPTER VI

The Ministry of Information

ON arrival at the British Embassy in Cairo, I was ushered into the office of a gentleman bearing the title of Head of Chancery. He handed me a telegram from Ivison Macadam,[1] Director General of Chatham House, the Royal Institute of International Affairs. The telegram asked when I would get back to London, as my services were required in the national interest. It was explained that studies were being started to provide Government with a Ministry of Information in the event of war. Ivison Macadam was in charge of this preliminary work and he desired to enlist me as a member of his planning group, covering Latin America.

My contacts with the Foreign Office had been few and I was nervous. However, I comforted myself with the thought that diplomats were but men (there were no lady consuls or ambassadors then), and my own previous negotiation with the Foreign Office had not been wholly devoid of its light side. It had occurred at a time when there was a lot of infighting among the various tribes and clans of the Jivaros, they who make the reduced human heads. I had discovered that some of this fighting was deliberately stimulated by civilised traders, so that they could sell the reduced *tsantsas* or heads in New York for Christmas presents.

This seemed unedifying and I arranged, by correspondence, to lay the whole matter before a committee of the League of Nations concerned with humanitarian affairs. Just before returning home on leave, I traded a reduced head into my hands as 'Exhibit A', but on arrival in London I took fright lest the Swiss Customs should find the object in my baggage and create difficulties. Customs people anywhere can be so pig-headed. The motives of anyone other than a museum-collector, wandering about Europe with a reduced human head wrapped in his pyjamas might be hard to explain convincingly.

So I wrote anxiously to the Foreign Office reporting the affair and

[1] Later (1955) Sir Ivison Macadam.

asking if 'my' head could be sent out in the diplomatic bag. The official who dealt with the letter promptly replied as follows: 'Sir, I am directed by His Majesty's Principal Secretary of State for Foreign Affairs to say that, having carefully considered the circumstances of your letter, he will be happy to put your head in a bag... I have the honour to be, Your most humble and obedient servant...' My head was accordingly so put.

On return to London I discussed things with Macadam and arranged to make time available. I turned up at one of the large houses in Chesham Place and made the acquaintance of some of my colleagues.

Later the outfit moved to Belgrave Square. At first it seemed like the Mad Hatter's Tea-party. Many in the plot were very learned academics, persons of higher intellectual distinction, and I was both rather afraid of them and uncertain why I was there. In those days there were not many people available with a thorough knowledge of Latin America, and among the blind the one-eyed man is king. Others were as confused as I was, not excluding the professional civil servants who were in the party. One day, being next to one of the Civil Service Commissioners, I wrote on a piece of paper:

> Nel mezzo del cammin' di nostra vita
> mi ritrovai per una selva oscura,
> che la diritta via era smarrita.

He replied:

> Ahi quanto a dir qual era è casa dura
> questa selva selvaggia ed aspra e forte
> che nel pensier rinnova la paura.[2]

After some thought, I represented that it was unreasonable to expect anyone, in a short time, to produce unaided information plans, estimates of local staff, proposals for the production of material and the rest of it, for so vast an area as Latin America. So I secured a very modest

---

[2] The opening stanzas of Dante's *Inferno*:
> Midway the path of life that men pursue
> I found me in a darkling wood astray,
> for the direct way had been lost to view.
> Ah me, how hard a thing it is to say
> what was thorny wildwood intricate
> whose memory renews the first dismay.
>   Trans. M. B. Anderson, World's Classics.

subsidy to allow the buying of the time of a few people whom I knew and believed to be knowledgeable. I discussed the whole question, in confidence, with men like Lord Davidson, Mr. F. Godber (later Lord Godber) President of Shell Transport and Trading, Sir Montagu Eddy of the British–Argentine Railway Committee and others.

Robert Marett was one of the first I recruited but he continued on the Shell payroll. He had been 'in oil' in Mexico just at the time of the expropriation in 1938. Early in 1939 he brought out an excellent work on Mexico[3] which greatly impressed me. I wrote to him 'out of the blue' and we met. He has given a lively account of the meeting:

> It transpired that, like myself, Grubb had spent a good deal of his early life in Latin America, mostly in Brazil, where as a missionary he had lived for several years in the backwaters of the Amazon, working among the Indians. He was the author of a number of books on Latin America. I took to him at once. He had a quick and lively mind and, despite his missionary background, there was little that I could detect of the pious do-gooder in his make-up. Even when he was most serious there was always a twinkle in his eye and he was quick to see the funny side of things. But underneath an easy and unassuming manner there was evidently a hard, determined streak. I felt that here was a man who would get things done . . .[4]

Be this as it may, I was acutely puzzled over the enterprise. There was a storm coming, and many would think that Latin America was on a sideline, remote, unconcerned and irrelevant. There were, it is true, valuable British interests there, and they had to be preserved by all means possible. In Brazil, and in Argentina and Chile, there were substantial minorities of Germans or communities of German origin, and they had to be watched and by subtle means hindered from acquiring influence. I had seen something of the Nazi penetration, tirelessly pursued in South Brazil, not least among the Lutheran clergy and not without success. There were essential supplies of raw materials and the freedom of the shipping lanes to be safeguarded. There were connections to be maintained with those whose task for the nation was to work in the shadow rather than the sunlight. And there was the vague but not

---

[3] *An Eye-Witness of Mexico*, Oxford University Press, 1939.
[4] Sir Robert Marett, K.C.M.G., O.B.E., *Through the Back Door* (Pergamon Press, 1968), p. 5. Robert Marett continued in the Foreign Service after the war and, prior to his retirement, was one of the members of the Service, admitted outside of the usual procedures, to reach ambassadorial rank.

unimportant factor of general and world public opinion. But all this did not add up to a very dramatic or exciting picture.

Our Latin American team worked well together. We did not have the advantage of the brilliant intellectuals who were to be found in other sections, but we did have men of long and intimate acquaintance with different republics, and who were thoroughly accustomed to transacting business. It transpired that no one, except myself, was acquainted with the whole area from Mexico to Buenos Aires, since the distances were truly enormous. It is forgotten today that formerly a Peruvian official from Lima appointed to a post in Peruvian Iquitos on the Upper Amazon, had to travel via Panama to New York, thence to Belém (Pará), and so nearly two and a half thousand miles up the river.

There is a superficial likeness between the republics, and Spanish or Portuguese will serve anywhere (except in Haiti which is French-speaking), but there is a world of difference between the 'Indian' republics such as Guatemala or Bolivia, and the wholly White republics such as Argentina or Uruguay.

So one of the first things I did was to take a few days off from work, and write, almost at one blow by sitting far into the night, a general survey of the area with separate sections dealing with the politics, economics, foreign interests, culture and sociology of each of the twenty republics, ranging in size from mighty Brazil to little El Salvador. This work came to be known, somewhat profanely, as 'the Bible', and indeed some 'books' in it were ponderous and intricate, and others simple and short. Throughout it, some endeavour was made to distinguish between the long and the short-term (i.e. 'for the duration') objectives of British publicity and information. It was obvious that if an efficient and not too expensive system of information work were set up in and for war it would prove its value, and there would be strong argument for its continuance in peace, and this was what occurred. This post-war phase does not belong to my story. There is an admirable account in Bob Marett's book of what did happen after 1945.

All planning had to be done in the knowledge that other bodies were concerned with similar issues and operations. No doubt in every modern war much time is taken up, particularly at early stages, with the mystic but also practical and necessary art of co-ordination. We who were working on Latin America had certain advantages, for I already knew well the persons mainly concerned among those invaluable, even indispensable allies, the British Council and the B.B.C. There were also other entities of a more mysterious and wraith-like order whom I soon identified and with whom I developed close and informal contacts. In the Latin American section of the Ministry of Information there was little that went on in that vast area which we did not learn at an early stage. Once having grasped what was needed, I usually found it possible to get the essential reins into my hands, not so much by authority, which I did not possess, as by tact.

War was declared and the Ministry of Information was set up. It might be amusing but would not be edifying to describe the initial confusion in the market-place with everyone bidding for the best stalls. It was due to several different causes. Since World War I there had been great developments in what today is known as 'mass communications'. No one could foresee exactly what type of organisation was needed to cope with all this. The permanent civil servants who inevitably handle the higher arrangements of a new ministry were themselves frequently at a loss to perceive the next step, although war presupposes quick decisions. Many different types of personalities and experiences were needed. Someone had to find the scholarly expert on some remote but key territory, the journalist with the right touch, the broadcaster, the advertiser, and many others from the publicity profession. Most of us indulged in an unscrupulous and crazy scramble to secure the best available people before they were snapped up, since everyone knew that war was bound to create a shortage of capable management types.

Nearly all concerned with overseas publicity were at first crowded into the famous Locarno room at the Foreign Office, working cheek by jowl at trestle tables under conditions which would sink a modern business without trace. The main organisation of the Ministry, the Minister and his leading officials, were installed from the start in the London University administration building in Malet Street, and most administrative controversies and struggles had to be fought out there. I was allocated to the Latin American Section under a boss whom I had met previously in Argentina. He was a man of undoubted ability, but the atmosphere was strange to him. Sitting, one day, on a bench in St. James's Park, he explained to me hopefully that he thought someone of a different temperament could better discover what we were there for. He left in a few weeks' time, and I was appointed Head of the Section. I met him once later, in Reykjavik of all places, and there lost sight of him. This Head of Section post was useful since it was in the Sections of the two big Foreign Divisions that the real job was done.

The overseas work was carried out in close consultation with the Foreign Office. This brought me into immediate contact with that august department of which I had previously had only such acquaintance as I have described. A whole new world opened up. One had to know broadly the difference between ciphers and codes. One had to learn what a Chancery was, when to address ambassadors as Excellencies, and when to invoke the really official style ('I am directed . . .' etc.). There were all manner of minor mysteries to be penetrated: for example, if you wrote the simple word 'saving' in the margin of a draft telegram, it meant that it was not a telegram at all, but for convenience was in telegraphic style. It went in the next 'bag', *en clair*. On the other hand, there were various grades of secrecy, the appropriate formula sometimes being very necessary, and sometimes being added by the writer purely to enhance his importance. My own mentors in these matters were first a highly intelligent and likeable young official from the Consular service, Roger Stevens, subsequently Sir Roger Stevens, G.C.M.G., Deputy Under-Secretary of State in the F.O., and later Vice-Chancellor of Leeds University, who had a natural flair for the work. Secondly, I leaned heavily on the admirable Mr. Leatherbarrow who was in charge of the registry.

Looking back a quarter of a century, I can see that I was disappointed with the Foreign Office. The years have passed on and there have been great changes in this venerable and crucial Department of State, and many improvements in training and in the transaction of business. It is just as well. I kept my convictions to myself, since good relations with the Foreign Office were essential for our task on the overseas side of the Ministry. There were unavoidable controversies. I studied carefully the personalities and eccentricities (there were many of these) of those officials with whom I had regular business, and I soon recognised their weaknesses as well as their strength. No doubt they sized me up with equal accuracy. Their industry and devotion were beyond praise; it was wartime and we all worked ourselves almost to a standstill. But for the most part they did not appreciate the crude market-place atmosphere of struggle and counter-bidding indispensable to the effort to assert and maintain our prestige in a neutral country, particularly when the war was going badly for the Allies. Often when I travelled abroad, east and west, among our ambassadors and high commissioners, inspecting and seeking to improve our organisation I encountered an atmosphere of slightly bored and detached interest.

It may be a little too easy to criticise the Foreign Office; it is a sitting bird; and often, to mix metaphors, has to suffer in silence for other men's sins. Guy Burgess and I met on frequent occasions, and after the War I knew Donald Maclean. It is hard to imagine anyone of sense and discretion opening up to Burgess but for some men he had a remarkable fascination. Maclean was a totally different character, a man with a rather weak face but a reasonably confident manner with something of a superior touch. To this day and in spite of the reams that have been written, I find it hard to understand how these two could come to commit treachery together. But the vital point, or one of them, is this: the kind of treachery of which they were guilty could probably be prevented, but only by a security system so tight that the man in the street would lift up his voice and cry out against it, since it would affect and limit the freedoms and rights of the individual; it would require a drastic revision of the traditional British view of the liberty of the subject, under law.

In one of the Latin American republics which I visited in the early part of the war, the Head of Chancery whom I had previously met handed me a file to study which ought not to have come my way. It contained a minute from him to his ambassador which advised the latter of my impending arrival. The minute was a very clear, model analysis of the matters which needed discussion. It also contained these words, 'Grubb is both a very nice and a very able man. It seems a pity that he should be merely occupied in improving our propaganda.' The exaggerated compliment was distinctly double-edged.

We arranged the Latin American Section in workmanlike style. Each 'specialist' was allocated a group of countries with which he was familiar and he was responsible for the administration of our affairs there. Each man, whatever his territorial responsibility, was also asked to sit down with one of the production divisions, let us say Films Division. The man immersed himself in the technique, suitability, availability and distribution of films for the whole sub-continent. By this means, and through regular meetings of the section, we formed ourselves into a strong and knowledgeable team, equipped to help one another, and able to cope with the many and novel problems that crowded in on us, with the minimum of delay.

All this would have been ineffective if we had not built up a capable local staff, either recruiting locally or sending out well-qualified men. The head of the local office was known as the press attaché, a term which stuck throughout the war, although something of a misnomer, for the press attaché and his staff, in some places quite numerous, had to deal with every branch of local information, such as buying time on the local radio, or organising 'whispering campaigns'. Later we established special production and distribution centres, in Buenos Aires and Mexico City, serving their respective areas in terms of the adjacent republics. Brazil, for reasons of language, its own special culture and its size, was a vast and well-defined area in itself. But Brazil, Argentina and Chile shared one characteristic already recorded, namely the presence of large, vocal and well-organised German minorities.

The necessity of such 'press' officers, now more appropriately called Information Officers, is taken for granted today in our large diplomatic posts. But in 1939 it was not so, there were only a very few attachés in one or two of the larger missions. Sir Charles Mendl in Paris was an example. They worked very much as individuals with a wide and invaluable range of influential personal contacts. The organised and well-staffed information office was not yet on the horizon.

When it arrived, a crop of difficulties sprang up, particularly because simultaneously a new planet had swum into the ken of the official universe, namely the Minister of Information. A competition of loyalties could not be avoided. The press attaché was appointed by the Minister, paid by the Ministry, and his home base and supplies were managed by a Section of the Ministry created for the purpose. Locally, the press attaché was also responsible to the Head of the Mission, viz. the ambassador or high commissioner, and his organisation was a part of the multifarious activities of the Chancery of a large embassy in wartime, all under the authority of the ambassador. The hoary and familiar threat of divided and possibly conflicting loyalties raised its unkempt head. It was exacerbated by the fact that the Foreign Office retained control of secret communications and the Ministry did not possess its own ciphers. It was mollified by assiduous attention to good relations between the Ministry in Malet Street and the Foreign Office, the Colonial and Dominions Offices in Whitehall. Generally a showdown was avoided by a face-to-face discussion leading to compromise and last-minute avoiding action. The only case where I can remember a violent clash of interests was over Madrid where the Ministry at one stage of the war took one view of the duties of the press attaché and the ambassador (Sir Samuel Hoare, later Lord Templewood) another and incompatible one. Hoare came to London and a meeting was held of all concerned. He put on his off-putting look which he could do very effectively and stared at us all as if we were chickens which had strayed from his backyard into his drawing room, and then remarked, 'If you do that, I shall go straight to the Prime Minister.' Brendan Bracken, who had been well briefed, replied serenely, 'Don't bother, Sam; I've already gone.'

This is to anticipate. The real struggle in the early stages was to persuade the Treasury that in Latin America it was not only necessary but thoroughly worthwhile to have any organisation at all, particularly because the republics were not in the sterling area, were remote from the war and were not, like the United States, of obvious and immediate significance to the Allied fighting cause. In the early months much of my time was spent in copious and apparently ceaseless argument over this, sometimes by minute or letter, sometimes in interviews or committees. I had an ally in the person of Sir Eric Bamford, himself a Treasury official, afterwards Deputy Director-General of the Ministry, and a man of unassailable solidity of character and unbreachable firmness of manner. That was in 1939–40. Years later he said to me in 'reminiscing' over the early years, 'Mr. W. (another Treasury man) and I used to say to each other, "We must really do some thinking; Grubb is coming for a talk this morning."' I was quite unscrupulous in presenting my case, knowing that I could turn the general ignorance of Latin America to advantage so long as I did not appear overweening and omniscient.

I could not get what I wanted, but I was determined not to be baffled. So I consulted Lord Davidson, a senior friend who in his early career had had much experience of the Civil Service, politics, and the Treasury in particular and who was connected with Argentina by family ties. He called together a group controlling large British interests in Latin America such as Lord Godber, the first Baron Luke, Sir Montagu Eddy, W. C. Warwick, and the heads of some of the old established British firms on the west coast, and of the Bank of London and South America.

The upshot was that a Commercial Relations Committee was formed, advisory to the Latin American Section of the Ministry, and I was elected to preside over it. It was not a generally popular move, being an unorthodox way of conducting the business of a wartime government department, but it was not officially interdicted. Later it led to the Commercial Relations Division of the Ministry. The action aroused immediate and corresponding interest among the British communities in Latin America. In Buenos Aires the members of the British Chamber of Commerce and the British Community Council, which then were very influential bodies, both led by Sir William Macallum, put up really substantial funds for information work, and the press attaché was able to develop a local organisation and very extensive activities. There were possibilities of a conflict of interests and loyalties, but by a little skill and the overriding concern of all to win the war, not only were clashes averted but understanding was established. Similar and more limited systems were promoted in Brazil, Chile, Peru and Mexico, and the funds flowed freely. After the lapse of years it is a privilege to record my obligation to the loyal British firms and individuals who made help available, and also supplied personnel with an intimate knowledge of the environment.

In 1940 I visited nearly all the twenty republics of Latin America, to meet the committees, see the press attachés, help smooth out difficulties, and discuss policy. It was a tense and anxious period of the war and I did not wish to be away too long. Bob Marett, who was then looking after information work in Mexico, accompanied me in Central America and the Caribbean area, and we worked easily together. In those days speedy air communications were difficult, and, in particular, facilities for night-flying and landing were only available in the very largest airports.

Yerex came to our rescue. He was a New Zealander who by sheer guts and energy had built up an air-transport line in Mexico, Central America and adjacent areas, known as Taca. He appeared in Mexico City and almost casually offered to fly us round the region, wherever we wanted. We settled with him at once, and we all tumbled into his little Ford Bellanca. It had a single air-screw which, if you managed the thing properly, went round and round in front. The availability of what was virtually private air-transport was an immense and time-saving boon.

In spite of the anxieties of war we had fun. Instead of 'goodnight', I would say to Yerex, 'James, we'll want the plane at 9.30 tomorrow.' Bob has since confessed that almost the only time he has ever felt really and acutely jittery in the air was when I took the controls. One Sunday we were flying from Guatemala into Honduras when I looked down and saw the vast Maya ruins of Copán, the greatest and possibly the oldest of the many Mayan cities. I recognised the place at once, having passed that way before on horseback from Chiquimula in Guatemala to Santa Rosa de Copán in Honduras. Being Sunday, I suggested to Yerex that we would be justified in coming down and having our lunch and a siesta. There was no regular airstrip there. Yerex flew one way down a field to scare the cattle, and then back to scare the small boys. Then he touched down.

Later that day we passed close to Momotombo, an active volcano not far from the Nicaraguan capital of Managua. Yerex, with a twinkle in his eye, asked if we would like him to fly into the crater. We declined politely. He then explained that he had flown round inside the crater of Irazú in Costa Rica. But this crater which I have ascended on a mule is a mile in diameter and the brute (that is, the volcano, not the mule) is moribund, or at least quiescent. Momotombo is small, sour and spiteful.

The stories about Yerex were innumerable: he was beyond question a 'character'. He had lost one eye and it was said that this was when he was hired by the Honduranean Government to fly up a consignment of arms which were lying at La Libertad, the port of El Salvador. His wife was a charming and cultured Honduranean girl, daughter or ward of a previous President. There were difficulties, so at least it was said, over the engagement, so Yerex brought a small plane down in the palace gardens, and off they flew to New Orleans where the deed was done.

One day, at the airport of Tegucigalpa, Yerex remarked meditatively, 'I've just been thinking what an admirable hearse an aircraft would make; it is just the right shape to take a coffin. People here, if they die in the capital, like to be buried in their native villages—a few airstrips and one of my smaller planes painted black, and there's money in it.' History does not record if he ever developed this line. Some years after these events, he sold out and retired.

By the time I had got down to the southern republics, Dunkirk had come and gone, Britain stood alone, things looked bad, and I was anxious for my wife and young children, for we lived in London. People were everywhere polite and sympathetic, but it was clear that few thought we had any real chance of winning through, although one well-known statesman in Brazil felicitously compared England to Athens standing out against the might of Persia. There were notable leaders of the British community, like J. W. Platt and Sir William Macallum in Buenos Aires, or Sir Eugen Millington-Drake and Hugh Grindley in Uruguay, in whom (as was said of Cromwell) 'Hope shone like a pillar of fire, when it had gone out in others.' I hurried on, working into the small hours, communicating constantly with the Ministry and making countless speeches, normally impromptu, in Spanish, Portuguese or English, and holding formal interviews with Presidents and Foreign Secretaries. At home Philip Guedalla took the oversight of the Latin American Section. It was not a popular appointment; Guedalla with his incontestable wit and brilliance somehow failed to engage the confidence of the solid men of affairs who by now and with their own experience of Latin America, had got a firm grip on their responsibilities.

The Latin American Section did its best work if it declined, as far as possible, to be drawn into the general policy discussions which raged up and down the Ministry. It is well known that the early weeks and months of the Ministry were chaotic. Although the lessons of World War I had been studied by the Planning Group, there was considerable uncertainty about the best approach to publicity and political warfare—the term 'psychological warfare' only came into use later. The Ministry was a haven for the most diverse types of men, including many of astonishing brilliance and verve; it was often dubbed 'a ministry of all the talents'. But an army of generals, or even colonels, is not the best instrument for war. There was a restless instability in the ranks, and it was easy for a man to transfer to another department. Talent was in short supply and hot demand, and since the most unlikely people were convinced they had a gift for propaganda, and then discovered that they hadn't, resignations were daily. There was an unnerving uncertainty about the Ministry's real place. There was reason for puzzlement, for the Departments of State, including the Services, continued their own public relations and information officers, and the Ministry of Food was particularly well-equipped in this respect. From my standpoint the really important thing was that the Minister did possess the right of policy direction and guidance of the overseas services of the B.B.C.[5] It also proved extremely important in practice that he was the Minister of the body known as the Political Warfare Executive, whose main direction was in the hands of Sir Robert Bruce Lockhart, Sir Rex Leeper, and General Sir Dallas Brooks. Similarly he later carried responsibility for the Political Warfare (Japan) Committee which met weekly and consisted of four or five of us under the chairmanship of Dallas Brooks.

Some aspects of the difficulties of the Ministry are illustrated in the changes of Ministers. There were six of them:

Lord Macmillan	appointed	4 September, 1939
Sir John Reith	,,	5 January, 1940
Mr. Duff Cooper	,,	12 May, 1940
Mr. Brendan Bracken	,,	20 July, 1941
Mr. Geoffrey Lloyd	,,	25 May, 1945
Mr. E. Williams	,,	4 August, 1945

[5] For a discussion of the wartime relations between the Ministry of Information and the B.B.C., see Asa Briggs, *The War of Words*, Vol. III of *The History of Broadcasting in the United Kingdom*, Oxford University Press, 1970.

At least two of these, Sir John (now Lord) Reith and Mr. Duff Cooper (later Lord Norwich), have left some account of their experience. In his memoirs[6] Reith gives his own version. He was Minister for the first part of 1940, and after a difficult start appeared to gain Neville Chamberlain's cordial support. He grappled with the internal organisation of his department, strove to establish its powers and functions in relation to other agencies and departments concerned, and secured the collaboration of the political parties. It remains a puzzle why, with his B.B.C. experience and prestige, he did not fully engage Churchill's confidence, and his war career was varied—Information, Transport, Works, Planning, and finally service at sea. He says himself that his departure from the Ministry was much regretted by his senior civil servants and the Press. In the Ministry as a whole he was not conspicuously popular. In the B.B.C. his authority had been unquestioned; in the Ministry he found a heterogeneous collection of men and women not accustomed to taking orders tamely. He says, 'Ultimatum procedure would have come easily and naturally to me; it would have been justified; it was hard to refrain...' but he denies that he used it.[7]

Duff Cooper's account is worth quoting for its retrospective judgments.[8]

> On the day of the outbreak [of war] the vast machine [the Ministry of Information] came into existence and 999 officials sprang to their office chairs. The result was formidable. A monster had been created so large, so voluminous, so amorphous, that no single man could cope with it. Within the mind of the monster there lurked as much talent, as much imagination and brilliance, and as much devotion to duty, as could ever have been collected in any one department of state. Ex-ambassadors and retired Indian civil servants abounded, the brightest ornaments of the Bar were employed on minor duties, distinguished men of letters held their pens at the monster's service, and all were prepared to work at any hour and without holiday in their enthusiasm for the cause. It was tragic to see so much ability, so much goodwill, so nearly wasted...
>
> It would be profitless and wearisome to enlarge upon all that was wrong with the Ministry. The main defect was that there were too few ordinary Civil Servants in it, and too many brilliant amateurs. Day after day admirable, although temporary, officials would come to me

---

[6] *Into the Wind*, Hodder and Stoughton, 1949. See especially pp. 351-5 and 522-5.
[7] Ibid., p. 360.
[8] *Old Men Forget*, Rupert Hart-Davies, 1957, the autobiography of Duff Cooper (Viscount Norwich). See especially pp. 285-8.

offering their resignation. And in every case they wanted to leave because their work was frustrated... Had they been regular Civil Servants they would have been neither surprised nor aggrieved, but not being accustomed to such treatment they were astonished and indignant.

Eventually, Duff Cooper quit, largely because, extremely unfairly, he became the target of public indignation over 'Cooper's snoopers'. This was a perfectly reasonable scheme for carefully studying the state of public opinion, and reporting where the shoe of wartime regulations pinched the foot of the average citizen. Anyhow, Duff himself had not been responsible for initiating it. But it became synonymous in the public mind with spying into private life which the Englishman detests. And the blame was piled on to Duff's unfortunate head.

Duff Cooper's analysis of his Ministry is not the full story. Civil Servants were not particularly useful in it; there were conspicuous exceptions, and no one questions their theoretical omnicompetence. Conversely, many of the experts and specialists had no idea how corporate business is conducted and by what processes decisions are reached. These brilliant individualists rebelled against such discipline. The transaction of business at the administrative level is much the same in the Civil Service, in a large firm, or in a big voluntary organisation. The difference lies in the fact that the end-product is more easily measurable in business: it is hard to measure in agreed and quantitative terms the influencing of opinion or the promotion of virtue.

Churchill's remarks on the transaction of business should also be laid to heart.[9]

> I am a strong believer in transacting official business by *The Written Word*. No doubt, surveyed in the after-time, much that is set down from hour to hour under the impact of events may be lacking in proportion or may not come true. I am willing to take my chance of that. It is always better, except in the hierarchy of military discipline, to express opinions and wishes rather than to give orders.

And he quotes his minute to the C.I.G.S. and Sir Edward Bridges, of 19 July, 1940: 'Let it be very clearly understood that all directions

---

[9] *The Second World War* (Cassell, 1949), Vol. II, pp. 16–17. See also in this work Ch. VII, pp. 143–4.

emanating from me are made in writing, or should be immediately afterwards confirmed in writing, and that I do not accept any responsibility for matters relating to national defence on which I am alleged to have given decisions unless they are recorded in writing.' As a lesser mortal I can only say I have found this practice not only clarifying but essential.

When Mr. Brendan Bracken (later Viscount Bracken) was appointed Minister in 1941 the main branches of the Department had assumed the form which they carried for the rest of the war, namely News and Censorship, Home Publicity, Overseas Publicity, and the Technical Production Services. Under Brendan Bracken, and particularly the Director-General, Mr. Cyril Radcliffe,[10] these branches were more clearly defined and their work, internally, was more smoothly and efficiently streamlined.

This was especially true of Overseas Publicity. Although the main lines had been laid down, the year 1941 was a time of both reorganisation and close and intense activity in positive achievement.[11] Each of the four main branches of the Ministry was divided into divisions and sections and each was responsible to a Controller who in turn cleared with the Deputy-Director General (Sir Eric Bamford) and the Director-General, and so with the Minister. The notable exception was the North American Division which for reasons of political delicacy stood apart, and on its own. It was directed in Brendan Bracken's time by the witty and lovable Robin Cruikshank, formerly editor of the *News Chronicle*. Francis Williams, Controller of News and Censorship, was also a former editor, in his case of the *Daily Herald*.

Sir Maurice Peterson, subsequently Ambassador in Moscow, was Overseas Controller in 1941 when Brendan Bracken decided to make some changes. I was summoned and informed that I was to assume this post. This was alarming; I was quite content with my Latin American job which I understood. When I asked why such an enormity was proposed, I was told that the work of the Latin American Section had aroused steadily increasing endorsement, and I had better pull myself together and exercise my energies in a larger sphere.

Bob Marett, in his clear, factual style has summarised the changes of this period as follows:

---

[10] K.B.E., 1944; Privy Councillor, 1949; Viscount, 1962; Lord of Appeal, 1949-64.
[11] For further details see mainly Francis Williams (later Lord Francis-Williams), *Press, Parliament and People*, Heinemann, 1946: and Marett, op. cit., especially pp. 35-51.

Mr. Cyril Radcliffe, as Director-General, brought one of the best legal brains in the country to bear upon the complex problems of war-time censorship and propaganda: with his ice-cold intelligence, he was a perfect complement to the exuberant Mr. Bracken. Mr. Francis Williams, an able and experienced journalist, had the right temperament and qualifications to inspire the confidence of his fellow journalists in his difficult post of Controller of Press and Censorship; and he was fortunate in his assistant, Admiral Thompson, the bluff, nautical and unstarchy Chief Press Censor who managed somehow to achieve the impossible task, in spite of the nature of the job, of becoming a popular and much-loved figure in Fleet Street. Mr. Kenneth Grubb . . . started the war as my immediate chief in the Latin American Section, but by sheer energy and competence was promoted over many disappointed heads to be the Controller in charge of all publicity except in the United States of America.[12]

At the time, I thought the exclusion of the United States from the Overseas Controllership was a mistake, but after some months I revised this view. My relations with Robin Cruikshank, and with Aubrey Morgan head of the British Information Services in New York were uninterruptedly close and cordial. The United States being well in the war after Pearl Harbor, this was very necessary. The British Information Services in New York were essential to the successful conduct of British wartime publicity elsewhere. So much was this the case that in Aubrey Morgan's organisation a special small unit under Hugh Mackintosh was maintained to assist British overseas publicity outside of the United States, not least in Latin America, and to work closely with the American Office of War Information and the Office of Strategic Services.

Shortly after being promoted I met Brendan Bracken by chance in the main lobby of the London University building in Malet Street, the Ministry's headquarters. He stopped me and said, 'I told the Prime Minister last night that I had appointed an ex-missionary as Overseas Controller of my Ministry.' 'Could I ask,' I said, 'if the P.M. made any comment which you are free to repeat?' 'Oh, yes,' replied Brendan. 'He said, "A very good thing, too; provided the man himself is up to it. If a missionary does not understand propaganda, what is he doing?" ' I afterwards met Churchill on several informal occasions, and once, either because of his excellent memory until his later years, or because someone

[12] Ibid., p. 37.

had briefed him, he reminded me of this, and, which was more important, presented me with cigars provided I smoked them and did not keep them.

On the overseas side of the Ministry there was still considerable uncertainty about function and purpose. I had long realised this, and at the risk of appearing arrogant, I assumed my new responsibilities with a perfectly clear idea of what I wanted to do.

The ideas which we proceeded to apply had been evolved in long discussions between a Mr. Rae Smith and myself. Rae was Chairman and Managing Director of the London company of J. Walter Thompson, one of the leading advertising agencies in the world, not excluding the United States. The directors of the parent company in New York, whom I also knew, were by no means sympathetic to the British, until the moment when America entered the war, but Rae Smith did not share their political outlook. He had fought in World War I, and wholly identified himself, right from 1939, with the Allied cause. A good-looking, very perceptive and able man, he was not everyone's friend. He was reserved and even enigmatic in manner, and at times sternly critical: one had not merely to know but to understand him. Much that went on between him and me, usually over dinner at Simpson's in the evening, was never recorded on official files, because in the early days there was prejudice against advertising men and much competitive jealousy between the various advertising agencies. Rae Smith was important not only as a man, a friend and an artist in his own craft, but because he was one of the few people, at one time the only person I knew, who was ready to enter into some of my basic ideas, enlarge them and then reduce them to a practical scheme. He died in tragic circumstances just at the end of the war.

The line I took as a result of our thinking was simple. One of the constant complaints on the overseas side of the Ministry was that no one knew what information policy was or ought to be. This was in any case dictated largely by the progress of the war and the nature of the 'target' area, but men felt the need to define or at least describe our main aims and objectives. At the same time, we all realised that the line to be taken in Spain was one thing, and in the U.S.S.R. another.

We set up a Planning Committee and Secretariat with a chief Secretary in the person of John Arrow (now deceased), then Director of the Overseas General Division which was concerned with the daily transmission of news, comment and guidance all over the world. He was assisted by Dennis A. Routh, a Fellow of All Souls. I wrote an Outline Plan for a fictitious Ruritania, and then the Planning Secretariat took over. Every plan followed the model outline. As a lead there was a brief statement of aims, valid whatever the local circumstances or state of the war. This was followed by a condensed analysis of the local situation, that is the state of public and official opinion in the target country, its significance to the war effort, the activities of the Nazis and a host of other considerations. Then there was listed a series of objectives which were to be pursued in that country. This was succeeded by a further section, written in close cooperation with the technical or production divisions outlining the various means, broadcasting, press work, visual aid, local organisations and societies and all the other instruments or channels by or through which the agreed objectives should be pursued. Theoretically, if you achieved all your objectives at once, you had done all that could be done to attain your main aims. But life doesn't work so neatly as that, this was a dream rather than a serious possibility. From a series of local or country plans, it was possible to produce regional plans covering large areas, such as the Near and Middle East, or the Latin American republics.

The Planning Secretaries consulted everyone involved. They started by sitting down with the Section concerned and writing a first draft. The Foreign Office, the Colonial and Dominions Offices, the Services, the B.B.C., the British Council and various bodies not to be defined, were all drawn into the process. The plan was then sent up to me, and provisionally approved for submission to the Overseas Planning Committee. This met once a week for a whole afternoon; representatives of such bodies as have just been mentioned were present with the Ministry's own staff, including men from its Finance and Establishment Divisions, and the plan (which by then had been sent also to the embassy and press attaché abroad for comment) was further discussed and amended. As Overseas Controller I presided at these meetings. The plan was then rewritten, submitted to the Director-General, and officially approved and issued to all concerned on his authority.

This simple process was not only invaluable as a means of clarifying functions and ends, but it served other useful purposes. It brought the production divisions into much more effective relations with the policy divisions and sections. It gave a sense of common purpose to all concerned, high or low. It enabled the Overseas Controller and his team of divisional directors and Heads of Sections to check at any time where we were all getting to. It also eliminated many occasions for disagreement and controversy between the press attaché and/or 'his' ambassador, and the Ministry itself.

This useful system would never have seen the light had it not been for the self-effacing insight of Rae Smith behind the scenes.

It was a real blow that in mid-1941 Harold Nicolson left the Ministry where he was Parliamentary Under-Secretary or junior Minister. He was an invaluable ally to all of us who were concerned with overseas publicity. He understood foreign affairs; was an instinctive diplomat and had started his career in the Foreign Office; had a wide knowledge of many countries; was well-known as a lecturer in the United States; and, above all, was an indispensable adviser on all things French. His departure from the Ministry was completely divorced from his capacities or suitability for his work and position; it was simply a political deal due to the Parliamentary Labour Party feeling that it did not have a fair share of Under-Secretaryships and also to a certain political prejudice against him. He would have been a very present help and strength in our overseas work. He was succeeded by Ernest Thurtle, Labour M.P. for Shoreditch, a rather dull man of great integrity but next to no knowledge of even the major tasks of overseas persuasion.

Harold Nicolson felt this very keenly. He carried himself at this difficult juncture with much dignity, but his diary throws a melancholy light on an understandable resentment.[13] His brief account is redeemed by one delightfully humorous note. He met Sir Gerald Campbell, then Director-General of the British Information Services in New York in the lobby of the Ministry's Duty Room. 'I hear,' he says, 'that you have been *thurtled*?' Harold's final comments wear an air of political gloom.

> Ever since I have been in the House I have been looked on as a might-be. Now I shall be a might-have-been. Always up till now I have been buoyed up by the hope of writing some good book or achieving a position of influence in politics. I now know that I shall never write a book better than I have written already, and that my political career is at an end ... Success should come late in life in order to compensate for the loss of youth; I had youth and success together, and now I have old age and failure.

---

[13] Harold Nicolson, *Diaries and Letters* (Collins, 1967), Vol. II, *1939-1945*, ed. Nigel Nicolson, pp. 179-80.

He was then only fifty-four, and he quotes the terrible comment by Tacitus on the Emperor Galba, which in 1936 *The Times* had used on the abdication of the Duke of Windsor, *Omnium consensu capax imperii nisi imperasset*—'Had he never been an emperor no one would have doubted his ability to reign.' But in these morbid sentiments of the moment Sir Harold Nicolson underrated himself. For many years he continued to delight a vast audience with his writing and broadcasting, and his official life of King George the Fifth (Constable, 1952) ranks with his best work.

It is a pity that so little is known and has been written of Brendan Bracken who died in 1958. To many, he was a mysterious and slightly daunting—even haunting—figure, particularly towards the end of his career when he withdrew from public life and did not take his seat in the Lords. There is no circumstantial record of his early years and he himself gave different accounts of them. He was born in 1901, the son of a Tipperary builder and at an early age was sent to Australia for schooling. He was next heard of at Sedbergh where he turned up armed with a cheque book and demanding admittance. He did not stay there long, and after some schoolmastering, he was introduced to Winston Churchill by J. L. Garvin, the well-known editor of the *Observer*. He won the difficult North Paddington seat for the Conservatives in 1929, and thereafter was intimately associated with Churchill.

He came from a background of journalism, or at least publishing, through his early friendship and connection with the Eyre family of Eyre and Spottiswoode. With them he formed a new publishing group in the 1920s, which came to control or own the *Financial News*, the *Investors' Chronicle*, *The Banker* (which, it is said, he established with £100 of capital, editing it himself), the *Liverpool Journal of Commerce* and a half-share in *The Economist*. After the war his group acquired the *Financial Times* which was amalgamated with the *Financial News*. Brendan remained chairman of the group; he gave much of his time to the Union Corporation, one of the City's leading mining finance houses over which he also presided. He was a founding father of *History Today*.

To many in the Ministry of Information he was rather a puzzle, tall and striking in appearance because of his boyish features and his mass of light reddish hair. He was so brimming with vitality and verve, that it was tragic to watch his decline in his last long illness. Here was a man who was always loyal to his friends, and kind without restraint to those in trouble. Not many penetrated his mask of good humour and sparkle. His skill and success as Minister of Information were soon recognised in Parliament, among his officials and in the country. He was born for the job, and it is worth quoting the words of Viscount Chandos about him in the *Sunday Times* of 10 August, 1958.

> The Ministry had formerly been the grave of reputations, and many men of high attainments had failed to manage it. Without appearing to work very hard he soon had picked the right people. He threaded his way with great skill through the labyrinth of public relations and avoided the pitfalls and sands. He kept his lieutenants in order with some astringent phrases. He ran the policy with a firm hand and left the details to others.

I took to him because he was clear-minded and decisive. The range of his knowledge and interests was astonishing. Many did not know that he was an expert on bishops of all things, or rather persons, if an expert can be imagined in so curious and tricky a subject. He took this role very seriously and his advice, presumably given direct to the Prime Minister, was to the lay judgment perceptive and usually sound. At times, his temper wore thin for the pressures of war were urgent. The nearest I came to a nasty quarrel with him was in a three-cornered showdown, to which Weizmann the well-known Zionist leader and I were parties, Weizmann having accused the Ministry of pro-Arab bias in its work in Palestine. But we reached agreement after some sharp words, soon forgotten.

He did not desire either a formal memorial, funeral or memorial service and by his wishes his papers were destroyed after his death. He maintained his affection for Sedbergh to the end, and left the school his valuable library. In him, time, the artist, 'had found a granite block on a solitary moor, and moulded from it a figure with at least one element of greatness —power.' Charlotte Brontë wrote those famous words of a very different and fictional character, but they apply well to Viscount Bracken.

It is no slur to his memory to say that the man without whom I could not have carried through my task, particularly in its early stages, was Cyril Radcliffe, Director-General of the Ministry. Some considered him a cold man, stern and unbending, magnificent in the isolation of authority, competence and confidence. This picture is false. I saw much of him in the war; indeed the Controllers met with the D.-G., the Service Advisers and others, every day of the working week for a brief 'Board' meeting, before the daily Press Conference which was taken usually by Francis Williams, the Controller of Press and Censorship. Every week I also had at least one, sometimes more, long discussions with him over our overseas difficulties and developments.

The odds were against this relationship being a success. I had an awe of professional men of high standing, having neglected my own education and having lived much alone in a very backward area. The cast of my mind was very different from that of this man who was to become ere long one of the most distinguished Law Lords and public servants of the country. I could perceive, at first contact, that here was someone who would go to the top, and a man of immense sincerity, perspicacity and impregnable integrity, capable of letting his mind range with equal percipience over a vastly varied range of problems. As the months went by I discovered another quality, namely an understanding, sympathy and appreciation which much encouraged lesser men.

I wondered if I could make such a man appreciate my strange world, one day coping with some nuisancey telegram from Nicaragua, another seeing how to help our representatives in Chungking, and a third seeking support in one of my recurring controversies with the Foreign Office. Radcliffe entered into all this, and I soon lost my shyness. He put his great weight and authority unreservedly behind the main reforms of the overseas side of the Ministry, and, in particular issues, once he was satisfied that your case was sound, he backed you right through, not least in the unavoidable arguments with other departments. But you had to know your stuff, and I usually did. I learned from him an art which has served me well in later life, although many today underrate it, namely a command of the English language whether on paper or in speech, precise without being clipped, and telling without the rococo elaborations of the ambassadorial despatches of those days.

The overseas side of the Ministry consisted of a series of territorial divisions and sections, and certain units which were essential as common services to all. Among the latter were the Overseas General Division, the Commercial Relations Division, and the Religions Division. The main duties of the territorial divisions and sections were obvious. They had to serve and supply their opposite numbers abroad, maintain close touch with the B.B.C., the Foreign Office, the Service Departments and other Whitehall offices, and clear their business with the establishment and finance divisions, the technical or production divisions, and indeed with all and sundry in the Ministry itself. In the early days there was a deal of talk of the need for liaison officers. I never took much stock of this. There are situations in which liaison men are useful but they are not numerous in general administration. After a first introduction, it is better for the principals concerned to clear direct which they can usually do expeditiously without shouting or bawling. When a new task requires the cooperation of many minds, what is needed is not a caucus of liaison officers but a joint meeting firmly chaired.

The Overseas General Division and the Planning system were essential to the operation. The former was a news-and-comment transmitter, a place where enemy broadcasts and press were studied and a bearer of many other duties. The operations were immensely complex; one illustration must suffice, the monitoring of the European press and radio.

There was a meeting from time to time in the Ministry of representatives of all sorts and conditions of war departments, chaired by the Overseas Controller. Here each department stated what intelligence it wished to have in addition to the general coverage. A list of subjects of special concern was compiled and cabled to the Ministry's listening posts, and when the material was received, it was edited into précis form and distributed according to the list.

Many besides the Ministry itself were concerned with the enemy's output and with whatever could be picked up in Europe, since a very careful scrutiny may reveal economic and political facts even when censorship is rigid. The 'listening posts' were in Stockholm, Lisbon, Berne and Istanbul, and together they employed some hundreds of persons. The busiest was in Stockholm and it was known as the 'Parrott House'. Cecil Parrott[14] who ran it, came from outside the Civil Service, like Sir Robert Marett, in his case from the world of education, and after retiring from a distinguished diplomatic career culminating in six years as Ambassador at Prague, is today (1970) Professor of Russian and Soviet Studies in Lancaster University.

The Commercial Relations Division was a small unit concerned with a large task, namely the mobilisation for publicity purposes of British business men overseas, and their encouragement, supply and support. Something of this has been recounted in regard to Latin America. It was also very helpful elsewhere, not least in India, especially after the Congress Party's critical 'Quit India' resolution of 8 August, 1942, passed on Gandhi's instigation. War publicity and information in India were at no time easy, and involved the closest cooperation between the Ministry's Empire Division and the Government of India controlling its own agencies.

[14] Later Sir Cecil Parrott, K.C.M.G., O.B.E.

The Religions Division was an unexpected outfit in the Ministry. The vigour of church life in the United States, the pro-Nazi sympathies of certain parts of the Roman Catholic Church, not least in Italy, Spain and elsewhere, and the special witness of the Confessional Church in Germany all required the closest study and appropriate measures where action was possible. The origin of the Division was peculiar. At the Planning Group which met in early 1939, there was a tendency to propose 'using' the Churches in ways which seemed quite out of keeping with their true calling and life. I said nothing but went direct to Archbishop Lang of Canterbury. He intervened, and this ensured that the religious question and the rôle of the Churches would be discreetly handled. The first director of the Division was the Rev. Dr. Hugh Martin C.H., a distinguished free churchman, and he was followed by R. R. Williams, formerly Education Secretary of the Church Missionary Society, and since 1953 Bishop of Leicester.

Another aspect of the work which required considerable attention was the arrangement of visits by selected groups of persons, often editors and journalists, but also men and women of other professions and vocations. They were shown war factories and other sides of the total war effort, subject to the limitations of security. This is either done well or best not done at all, and the visit of a party required careful preparation jointly by overseas and home divisions. For reasons I cannot now recall one of these visits included Portuguese firemen: many Portuguese had individually been of great help to us, and some had been in prison because of their work in the Allied cause. The firemen made quite an impression in the course of a few hours spent, I believe, in Leeds, and the common phrase 'visiting fireman' is said to have originated there.

An amusing incident occurred on the occasion of a visit of Turkish editors at a crucial stage of the war. At the farewell reception I asked one of them if he had seen all that he had hoped. He replied gratefully—his French was excellent—and then manoeuvred me into a corner. He explained that he had been a life-long admirer of British detective and police skill, and he would much like to leave some flowers at No. 221b Baker Street, the home of the immortal Sherlock Holmes. It was obviously a moment not of truth, but of resourcefulness. I thanked him profusely in my most copious French, and explained that that area of London had suffered sadly from bombing. A visit, therefore, would be pointless, but it would be much appreciated if he would write to the Commissioner of Metropolitan Police and express his sentiments. By the time the Commissioner had received the letter, I had phoned and explained, and my friend received an effusive and grateful reply.

The variety of matters that came to the Overseas Controller was baffling, and one had to work long hours to cope with the daily inflow of files and telegrams, often presenting complicated proposals which required immediate decision. They ranged from the building of a new radio station in some distant part of the Commonwealth to the content and meaning of the formula of 'Unconditional Surrender'. I held strongly to two simple principles: to be truthful, and to be consistent.

Asia and the Mediterranean were the scene of many of our difficulties. Cairo was a major centre, a miniature Department of Information on its own capable of mounting considerable operations. At the end of 1941 Sir Walter (later Viscount) Monckton, previously Director-General of the Ministry of Information, took charge, and his standing was of great service to the Ministry. The Near and Middle East was a ticklish theatre of operations. Turkey hovered in the balance, Iran (Persia) was nearly taken over by the Germans. Always important to the Allies, it became doubly so when Russia entered the war. There was a propaganda battle almost everywhere with both the Germans and the Italians. Baghdad was a focus of intrigue, and the conflict between the Free French and the Vichy French became acute in Syria and Lebanon. The Jewish-Arab struggle over Palestine was with difficulty kept from erupting. The German invasion of Greece and Crete in 1941, and the whole grim year of 1942, with Pearl Harbor and Singapore, and the second British retreat in the western desert seemed almost too much to bear. As one travelled around, visiting our agencies and posts, it was easy to read men's anxieties in their calm as much as in their questions.

The Middle East activities of the Ministry attracted some of the liveliest and ablest of those who served it overseas. Owen Tweedie in Cairo was a tower of strength. Ann Lambton in Persia, a rare and rather solitary character, later Professor of Persian in the London School of Oriental and African Studies, was known even in remote villages. Stewart Perowne in Aden and Baghdad, son of a bishop, a man with pre-war knowledge particularly of Palestine, witty, brilliant and engaging, was the only member of the Ministry who could subsequently claim to be the discoverer of a lost city (Aziria). In Istanbul and Ankara Leigh Ashton (later Sir Leigh Ashton) was Director of Information, and, after the war, for a full decade the boss of the Victoria and Albert Museum.

Although I had travelled in the Near and Middle East before the war,

I did not profess knowledge of it and did not speak Arabic. I had read the Koran at least twice, several histories, some modern studies and the stories of the earlier travellers, Persian poetry in translation, Haji Baba, and that was about all. I recollect on one of my war journeys being invited to a house where 'whirling Dervishes' were dancing. It was extraordinary to see a boy rotate steadily with his arms akimbo, at a high speed, for ten minutes or more, and then walk to his seat without any sign of giddiness. The performance was followed by speeches, coffee and sweetmeats. On going out my host spat in a spittoon; I did the same, being uncertain whether it was a part of the ritual. I missed, but a hungry dog did the necessary, and I was saved from disgrace.

A slightly similar incident had come my way in one of the smaller Latin American republics. I called on a Very Important Government Potentate. He sat in a large office whose floor was inlaid with blocks of a beautiful hardwood which took a high polish. On entering I caught a spittoon with my foot; it glissaded across the floor and came to rest by his desk. He clearly thought that an English custom was involved, for he stepped round the corner of the desk, shook hands, and, bowing slightly, said, 'Have the goodness to spit first.' I did so, accurately this time, although I have never claimed any skill in spitsmanship.

That floor was something to be proud of. It reminded me of the remark attributed to Sydney Smith when he was told of the proposal to pave St. Paul's with wooden blocks: 'Let the Dean and the Canons lay their heads together and the work is done.'

Freya Stark, irresistible in her charm and vivacity, was the best known of a lively team. It often occurs that women, with their particular sympathies and sensibilities, make the best practitioners in the information field, and this was one of the main reasons why I had appointed Miss Monroe (Mrs. Neame) to direct the Middle East Division. Freya Stark early grasped that the conception of 'propaganda' would not do. In the Middle East the emphasis was on persuasion and the strategy that of promoting interest by appealing to the other man's self-interest.[15] In spite of serious bouts of ill-health, and of difficult and intrepid travels, she always maintained her courage and, to the delight of thousands of readers, obviously found solace and cheer in her gift of vivid and beautiful description, and her lively correspondence. She showed films to harems in virtually forbidden countries like the Yemen. She kept her

[15] She has given a full account of these years in *Dust in the Lion's Paw, Autobiography 1939–1946*, John Murray, 1961.

The C.C.I.A. calls on the High Commissioner for Refugees in Geneva: (*left to right*) Dr. Elfan Rees, the late G. J. van Hoeven Goedhart, K.G G. and O. F. Nolde

With Dr. O. F. Nolde of the C.C.I.A. at an Asian Conference

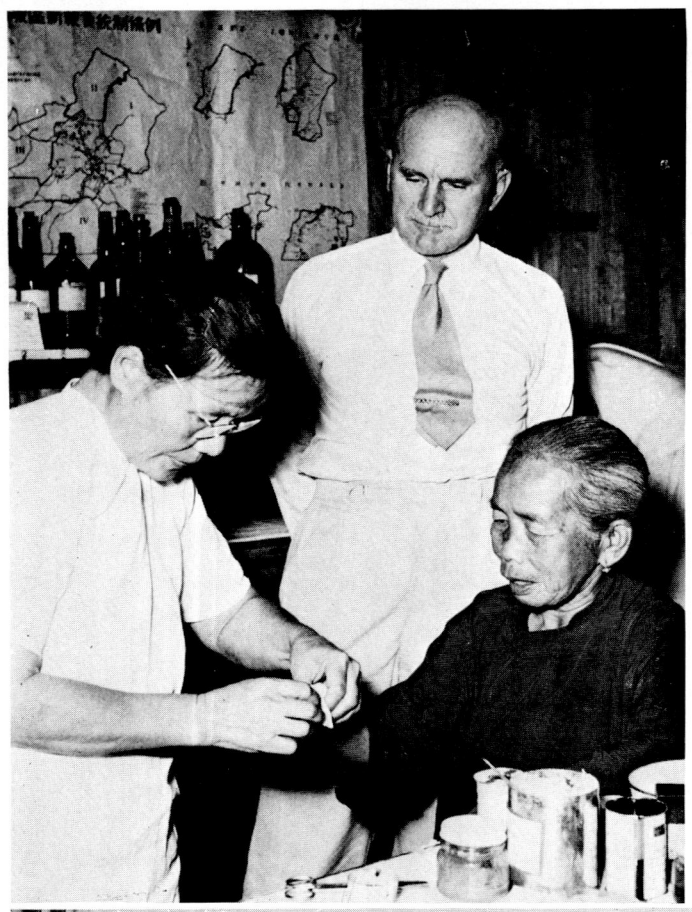

At a clinic in Malaya, 1955

In Athens in 1955 with (*left to right*) Mrs. K. Bliss, Dr. Liston Pope and Dr. John Baillie

head amid the complicated and risky intrigues of the mid-war period in Baghdad. She travelled in Persia and overland to India. She swayed the most improbable people and found an entrée where all hope had been abandoned by others who would enter there. She knew Italy well for her home was near Treviso, and later she did valuable work there, as well as a tour in the United States made very difficult for her by the heat of the Zionist controversy. Her finest achievement was the building up of the 'Brotherhood of Freedom' to a membership of 60,000, an operation based on her sound conviction that the right, if not the only effective approach to 'persuasion' in the Near and Middle East, was through the active interest, work and association of declared friends. The Brotherhood naturally declined after the war, and following the establishment of the State of Israel, but it survived in tenuous form until the British invasion of Egypt destroyed any last traces of the conviction that Britain was a friend of the Arab world. Freya married Stewart Perowne in 1947.

John Lawrence (later Sir John Lawrence, Bt., O.B.E.) was Press Attaché and Information Officer in Moscow. He had a tough task. He started in misfortune, since the convoy taking him to Russia was attacked off Norway and he was fished out of very cold water and eventually decanted in Murmansk. Once installed in Moscow, he soon won respect for his general competence and his ability rapidly to improve his knowledge of Russian, of the country and of the Revolution. Considering the slow progress before the war of Russian studies in British universities, he built up a very competent and lively team. Conditions were not propitious. It was the period of the German invasion of Russia, involving the evacuation of embassies from Moscow to Kuibyshev and culminating in the tremendous defeat of von Paulus at Stalingrad. Later he had to cope with the constant Russian harping and carping about the Second Front. Always he was faced with the abysmal Russian ignorance of all the battles and struggles except their own.

Given the trickiness of the setting, Lawrence and his colleagues built up, with great care and skill, a surprisingly large circle of influential contacts. At a British Embassy reception, nearly all the guests not actually from Russian government departments and services appeared to come from the press attaché's list, and the most famous Moscow writers and journalists were on easy terms with him.

Walter Monckton visited Russia early in the war and later I was despatched to Moscow. I flew to Teheran and stuck; and then to Baku and stuck; and then to Astrakhan and stuck. It was the beginning of winter and bitterly cold, and the Caspian and the mouths of the Volga were freezing. We spent several days in a rickety boarding-house in Astrakhan, and I passed the time, either pacing the streets in my overcoat, walking round and round the local Kremlin, or playing chess and losing, in my dressing-gown. Astrakhan was a dull place.

From there another plane presently took us on to Stalingrad. There seemed no accommodation at all there, and this was not surprising. It was not long after the tremendous fighting and the desolation was terrible. Our party, which included two Ambassadors going *en poste* to Moscow and my own Secretary, was parked in a wooden barrack on the edge of the airfield some distance outside the town. The cold was not so bad as the mud when it thawed. The Russians were very friendly, but even vodka and caviar were hard to come by. One afternoon the secretary of the local Communist party came out, packed us all into an open lorry and took us round the ruined city explaining in tolerable German the main features of the fighting. There were German prisoners-of-war everywhere; some of these were rounded up, and I was asked to address them in German, telling them what a fearful thing it was to be a 'fascist beast'. I did make a little speech, but not quite in such terms, and fortunately a sudden and heavy fall of snow gave me an excuse for abbreviating my discourse.

In Moscow I was warmly received and installed in the National Hotel. I was delayed in the great city for longer than anticipated owing to the cancellation of flights in the wintry weather. Sir Archibald Clark Kerr (later Lord Inverchapel) was at the Embassy and John Lawrence had his department excellently organised. He was already well-known, in so far as anyone in such a position could be in Russia, and his regular publication *The British Ally* (*Britanski Soyuznik*), excellently produced, had quickly achieved the maximum circulation the Russian authorities would allow. A full quarter of a century later there came into my hands some unpublished notes which Lawrence had made about my time in Moscow where I was soon known as 'The Revisor', viz. the 'Inspector-General', the title of one of Gogol's well-known plays. 'Kenneth,' he writes, 'had come out to inspect the work of the press department and got caught in Moscow for longer than he intended, since there was no flying weather for about two weeks. In consequence I got to know him pretty well . . . he is shortish and bald but very wiry and never ill. He is shy and never looks at you . . . at first he seemed enigmatic, but after ten days close acquaintance and collaboration I feel sure that he is honest and human as well as brave, crafty and penetrating. A sort of Christian Odysseus.'

John Lawrence, at that time, was not interested in Christianity. After the war he came back to the faith with a leap; he has given his own account of his spiritual experience.[16] He was later a chairman of the Executive Committee of the Church Missionary Society and an active member of the Church Assembly. He has been editor of the review *Frontier* for more than a decade, creating an admirable spiritual and intellectual achievement which could quite easily have become a pedestrian piece of periodical print.

This brief account of the Ministry's overseas concerns could be multiplied by examples stretching out to the crack of doom, but this would serve little purpose. Similarly, much could be written of the distinguished service rendered by the B.B.C., not only in their German or French broadcasts, or in their Empire service which was so highly appreciated, but in all the fifty or so languages in which they broadcast. Or again, there is a whole story to be told of the information and political warfare activities of the Governments-in-exile, of the Free French, and the formation of the Interallied Information Committee. Such matters threw up negotiations which required tact, clarity and understanding to sort out, and in which some knowledge, at least of European languages, was a great help.

The darkest hour was early 1942, but much of that year was depressing. 'In an hour', cabled Churchill on 19 January, 1942 to Curtin, Prime Minister of Australia, 'the American naval superiority in the Pacific was for the time being swept away. In another hour the *Prince of Wales* and *Repulse* were sunk.'[17] The fall of Singapore followed within a month. Such disasters are not helpful for information work, persuasion, propaganda or political warfare—a statement which could be put more strongly without exaggerating. But we were fighting in a just cause and at night, sleeping in my office, or on Home Guard, I used to repeat to myself the concluding lines from *Prometheus Unbound*:

> To suffer woes which Hope thinks infinite;
> To forgive wrongs darker than death or night;
>   To defy Power, which seems omnipotent;
> To love and bear; to hope till Hope creates
> From its own wreck the thing it contemplates;
>   Neither to change, nor falter, nor repent;
> This like thy glory, Titan, is to be
> Good, great and joyous, beautiful and free;
> This is alone Life, Joy, Empire, and Victory.

[16] See Dewi Morgan, ed., *They Became Anglicans* (Mowbray, 1963), pp. 85-92.
[17] *The Second World War* (Cassell, 1951), Vol. IV, p. 15.

After the war the greater part of all this organisation was dispersed, but the principles and, on a much reduced scale, the practice of overseas publicity remained. The Ministry of Information closed. The essential production and distribution services went to the Central Office of Information. Special units were set up in the Colonial and Dominion Offices and in the Foreign Office which for long had had a small but skilled press department of its own. My last act at the Ministry was to hand over to Sir Ivone Kirkpatrick (later Permanent Under-Secretary of State at the F.O.) with whom I had had so many dealings during the previous years.

It is hard to evaluate the worth of this work which occupied some seven of the best years of my life. But wars must be won and I wasted little time in morbid reflection. The main argument which went on, all those years, was familiar, what are we fighting for? What are our war aims? It was contended that war publicity and persuasion could not be effective unless this was answered. The easy reply was that we were fighting for safety, existence and freedom, and then for democracy, for one world, and all the rest of it. This did not seem good enough to some thoughtful people. The argument, or as people say today, the dialogue, became more acute when the U.S.A. entered the war. The Americans disliked colonies and monarchy, but liked themselves and the 'American way of life'. They thought that the United Nations could be much more successful than the League of Nations. The Russians wanted a Communist empire, which they got, the cheap labour of millions of Germans, and security. The administrator can spend an immense time on these discussions, usually conducted by exchange of minutes, when in practice the best thing to do was the next thing. But I had to discuss at length with Elmer Davis of the O.W.I. (Office of War Information of the U.S.A.) and his officials, and the Office of Strategic Studies people. It all flared up when the formula of 'unconditional surrender' was announced. On this, it pays to read again Churchill's own account,[18] and to note in particular these words, 'Unconditional surrender means that the victors have a free hand. It does not mean that they are entitled to behave in a barbarous manner, nor that they wish to blot out Germany from among the nations of Europe. If we are bound, we are bound by our own consciences to civilisation. We are not to be bound to the Germans as the result of a bargain struck. That is not the meaning of "unconditional surrender".' It cannot be contended that the Western Allies have acted towards Germany 'in a barbarous manner'.

[18] Ibid., Vol. IV. pp. 613-18.

The Ministry of Information disappeared on 31 March, 1946, and to tell the subsequent story is no part of this book since I was not connected with its successors. In 1965 the Royal Institute of Public Administration issued a general study done through a well-equipped Study Group. The chapter on 'From the beginning to 1945' ends with this paragraph.

The wartime experiences of the working of the Ministry of Information, and the rest of the information machine, greatly influenced the kind of information services which were to develop after the War. For the future, the most important aspect of the wartime organisation were not so much the coordinating functions of the Ministry of Information, as the build-up of personnel and experience at departmental level and the experience of providing common services and publicity materials for the use of departmental public relations divisions. The other valuable experience proved to be the habit of using government machinery to collect information on which policy and administrative action could be based.[19]

* * *

This is the best place to say something about the Hispanic and Luso-Brazilian Councils of which Lord Davidson was in large measure the creator. He had himself been Controller of Production in the early period of the Ministry. Later, in 1942, he made a long journey around South America which proved of immense value to building up Britain's national standing and a fuller appreciation of her immense effort in the war. Throughout the war years, I had worked very closely with the leading interests of our overseas trade. This connection and support were recognised as particularly valuable in Latin America.

Already, during the war, Davidson had begun to collect contributions for the purpose of establishing an institution to be a centre of Anglo-Latin American cultural and commercial understanding; Professor E. Allison Peers (deceased) of Liverpool University was encouraged and assisted to promote the wider teaching of Spanish in the country.

After the war I was invited to head up the scheme under Davidson's leadership. I started in a single office at River Plate House and proceeded to raise the considerably increased funds necessary. Very soon afterwards,

---

[19] Marjorie Ogilvy-Webb, *The Government Explains: A Study of the Information Services* (Allen and Unwin, 1965), p. 66.

we engaged the services of Mrs. Maria Louisa Arnold (later Mrs. Fordham, C.B.E.) as social secretary and hostess. Of Mexican birth, she had worked with me in the war and we knew well her brilliance of mind, her sparkling personality, and her unrivalled knowledge of the Latin American *milieu* in London, particularly the Embassies. She continued with the Councils until the end of 1969.

The twin Councils first acquired a short lease of No. 4 Upper Berkeley Street, and later moved into No. 2 Belgrave Square. The funds for acquiring this second lease (since considerably extended) were raised by careful management at Upper Berkeley Street, extra contributions from member-firms, and a munificent donation from a fund established in the war by Sir Eugen Millington-Drake, K.C.M.G., who, in the course of an enterprising career, was Ambassador at Montevideo at the time of the *Graf Spee* 'incident'. The new headquarters were called Canning House, after the famous foreign secretary George Canning who 'called a new world into being to redress the balance of the old'. All the departments of the work, social, educational, information, and the valuable library were established there. Years later, in 1969, the library, indispensable for an institute which was not only a social centre, but engaged in study and information and in the promotion of Spanish and Portuguese teaching throughout the country, was splendidly rebuilt through a donation of some £40,000 from the Gulbenkian Foundation to the Luso-Brazilian Council. Mr. G. H. Green has been Librarian from the beginning.

As Secretary-General from the start until 1954, I cannot speak too warmly of Viscount Davidson and, indeed, of Lady Davidson, M.P. for Hemel Hempstead from 1937 to 1959, and later a Life Peeress, Baroness Northchurch, in her own right. Both were always ready to help, and nothing was too much trouble for them. The relations between Lord Davidson and myself were always most cordial, indeed all that could possibly be desired. His experience of public business, natural shrewdness and vast range of contacts were put unreservedly at the disposal of the enterprise. He commanded respect both for his qualities of mind and heart and also for his impressive appearance, in his great years; he was one of the most handsome men I have had the fortune to know well. His family had been connected with Argentina for over a century. He continued as President of the Councils until 1969,[20] when long illness compelled his resignation, and he was succeeded by Lord Erroll.

[20] See Robert Rhodes James, *Memoirs of a Conservative: J. C. C. Davidson's Memoirs and Papers, 1910–1937* (Weidenfeld and Nicolson, 1969), Epilogue, p. 426.

Canning House must be carefully distinguished from the Canning Club. The latter, with which I have also long been associated, is the successor of the former Argentine Club, founded sixty years ago. The difference between then and now is that today the Club makes its membership available not simply to 'clubbable' persons connected with Argentina, but to those interested in any part of Latin America, Spain or Portugal, and to the citizens of all these countries.

CHAPTER VII

The Church Missionary Society

IN 1944 I accepted the Presidency of the Church Missionary Society (C.M.S.). The reasons for my decision were simple. I was flattered by the approach made by the General Secretary of the Society, the Rev. M. A. C. Warren,[1] but flattery is not enough. Most men feel elated when offered a position of respect and leadership. If they know a little, they also realise that this agreeable feeling will evaporate in about a fortnight, and then there may follow years of hard slogging. By 1944 I knew quite enough to perceive this.

It seemed, and still seems to me, a surprising invitation. I have since learned that Dr. Warren, in addition to proceeding through the Society's usual mechanism for choosing and making such appointments, had taken the advice of senior men who knew me well, had survived this experience but had not accurately reported my failings.

For once I felt misgivings. My customary decisiveness evaporated, and prudence which has saved me from many mistakes afforded no help. I prayed and thought, and then consulted William Temple, Archbishop of Canterbury. It was during the short time of his 'reign' and we already knew each other well. The main difficulty was the standing and nature of the job, and the claims which it would make in an age of post-war flurry and restless reconstruction.

One of my worries was that the post ought to be filled by someone eminent. The Society had been founded in 1799; it did not appoint a President until 1812. Since then there had been only five, and I was proposed to be put in to bat sixth. One, the Earl of Chichester, had served for fifty-four years. I reflected with pain that if I lasted that long I would not escape until I was ninety-eight. Another died after six months only in office, and if I did likewise, it would be hard on my wife and children.

Temple was emphatic that all this was irrelevant. He perceived very clearly the equalitarian nature of the times. He was confident that the

[1] Now (1970) a Canon and sub-Dean of Westminster.

Society should not seek a President who was actively identified with a political party, like my predecessor Sir Robert Williams. He talked much of the new type of competence which the Church must seek in its practising laity, and he urged me to accept.

After I had done so, he summoned me again. He said that for some time after the war it would not be clear who would emerge from the laity with the time and the disposition to serve the Church actively. He urged me not to limit myself to the C.M.S. but to accept other posts if such came my way and engaged my interest. I pointed out that I had no personal fortune at all, children to educate and a home to maintain. His reply, roughly, was, 'You have the native energy and skill to earn your living and at the same time to serve the Church. You will not be rich, but you will be satisfied.' The first of these two latter prophecies is true; as for the second, something in one's depths 'doth glow, too strange, too restless, too untamed': satisfaction ever eludes me.

Dr. Warren's invitation was decisively endorsed by William Temple's comment. I accepted the invitation, and had to face the implications of the comment. It was agreed that the Society should make an important change in the tenure of presidency. Traditionally this had been a life sentence, but in these uncertain days this was no longer appropriate. The laws of the Society were altered and it became a five years' post, the tenant being free to offer himself for re-election. In the end I served the Society for a quarter of a century. The English are incredibly conservative in these matters.

Although the post was far above my deserts, nevertheless it was within the family tradition. The heroes of my youth were such men as Barbrooke Grubb of South America, Grenfell of Labrador, Temple Gairdner of Cairo, and at a later date such men as John R. Mott and William Paton. Since both the latter had a decisive influence on my outlook and career, a few words must be said of them.

I first met Mott in Atlantic City, in 1926. It was a hard winter; I had just emerged for a few weeks from Amazonia; the sea along the beach was frozen and it seemed a strange environment. Mott addressed an assorted collection of religionists, professional leaders of the great American Churches and missions assembled in a large hotel. I knew his reputation well, and the religious world had for nearly two decades associated his name with the Edinburgh Missionary Conference of 1910, usually regarded as the pioneer of modern ecumenical conferences. He chaired this, by common consent, with consummate wisdom and skill. It was a missionary conference on the evangelistic extension of the Church through the proclamation of its message, even more than an ecumenical one. The word 'ecumenical' was not much used then, or for many years afterwards, but Mott's watchword, 'The evangelisation of the world in this generation' was widely known and discussed. The ecumenical movement of today likes to claim the conference for itself; it would be more justified in doing so if it were inspired by a like evangelistic fervour.

I met Mott on many subsequent occasions, but remember him particularly at the Madras (Tambaram) Conference of the International Missionary Council in 1938. When I was elected to office in the C.M.S., he at once wrote in terms of remarkable cordiality and encouragement. After the war I saw him often both in the preparations for the World Council of Churches, and at its first two World Assemblies. He died in 1955 at the age of eighty-nine.

His commanding presence and complete mastery of the details of public business were equally impressive. He was an indefatigable worker and tireless traveller. He had the gift of interesting wealthy and generous benefactors in the promotion of his schemes. He failed in little, and succeeded in much.

His vision and courage were unmistakable. His public style was suited to the times, and his sonorous, fervent and often solemn oratory captivated the attention of thousands, young and old. Like all such men he had his well-known mannerisms and turns of phrase which endeared him to all who had the merest glimpse of the integrity and consistency of his outlook and the depth and faith of his mind. In the period covered by his great years men who believed at all harboured fewer doubts than today. The hope of world evangelisation fired the imagination even of ordinarily unconcerned Christians. You could not but be stirred by the breadth of Mott's vision in an age when internationalism was in its infancy and contacts between east and west relatively few. In his every evangelistic utterance, you could read his faith, and not merely his fancy that the day was coming when many would flock from the east and the west and 'sit down in the Kingdom of God'. He was a man of mission and for him this meant men and women dedicated to the proclamation of the Gospel. He often repeated before large audiences one of his favourite rhymes, despised by some for its simplicity, welcomed by many for its urgency—

> The task which centuries might have done
> Must crowd the hour of setting sun.

Mott was an apostle of *greatness*. He responded to the greatness of the Gospel. He set no limits to what he believed God could do through ordinary people. He felt and measured the greatness of the Christian heritage and the magnitude of the Christian task. He was undaunted by obstacles. When he was harassed he was still great in his prayers and in his words, and when the light shone on his horizon he was already breaking camp to advance to greater explorations of faith.

I counted it a privilege to be one of the speakers at the symposium organised in Cornell University, Ithaca, in 1965 to mark the centenary of his birth.

William Paton's career was shorter but notable for solid achievement. He died in 1943 at the early age of fifty-six, his powers still to be fully deployed but his energies fully employed. He passed his early years as a secretary of the Student Christian Movement and later worked with the Y.M.C.A. in India, subsequently becoming Secretary of the National Christian Council there. His service with this body was effective and energetic. He had a lot to do with the early repatriation of German missionaries to their posts after World War I, and he was the main agent behind the Lindsay Commission which had a decisive influence on Christian higher education in India.

Later he returned to London to take the key post of Secretary to the International Missionary Council, and was much concerned with the organisation of the Jerusalem World Assembly of this body, and the similar occasion ten years later at Madras.

I knew him for many years, and when in London frequently saw him. I served on various committees at Edinburgh House, where were the offices of the International Missionary Council and also of the Conference of British Missionary Societies. The chairmanship of the standing committee of the latter body was the first such post of any wide influence which was offered to me. This was in 1938. Owing to World War II, I was unable to take it up.

I was in close and frequent touch with William Paton when the preparations for the Madras meeting were being made, and he was involved in the work necessary for setting up the Oxford and Edinburgh Conferences on 'Life and Work' and 'Faith and Order', and the British and World Councils of Churches. During the war he was closely associated with George Bell, Bishop of Chichester, in his efforts to secure reasonable treatment for refugees of German origin, particularly non-Aryans, and, in addition to many other duties, he was Secretary to the Peace Aims

Group. This was a small informal body which met under the chairmanship of William Temple. It included some very distinguished members such as Bell himself and, for a time, Arnold Toynbee. Although on a small scale, it was the British counterpart to Dulles's Commission on a Just and Durable Peace, and it was in the Group that I first met John Foster Dulles. I attended whenever I could, but official war duties were exhausting and the Group was boring. There was an atmosphere of too much peace when what was needed was more effective war. The fallacy in this argument was obvious, but to those serving in the war machine, unofficial talk about peace in the early years of the war seemed unrealistic.

Paton's life has been written[2] by Miss Sinclair who knew him well, since for years she worked with him as an editor of the *International Review of Missions*. Valuable though it is as a source of facts and a connected account of his career, somehow it just fails to put him in a really lively light, and Paton was nothing if not lively, original, and stimulating.

He died before anyone had raised the question of the Presidency of the C.M.S., but his influence with me was more decisive than that of John R. Mott or William Temple. I could not but like the man although he was not an easy man to know and some did not find him easy to like. He was forthright and frank to the point of ignoring the sensitivities of others and causing offence. He simply could not see why the minds of others did not move as quickly as his own. He neither suffered fools gladly nor did he gladden suffering fools. He appealed strongly to me. One did not have to repeat anything to him twice. He seized immediately on the real point in a debate and unmasked the half-truths, the intellectual nudity of which verbiage is the customary and useful cloak. This was one reason why he was by no means always popular, either in India or in the West, but men of worth knew his sterling capabilities. He did not always have time to make friends and influence people, and many resented the almost arrogant air which he sometimes chose to assume. I can see him today on the platform of the Madras Conference, telling us all, from scores of nations, East and West, how to behave.

During the early years of the war we met regularly, usually in a London club, and his interest and advice were most stimulating. The man himself had a vitality and punch which were irresistible. He made some conspicuous mistakes—which of us has not done so?—but he was also a dangerous marksman. In his guerilla wars of argument and policy-making, he shot well and accurately. He used his side-arms with

[2] Margaret Sinclair, *William Paton*, S.C.M. Press, 1949.

admirable thrust, and if sometimes he winged and wounded the wrong man, I provided the balm when the controversy was over.

He constantly encouraged me to take the world mission of the Church seriously, and I listened to him with the greater attention because he entered into my own difficulties. He frequently opined that I should give my whole time after the war to the ecumenical movement with which he was deeply preoccupied, but that was not to be. We discussed this over dinner with all the gravity which I could focus on my own affairs, which is not much, on the night in 1943 when he left London for the North and for Scotland. A few days later I turned on the radio just in time to hear the news of his unexpected passing through a sudden illness. In those bitter war years the angel of death was abroad in the land and you could almost hear the beating of his wings. The household of God accepted its share, and not least in my own little circle, in William Temple and William Paton.

The years have melted away and time has brought its healing compensations. When the Missionary and Ecumenical Council of the Church Assembly was set up twenty years later, in 1963, William Paton's son, David, was appointed Secretary, and I became the first chairman, holding the office for five years until health compelled me to give it up. Thus towards the end of a long career, I renewed a family contact which I had profited so much from in earlier years. We worked closely and happily together, in mutual confidence and appreciation. Canon David Paton had himself been a C.M.S. missionary in China, and the twin causes of mission and unity found as devoted expression in David as they had in William. It is pleasant to record so faithful a succession, for in the corrupted currents of this world, much is forgotten which for the common enrichment should be remembered, but,

> Time hath, my Lord, a wallet at his back,
> Wherein he puts alms for oblivion.
> A great-siz'd monster of ingratitudes...

William Temple's views were disturbing. I had been looking forward to some years of moderately profitable occupation which would keep the wolf from the door, provide for family responsibilities and retirement, and afford some leisure and home life. I attached importance to the latter, since I had already spent a long time abroad, away from my wife and children. In the 1950s and 60s my journeys were generally shorter and my wife often accompanied me in Asia, Africa or Latin America. At home it was difficult to get any leisure. Occasionally my diary shows a vacant evening when we went to a theatre, but for months at a time there was no relief, even at weekends. If I were not speaking, then I was wading through pages of accumulated minutes or memoranda.

Even travelling, it was often impossible to enjoy the view. I kept my seat-belt on all the time in the plane, in case I missed the warning announcement while absorbed in some complicated drafting. This habit saved me a nasty knock. We were crossing the Andes and the usual announcement was made. I did not hear it; I had not even realised that the weather was bad and the peaks were just below. Suddenly, the plane dropped. A passenger in front who had ignored the warning, quit his seat abruptly and vertically, hit the cabin roof with his head, cut that article badly and was for some time unconscious. There was some good cognac aboard, so my sympathy, although profound, was of limited duration.

So if you maintain yourself and your family, provide for retirement, make a hopeful Will, work voluntarily for large bodies, travel, and speak for them, it is well to acquire certain qualifications. You must be alert and energetic, decisive but not *too* hard to get on with, clear-minded so as not to reply to the Secretary of the C.M.S. as though he were president of the Rationalists' Association, patient in the chair or else your nerves will catch fire, and capable of eating a lot or ignoring whole meals in succession. And see to it that you have the best financial and investment advice which you can afford.

It is also well to remember, whether dealing with churchmen or great train robbers, that 'there's no art, to find the mind's construction in the face'. A senior and close friend, now deceased, whom I saw regularly and frequently for many years, Sydney Walton,[3] used to say 'Distrust a man who tells you that he is a good judge of people.'

At the C.M.S. I worked with two General Secretaries, Canon M. A. C. (Max) Warren and Canon J. (John) V. Taylor, still (1971) in office. Max Warren succeeded the Rev. (later the Rt. Rev.) Wilson Cash in 1942, and held his high office until 1963. John Taylor followed him in the same year.

I had known Max Warren off and on since about 1921, but more the former than the latter. He came to headquarters from Holy Trinity, Cambridge. When he approached me about the C.M.S. presidency, the one question which it never occurred to me to ask myself was whether

[3] Sydney Walton, C.B.E.; died 12 December, 1964.

THE CHURCH MISSIONARY SOCIETY

I liked him, or my advisers whether I could get on with him. I simply assumed that this would be so, and although I have had my quarrels and graceless showdowns, generally I have found it possible to work with disagreeable persons, and easy to do so with agreeable ones.

Warren impressed me for a combination of qualities. He had been a missionary in Africa, but he never enjoyed robust health either there or at home, and it seemed doubtful whether he could face an exacting career. But he did so, and with exceptional flair. He was resourceful as an organiser. His personality and attitudes, as much as his actual words, both inspired and persuaded. He was and still is a prolific writer, theologically capable, with an acute insight into the meaning and lessons of the past and a brilliant vision of the dangers and challenges of the future. No man of my acquaintance, in successive post-war governments or in business or public affairs, made a more accurate and realistic estimate of the courses which the newly independent countries would take in politics or in religious attitudes, and in the event have mostly taken. And he had the courage to commit himself publicly.

His public speaking varied in its appeal. The quality was always high. Nearly all men have their 'off' times on the public platform. Toothache and the weather, home quarrels, the number and responsiveness of the audience, the rough work of the day — all these and many other things affect most of us. Even Winston Churchill once broke down in Parliament as a young man and was unable to continue his speech.[4] I have never mastered the art of public speaking, which, indeed, is very different today from the style popular fifty years ago, at least among religious people.

Administratively, he dominated the job and the rest of us, petty men, walked under his huge legs, and peeped about 'to find ourselves dishonourable graves'! The general secretaryship is not an easy post, because, by tradition, the unhappy occupant is *primus inter pares*, and not a dictator-boss. He must secure by guile what he cannot effect by command. Max juggled admirably with committees, and smiled very sweetly at obstructors.

He has himself commented on aspects of the relationship which developed between himself and the president in the post-war years. The correspondence which passed between us was copious. It was conducted by minute and supplemented by telephone. It is surely the experience of most men who have a part in the direction of affairs that business is better thus handled. It is not simply a habit of the Civil Service, or of

[4] See Randolph S. Churchill, *Winston S. Churchill* (Heinemann, 1967), Vol. II, *Young Statesman*, p. 79.

Chanceries; it is necessary both to define understanding and avoid misunderstanding. The telephone is indispensable for exchange of views in moments of crisis, for fixing engagements, and for reaching a general approximation of individual conceptions. The spoken word has its own special function; it cannot supplant the carefully drafted text. If, as often happens, what is broadly said be not what is precisely meant, then what ought to be done may be left undone.

The exchange of minutes with Max Warren across London (my private office being near Park Lane and the Society's headquarters then at Salisbury Square, near Ludgate Circus) was a feature of our cooperation. It would be quite common, when not abroad, to receive two, three or four minutes from Warren, every working day of the week, sometimes accompanied by a luxurious undergrowth of papers which required careful exploration. On certain occasions, I had enquiries of my own to institute or proposals to be examined.

I cleared minor matters at once; major ones were reserved, unless immediate, for a few days' consideration and more detailed consultation. If the General Secretary so desired, a particular matter would be pursued with the Home Secretary, the Asia Secretary or any others of the team. I find it harder than many people to dictate correspondence, and, although a copious user of dictaphones, I always drafted a serious comment by hand and sometimes revised it several times before despatch.

If there is one criticism of Max Warren which I may venture, it is that he was prone to over-argue his case and to appear right when he was wrong. The fellow was, and is, so clever that the rest of us were intellectually annihilated by his single broadside. He could tease an elephant out of a flea by sheer argumentation, whereas I knew from my Amazon days that the only thing I was good at was teasing a flea out of an elephant, or at least a tapir. But a broadside does not win a war, and it was both tactical and tactful to *recueiller pour mieux sauter* and try again another day. On a matter not requiring public decision, it may be best to allow a clever man to assume one's mild consent, so that he may later discover that he has not carried one's conviction. After the skirmish the commanding heights can be regained.

But this intellectual dexterity, coupled with a very practical Christian understanding, served Max Warren well in one of his most notable sustained achievements, the writing, month after month, of the invariably refreshing C.M.S. *Newsletter* which Taylor has continued at the same level of excellence.

With H.M. the Queen Mother at St. Mary's College, Cheltenham

Laying the foundation stone of the new C.M.S. headquarters in 1964: (*Left to right*) Canon J. V. Taylor, K.G.G., Arthur Bailey, the architect, and the Dean of Windsor

K.G.G. with the Cardinal Archbishop of Bogotá in 1963

At a party in honour of the Brazilian Ambassador (third from right)

Both Canons, Warren and Taylor, carried in their psychological pharmacopoeia a handy mixture of subtlety and spirituality. Since both are Doctors (of Divinity) one assumes that this is what the doctor ordered. They utilised these stimulating dosages in different degrees and for different purposes. Taylor is an excellent successor to Warren. A mind such as Warren's was needed to cope with the massive reconstruction of the Society, a body with a longish history and baffling ramifications. A mind such as Taylor's has been of incalculable value in estimating modern desiderata of policy, the quality of missionaries needed, and the further and crucial adjustments of outlook, spiritual and ecclesiastical, which the passing of a generation required.

My relations with Dr. Taylor have been different from those with Dr. Warren. Max Warren is only four years my junior: by a foreseeing disposition of Providence we failed to overlap at Marlborough, for no sane man who had known me there could have really wished to know me elsewhere. There is a gap of fourteen years between John Taylor and myself. It is not merely whether I judge them differently: that is natural. It is whether it is the same 'I' who makes the judgment. It is the old story, sparked off by Heracleitus. It is not only that a man never looks on the same river twice, but the same man can never do so.

One of John Taylor's engaging qualities is that he flows, but in a sense different from what the verb usually implies. He does not utter unceasingly like Mr. Micawber; he does not seep silently from room to room like a gas, a quality ascribed to Jeeves. But he consistently and quietly filters his own convictions into the stream of prayer, thought and debate which mould the policy of a responsible religious organisation. It is a puzzle how this is done; it is a costing process to the doer, but deeply impressive to the spectator. It is a sign of a mature mind, well founded in truth, content and patient in the turmoil of affairs to rely in the end on the divine charity, 'l'Amor che muove il sole e l'altre stelle'.[5]

This has given John Taylor's approach a distinctive touch and healing quality. It is evident in the fundamental rightness of his main proposals, not least in the field of inter-Anglican and ecumenical relations. In my final years with C.M.S., which overlapped John's general secretaryship, this was an ocean of thought and action which needed a skilful hand at the helm. Inter-Anglican relations, the Lambeth Conference of 1968, other international meetings, the British Council of Churches and World

[5] 'The love that moves the sun and the other stars.' This is the last line of Dante's *Divine Comedy*.

Council of Churches, by their words (when few and good) and their actions (when few and wise) all concern the Society. To steer a sound course in these inadequately charted waters has required sensitivity in the helmsman. John Taylor has this—and also a star to steer by.

He spent nine years in Africa, four with the Research Department of the International Missionary Council, and then four as Africa Secretary of the Society, and brought with him a first-hand knowledge of the Church overseas and the Society. But the institution has never smothered the man. One can smother Little Princes or even a Desdemona, but not John Taylor. He is too individual a character. He has too much of the taste of the aesthetic and the perception of the creative critic. He brings to his theological writing and to his total outlook on work and leisure alike a quota of originality, sometimes expressed in a lively and gay wit, sometimes in a startling novelty of ideas and vision, and sometimes in a solemn silence which is always significant, if you can interpret it.

The Honorary Treasurer of the Society, Mr. S. Kingsley Tubbs, of a well-known firm of City Accountants, was already in office; he completed thirty years of service in this capacity in 1969. Naturally we knew each other well; I always admired his succinct and concise exposition of the state of the Society financially, and his willingness to rally round when special business demanded urgent attention. After the war, the financing of the Society needed close and careful attention, and it received this from Kingsley Tubbs and successive financial secretaries who worked under his guidance. During the post-war years the Society's income from various sources, including legacies, rose from just over £400,000 to well over a million pounds per annum. These figures take no account of the moneys earned, contributed and used abroad and not remitted to headquarters.

Both in the first chapter of this book and early in this one, I have referred cursorily to my family connection with evangelical causes. All their lives my parents had been deeply interested in the Society, and my father served for a short term as an assistant secretary and as acting Home Secretary. I recall as a child, in a velvet suit, being taken to see Dr. Eugene Stock, one of the great lay patriarchs and the historian of the Society, then living in retirement in Bournemouth with his wife Sarah and a skull-cap. Background has certain advantages even in a revolutionary age. *Autres temps, autres moeurs*, certainly; some wit has said that the difference between a groove and a grave is only a matter of depth. But a sense of direction depends on the starting point as well as the final goal.

It is a case of the Irishman's reply, 'Well, if I were going to Limerick, I wouldn't start from here', or, as an Englishman has put it more gravely:

> For who can always act? But he,
> > To whom a thousand memories call,
> > Not being less but more than all
> The gentleness he seemed to be.

Both from family circumstances and from experience, I knew in my bones, which with me are sounder than brains, what the feel of an evangelistic situation was.

The outlook or ethos of the C.M.S. was congenial to the faith which was traditional in the family. Our home was not a theological cockpit. Father was a man of broad outlook and scholarship, *and* — I nearly wrote 'but' — both mother and he were of deep individual devotion and the highest practical standards of Christian life, upright and loving, active in good works, but never patronising or censorious, imbued with the vision and passion of world evangelisation and never parochial, humble but joyful in their Christian vocation. Mother had been very active in a smaller, but sister Society, the Church of England Zenana Missionary Society, which, after the war, merged with the C.M.S. It is said that its separate existence was due mainly to the pigheadedness of the C.M.S. in the later nineteenth century, in refusing to accept women as missionaries, except in the roles of nurses and teachers. Several traditions, the theologically conservative, the individually devotional, the reverence for the best biblical scholarship, the personally sacrificial, and the passion for educational, social and medical service to the underprivileged, had traditionally flourished in the Society, as they still do, cemented by the common call to evangelism and Church growth. All of this, with the emphasis sometimes here, sometimes there, was familiar ground in the family.

The post-war decades have brought a peck of troubles for most of us, and this is certainly true of the Churches. What is the primary task of the Society? Is it to proclaim the Gospel of Jesus Christ, God made man, and the finality of God's revelation of Himself? Or does not this smack of impertinence, in a world where many hold that all faiths are of equal truth and relevance, or of none? If the Gospel is not unique, is not its mission discharged by helping to meet the world's need for food, homes, and progress? Is there any real difference between a Christian mission and a technical aid mission? Why are mission bodies short of missionaries, men and women? Might it not be best to shut up shop and let volunteers go to the development agencies?

If a Christianly positive answer can be given to these questions, there are others which concern the polity and arrangements of the Church. Why must there be Missions; why not rely on a selected number of conscripts or of volunteers starting with members of the General Synod or the Diocesan Synods? What is the particular concern of the Church of England? Is it to insist on doing a lot of things on its own, when it ought to do them in association with others? Or, indeed, why not leave it all to the Vatican? Where does the ecumenical movement come in? What is the role and place of the laity, assuming that they can at least be regarded as harmless?

Answer all that, and there are a pack of puzzles about the consequent organisation of a Society like the C.M.S. Is the committee system right? Are we well organised to make an impact on the home Church throughout the land? Do we have the right relations with the Churches overseas, originally founded through the Society? Is our literature up-to-date? Are the laws, by-laws, rules and conditions of service suitable for modern times?

What between the peck of troubles and the pack of puzzles, there has been work to do. A detailed answer to all these questions belongs to a history of the Society; a temporary actor who struts and frets his hour upon the stage, and then is heard no more, can but make some cursory comments.

The primary task of the Society is to proclaim the Gospel to all creation. This Gospel is that 'Christ died for our sins according to the Scriptures; and that he was buried, and that he rose again the third day according to the Scriptures . . . so we preach' (I Cor. 15: 3, 4, 11 A.V.). This and not the urgent tasks of development or the cure of poverty, is the prime essence of the Gospel. Men of goodwill will serve and help men in their ignorance, hunger and poverty, and among them there will be many Christians. But only Christians who have the root of the matter in them, who 'know Christ, and the power of His Resurrection and the fellowship of His sufferings' can proclaim this Gospel. This is the faith of the Church, and it is not for missions to quarrel with it, but to proclaim it. This is the saving message of God to all mankind.

This 'saving' or salvation is not for the soul alone, whatever that word might mean. Christ died for man's whole personality, the just for the unjust, that He might bring us to God. Mind, spirit and body, men's thoughts, emotions, and physical powers must be claimed for Christ, for they are most surely claimed by Him. Missions have been among the first to realise this and to act accordingly, a fact which their critics easily forget. Evangelism, education and medicine became at a very early stage, standard activities of mission, and in some countries of Africa, mission was the sole agent in education, medicine and other means of progress. To hear some people talk today, you would think that our 'moderns' were the first to discover the poverty of the underprivileged. Missions branched out into practical social welfare in the towns and rural 'reconstruction' in the countryside long ago. William Wilberforce is a standing example of all this. His greatest memorial is his long and ultimately successful struggle against the slave-trade and slavery itself, the most crying social evils of the time. But he was also among the original promoters and founders of the C.M.S. and the Bible Society.

It is untrue that missions have only cared for the 'souls' of Africans or Asians. They seek the re-creation of the whole man. It has been estimated that they spend on 'welfare' work, as distinct from evangelism, about $100 million per annum, year after year.

In the nineteenth century and the early part of the twentieth, they were about the only agencies doing this work. They knew the searching word 'Inasmuch as you did it not to the least of these my brethren, you did it not to me'. But they also knew that the Lord had said 'Except a man be born again, he cannot enter into the Kingdom of God'.

In the last century, if a man wanted to serve his fellows in Africa, Asia or Latin America or the South Seas, missions provided one of the few channels by which to do so. If he wanted to take the measure and plumb the depths of human ignorance, poverty and suffering, mission work afforded one of the few channels for such devotion. It was hard work because the imperial governments, and often the peoples themselves, did not see the point. If they did and got big ideas, then they were often doomed to disappointment, for the means of cleaning up a marsh were not available, science had not got that far; you could not spray a bog from a helicopter, you could only swat a mosquito with a fan. Well into my time there were great days for the anopheles.

Then came the development revolution. It started rather slowly after the last war with the colony-holding countries voting sums which then seemed generous, with the United Nations and wealthy governments like that of the U.S.A. (but hardly to any extent the U.S.S.R.) doing the same, and with the creation of a plethora of specialised agencies and international organisations. Voluntary funds such as Christian Aid and Oxfam grew rapidly. Clearly, missions had to think.

In the C.M.S. we never had doubts of three things. First, we contracted our operations. We were too far-flung. Simply because human need touches human hearts, there had grown up under our aegis a great number of institutions which were not good enough for the modern technical age. Achievement of quality depends on being able to say 'No' and missionaries are not good at that. Hundreds of properties were held by or on behalf of the Society. An operation devoted to quality rather than quantity, a bid for compactness rather than ramshackledom, was mounted. Institutions were handed over to the local church or to civil authorities, or were closed. The process took years; indeed it still goes on.

Secondly, we faced the fact that mission would no longer inspire many useful and Christian young people; they would find their vocation, often as short-termers under voluntary or official aid schemes. Therefore we had to plan new methods of recruitment, and, because of the widespread decline of religion in Britain, new training in the fundamental spiritual and theological equipment indispensable to those who go out in Christ's name to serve man in the wholeness of both his nature and his need. An African bishop said to me in Uganda, 'Send only those who know what they don't know.'

Third, we realised that in the scramble for independence and the heyday of nationalism, the attitude particularly of the older missionaries, would often be regarded as paternal and patronising. This natural suspicion was soon to be inflamed by the sinister flare of racialism. We worked out a whole series of new arrangements with the Churches overseas, usually based on the principle that we would only send out missionaries whom the Church on the spot specifically requested from us for special tasks.

Most of us associated with the guidance and leadership of the C.M.S. realised all this early and vividly. But we knew how simple it was to pop over the horizon out of the sight of our followers who bore the burden and heat of the day. I carried the struggle into other spheres and it was not always easy. I well remember, at a committee on the Continent shortly after the war, arguing that racialism was bound soon to become one of the grim 'running sores' of the world; and for the Christian Church where was 'neither Jew nor Greek, bond nor free', this was a serious challenge. I begged that it should be a major subject at the First Assembly of the

World Council of Churches in Amsterdam in 1948. Dr. Visser 't Hooft, the General Secretary, agreed, but others did not. The subject was certainly mentioned, but it was not until the Evanston Assembly in 1954 that a special section was set up to study it and issue a statement.

Previously (1952) I had identified myself with Lord Hailey, H. V. Hodson, Philip Mason, Miss Margaret Read, Kenneth Kirkwood and quite a few others in promoting a special Committee at Chatham House for the serious study of race. This presently became the Institute of Race Relations of which I was a vice-chairman and latterly vice-president. Its steady work has won for it a place of much influence both general and at specific crises, particularly in Britain itself. It has owed much to the generous support of the Nuffield Foundation, to the wise leadership of Alec Carr-Saunders,[6] to the devotion and expertise of its director, Philip Mason, and not least to the later chairmanship of Dr. Leslie Farrer-Brown, himself formerly Director of 'Nuffield'.

Similarly when the subject of aid and development began to arouse a growing concern, I was not satisfied with the attention such bodies as the British Council of Churches and the Conference of British Missionary Societies gave to it, let alone individual Societies or the government itself, so I followed my usual tactics of selfishly going my own way. I joined with a group of men called together by Sir Leslie Rowan,[7] to form the Overseas Development Institute, of which he was first chairman and later president, and served on its Council through the years until I began my general retirement from such affairs. Later the Churches produced one of the best of the many studies then available, namely, 'World Poverty'. It came from a special group set up by the British Council of Churches, and chaired by the Rev. Alan Booth.[8] The story is always the same: a few far-sighted pioneers get together, risk their credit and sometimes their cash, draw on what confidence they enjoy from their friends, and are prepared to be told by critics that they are wasting their time. Then the years pass by, as they have a habit of doing, and very clever people suddenly discover the subject, perceive its importance, and launch their literature, speeches and broadcasts. Governments bestir themselves and conferences are held. But *il n'y a que le premier pas qui coûte*, which is not quite true. Doubtless it was wholly true in its original use by the Marquise du Deffand who made the observation to d'Alembert in

---

[6] Sir Alec Carr-Saunders, K.B.E., formerly Director of the London School of Economics.
[7] Sir Leslie Rowan, K.C.B., lately Chairman, Vickers Ltd.
[8] *World Poverty and British Responsibility* (S.C.M. Press, 1966), 1st ed.

commenting on the legend that St. Denis walked two leagues carrying his head in his hands.

In Dr. Taylor's time at the C.M.S. we came to recognise that many Christian men and women felt called to express their Christian vocation to proclaim the Gospel in the setting of their ordinary job, as, say, a university professor in Nigeria, or a government agronomist in Uganda. These were missionaries as much as others, and we had a responsibility to keep in touch with them, help them if we could in their Christian witness, and learn from them. This conception of the missionary vocation is still being actively worked out in the light of growing experience. It has a special importance for a Society which has always emphasised the role and witness of the layman.

Certain deductions can be made from all this. One is that the thinking of those actually responsible for mission overseas is miles ahead of that of the man in the pew, or even, if truth be told, of many members of the Church Assembly or Synod. Missions are partly responsible for this: they must raise their budget and the facts and arguments that best do this are popular rather than strategic. Another is that this process, pursued without fuss, was infinitely complex and required a firm sense of policy and patient attention to details. I had some part in it, but the real thanks must go not in the first place to the officers, but to the Secretaries, and to the understanding and support, given discerningly, critically, but constantly, by the members of our many committees.

There were frictions and difficulties. For example, at an early stage we decided to separate off the west African bookshops from the C.M.S. They belonged to the Society and were to be found in scores of the towns and villages of Nigeria and other African countries. They not only sold Bibles and books on the Christian life, but educational texts, stationery, school equipment, and other miscellanea. The enterprise was so considerable, and so like a trading venture, that we constituted it as a company outside our jurisdiction, although, because of the popularity of the mere letters C.M.S., it was insisted to our embarrassment, that the title should be C.M.S. Bookshops Ltd.

About this time, I was in Nigeria and a lady called on me in Onitsha to protest. She said that the bookshops were selling toilet rolls and this was not dignified. I asked if she wanted a text from Holy Writ printed on each sheet, but she denied this. It would have been profane to have descanted on the importance of having a sound bottom to navigate the seas of life. So I defended the policy in general terms and observed, 'One touch of nature makes the whole world kin.' I was much tempted to invite her to find these words in Holy Scripture, but I resisted the temptation.

Another deduction is obvious. The special situations of those post-war years were common to all. They were not peculiar to the C.M.S., or the Church of England, or the Anglican Communion. They derived from the modern interaction of religion and secularism, culture and politics. In the face of all this, our ecclesiastical divisions are not merely a nuisance or an 'expense of spirit in a waste of shame', but their irritating irrelevance is only exceeded by their handicapping incumbrance. No wonder that the Churches of Asia and Africa are either bored or frankly infuriated by them. Alexander the Great, when, told during his mighty conquests in Asia, of the continuing squabbles of the Greek city states, described them as the battles of frogs and mice. The divisions of the Churches must appear in that light to those who command the powers of the modern world. It was Burke who remarked that he admired virtue in any company, except in the contemptible company of weakness—not precisely a Christian, but a practical, point of view.

Anglicans could do much more good in the world if they dropped the idea that they have got something particular, wonderful and incomparably special to contribute to the common life of the Church.

However, the general temper of relationships between churches engaged in mission has improved remarkably. The number of actual missionary bodies, whether the Orders of the Roman Catholic Church, or the societies and boards of the Protestant and Anglican Churches, is of no great significance. Events force mergers, while special tasks demand specialised teams. In the Church of England, missionary societies have made their common contribution to the building up of churches of a historic episcopal order, including the Church of South India, and progressive Anglicans are ready to face the likelihood that Anglicanism as such may disappear, so that the enriched and unified church may grow and flourish in every place.

The existence of different societies is not sacrosanct. When the subject is raised in the Church Assembly or in the dioceses, it is argued that the Church should be its own missionary society. So it should be, but it failed to be interested at crucial moments of its history when it had the chance, and the like-minded, who felt deeply and seriously called to proclaim the Gospel, united in a common fellowship of endeavour, a Society. I suspect that if the Church of England were its own missionary society today, if missions became a single and official Board of the Church, much useful flexibility, inspiration and initiative would be lost. Whenever general economies should be demanded, one may guess that missions would suffer first. In this whole line of argument there is a good measure of bureaucratic power-seeking, an urge for centralisation for its own sake and not for the sake of the 'fields ripe unto the harvest'. The Church of England is a noble and nice body, but it does not strike me with irresistible force as an enterprising or an enthusiastic one, ready to spend and be spent in the worldwide extension of the Kingdom of God.

My years with the Society have involved unprecedented changes. Sometimes it has seemed that the fountains of the great deep were broken up, and mighty earthquakes were transforming the entire landscape. I remember knocking up a friend in Central America whom I had not seen for some years. After tying up my horse I stood in his porch and congratulated him on the beauty of the view. There was a jolly little volcano a few miles away, with a perfect cone framed between the entrance pillars. 'Oh,' he said, 'thank you; but it isn't really my fault; it wasn't there when you passed this way before.' Yes, indeed, I reflected that night (according to my diary), it is no longer a world of quiet pastures, but of one volcano after another.

The work brought a lot of fun. From the middle of the 1950s I managed to travel a good deal for the Society, often accompanied by my wife. Some journeys arose out of special events, such as the Niger Mission Centenary in 1957 largely commemorating that great African Christian, born in slavery, Bishop Crowther, or the Jubilee of the Diocese of Iran, or the need to discuss the problems of religious liberty, Church and State, with potentates and chief Ministers. Others were broadly in the interest of the cause, such as the journey of 1955 to Singapore and Malaya, Hong Kong, other places in East Asia, and long visits to sister societies, the C.M.S. in Australia and the C.M.S. in New Zealand. These trips can be exacting because of the speeches that are demanded on every occasion, often with little notice. Even if the event was formal, little warning might be given, and I sat up far into the night writing out the wretched stuff. If it was informal it was even harder to cope, since I am not a natural orator.

In Australia and New Zealand I spoke on an average two or three times a day in a seven-day week. The appetite for oratory seemed as incredible as it was insatiable. The tired must become weary, and the weary exhausted.

Travelling in Africa always had a fascinating flavour. One visited and spoke, laid foundation stones and cut tapes. In west Africa I was fascinated by the theological (?) titles or labels on the local buses, a habit which does not exist in Latin America. Thus (in large letters): 'One with God is a majority', and just underneath 'Maximum 37 persons'. Or there was that other bus stuck in a ditch near Port Harcourt, bearing the legend 'Always the Will of God'. I reflected that it was hardly possible to criticise since too often the Church spent its time in the ditch, whether it was the will of God, or not.

The approach of independence in the parts of Africa where the Society worked entailed additional responsibilities. As President I gave regular receptions to the delegates who arrived for the constitutional conferences. I also made a point of inviting individual delegates to lunch or dine with me in a club of standing, ensuring that they would not be embarrassed and would receive exactly the same courtesies as I extended to any of my acquaintances. The Society's reception for the Kenya delegates played (so I have been told on high authority) a decisive part in avoiding a breakdown of the conference. All the participants met on an informal footing just at the time when they had begun to refuse to meet around the conference table, and a crucial corner was turned.

Following this special variety of pilgrimage was the call to join with my wife in representing the Society at independence celebrations in several countries of east and west Africa. It is invidious to pick and choose, but Nigeria was the most splendid of these occasions, and Uganda perhaps the most pleasant. The capitals were crowded with special guests from almost all the countries of the world. There was a general pattern discernible. The Royal Visitor appeared on the appropriate occasions. There were the State banquet and the State ball. The actual independence ceremony was held at midnight in the floodlit stadium, complete with its special lying-in clinic behind the scenes. The Union Jack came down, the new national flag went up, and the new national anthem was sung. The next day there was the handing over of the constitutional documents, and the stately and colourful opening of Parliament with the Speech from the Throne. There were endless parades of troops and air displays, young people's and children's pageants and demonstrations, concerts and feasts, and solemn services in the Cathedral. One usually had to travel with full evening dress and decorations, morning coat and grey topper, as well as academic robes.

The organisation was superb. At one independence celebration, there was a clock tower erected at the end of the stadium. The official dinner had run over the due time, and I began to wonder how we would get through, especially because the traffic was jammed almost solid. However, just as midnight was striking, all was in order, the governor-general and the new prime minister marched out to the centre of the stadium and the deed was done.

A few days later, I met the officer who had been in charge of all the arrangements. I congratulated him on his timing, and then seeing that he had a hint of a twinkle in his eye, I said to him, 'I suppose you had a man in that Clock Tower.' 'Sir Kenneth,' he said, 'I will tell you a State Secret; there are two hands to a clock, we had two men.' Now and then there was a very understandable misuse of the English language. In another country, a part of the programme one night in the stadium was the singing of 'Lead Kindly Light'. A note on the order paper read 'Recommended to be sung by the Prime Minister.'

These great occasions were fitly, indeed magnificently, done. Britain herself has never known an independence. Our fathers worshipped their stocks and stones, were conquered by Roman, Saxon and Norman, mingled with their conquerors, and grew up through war and peace and civil strife. We formed and framed our laws and institutions across the centuries. The nations of Africa, where, all though the early decades of the C.M.S., slavery and dire cruelty stalked the land, have now moved on into this solemn and yet joyous responsibility, and all of us rejoiced with them. Church and mission had played their part, the new leaders paid generous public tribute to their work. For our part, we were glad with our African brethren, knowing that happy is the nation whose God is the Lord.

All this was the decorative aspect. But after the dance and the feast comes the cold reality of dawn.

> Not till the hours of light return
> All we have built do we discern.

The long road of nation-building winds uphill to the very end.

The life of a C.M.S. President is not all beer and skittles. I had frequent occasion to use my contacts, built up largely in the war, with statesmen and politicians, not only of Britain but of other countries. It would be churlish to omit here a word of gratitude to many British ambassadors, governors and high commissioners, and many other distinguished men of other nationalities, who have smoothed my path with advice and help, and, incidentally, afforded to my wife and myself, most refreshing and welcome hospitality. Something of this is said in my record (Chap. VIII) of service with the World Council of Churches, but it must be repeated here. My predecessors in office had all given their attention to these duties. But the situation had changed. The Church and its missions were no longer in such close touch with the State; the tolerant secular age had arrived; and the range of responsibilities laid upon governments and on civil servants, had vastly expanded. Mission stood in a different place, but I always encountered a sympathetic understanding. There are only a very few hints which I pass on to others who undertake similar duties: don't overstate your case, don't overstay your welcome, keep confidences and acquire a reputation for doing so, and always, if you can, return hospitality shown to you.

As the years went by, my interest in the Society, always deeply sincere, increased. I have Dr. Warren's permission to quote the following paragraph from a communication he wrote to me in 1969, 'Only a General Secretary coping with as complex an organisation as the Society, at home and overseas, can estimate what it meant that you gave so generously and ungrudgingly of your time.' This is exaggerated, but I find the words rewarding now that I am old and worn and cast-off, because few men were so well-placed to identify and deplore my notorious weaknesses. But I had advantages. I knew what it felt like to be a missionary, and I understood the different types of Christian outlook, particularly in the Church of England. Moreover, government and official contacts apart, I had a large acquaintance in the world of general and international affairs, and knew how to check one's judgment and enlarge one's views.

The C.M.S. is often said to be a 'lay' Society; no one seems sure exactly what this means. In its beginning, in 1799, it grew out of the deliberations of a body of men of whom many were laymen. On the first committee of twenty-four, there were thirteen clergymen and eleven laymen, and the seven first vice-presidents were all laymen. The President and Treasurer must be laymen; the Chairman of the Executive Committee can be of any cloth but has customarily been of the laity. The General Secretary is a clergyman, but in the Secretarial team there are always lay secretaries, men and women. The more significant meaning of the word 'lay' is not to be found in these statistics. It resides more in the fact that the Society always has taken the laity seriously both in their rights and their duties as the people of God along with the clergy. Many of its missionaries, not only women but also men, are lay people, and the layman on a C.M.S. committee feels that his contribution as a Christian man of prayer and thought counts. There are no stupid antagonisms between laity and clergy; all recognise that the command to proclaim the Gospel to all is laid on all, and not on the clergy or bishops alone.

Far-reaching changes were made at the headquarters of the Society, and in its outreach in the country. Here we owed much to the competence of the secretarial team, and it would be unfair to overlook the immense contribution as Home Secretary made by Leslie Fisher, now Archdeacon of Chester. The membership structure was reviewed, literature production was modernised, and other forms of 'communication' were brought up-to-date. The team of area secretaries was built up after the long war years, and the life of the Associations received a new injection of vigour.

The Society's policies were discussed in the informal monthly meetings initiated by Dr. Warren. The General Secretary, the Chairman of the Executive Committee for the time being, the Treasurer and the President met for dinner, and spent the evening together once a month. The ostensible purpose was to consider the agenda for the Executive Committee on the following day, but occasion was taken to review the developments pending in the Society's life and work. This practice continued throughout my presidency. The meeting had no status; it did not officially exist; and nothing said between us could be quoted. It was quite invaluable to its members in forming their own opinions and challenging policies and views before they became expressed in some document, difficult to revise. The members of this small dining party have been astonishingly regular in attending over the years, and the value of the group has grown accordingly.

The Executive Committee, which is the main governing organ of the Society, was carefully studied, and some really excellent men and women were brought on. To refer only to the laity, these included Sir Maurice Parsons, M. G. Talbot Rice, Sir H. Mance, E. Gumbel, Miss Diana Reader Harris (now President of the Society), D. R. Wigram and Dr. Violet Grubb, a group which among them have produced a Chairman of Lloyds, a Deputy Governor of the Bank of England and later Chairman of the Bank of London and S. America, two past Presidents of the Association of Headmistresses and one of the Headmasters' Conferences. The times of meeting were changed so as to suit best the convenience of both clergy and laity. The cry is constantly raised that 'We must have younger men on our committees.' The way to do this is to chance one's judgment, go out and find them, and tell them that you don't expect them to give very much time while they are still very young. As the years go by several things happen. They get older, and this cannot be prevented. They acquire promotion and responsibility in their own businesses and therefore an easier command of their time. They have picked up invaluable experience both of the world and of the Society. Finally, just at the time when others want to lay violent hands on them for something else their loyalty has been fully engaged. I gave much time to identifying such men and women. On the whole, the Executive Committee of the C.M.S., although large (fifty-three members) is the best of such bodies I have known. It has its own Chairman; the President usually attends, but is only expected to behave with tolerable propriety.

The General Committee was reorganised in order to make it a forum for the Associations which send their representatives four times a year. They are supplied, months beforehand, with one or more leading questions which they are expected to discuss with their local committees, and bring to the General Committee their authorised comments and answers. This they did with such vigour that it was usually impossible to take all those who wished to speak from the floor. It was a lively show and an excellent occasion on which to judge the general feeling of the Society's members about policy questions. The Committee also retained certain decisive voting rights on important matters sent up by the Executive Committee.

During these decades, there was much ebb and flow, coming and going, cross currents and tidal streams, on the nature of the Society's task today, the fundamental meaning of Mission and the Society's relationship to other such bodies both in the Church of England and outside it. There was a constant 'sniping' at the Society in some influential quarters of the Church. There was a whole set of teasing questions about the right functions of the Conference of British Missionary Societies, the International Missionary Council (a body which has never received the tributes which are its due); and the Society's relation to the ecumenical movement.

I had a share in all of this. The Secretarial team and the committees concerned were fully competent, but it was useful to have some one, detached from the tactical decisions of headquarters and studying the prospect with an eye on the strategy. It was a part of my deliberate approach, as it is a part of my nature, not to be too matey but to keep a certain distance, a terrible thing to say in these backslapping days. It was just as well that this role should be carried by a President who had his independent standing in the Church Assembly, the International Missionary Council (whose European Committee I chaired for many years), the British and the World Councils of Churches. When men's minds are confused, it is often reflected in the exacerbation of personal tensions and quarrels which require the intervention of a detached personality. Christians are not exempt from all this. Similarly, experience in the Chair and ability to summarise a debate, at times even to dominate an assembly, are very useful. There is excellent precedent for this, because Beelzebub himself worked in this style:

> With grave
> Aspect he rose, and in his rising seemed
> A pillar of state. Deep on his front engraven
> Deliberation sat, and public care . . .
>   (*Paradise Lost*, Book II).

The President of the C.M.S. has other duties, either required by the laws or by custom. Naturally, he presides at and addresses the Annual Meeting. He also presides over the appointments committee. This is sometimes rather a tricky responsibility, involving time and attention outside the actual meetings. Senior appointments at the Society's headquarters and at home, positions of honour and recommendations for Committee membership, are nominated by the appointments committee to the Executive. One had to take pains both to know what qualities were required for the vacancy, what were offered by any applicant, what kind of a long or short list was in prospect, and one had to be entirely fair. On any appointments committee it is also advisable to know the peculiar likes and dislikes of the members. I cannot recall that in my time the Executive Committee turned down a single recommendation from the appointments committee.

Many other duties had to be discharged. One of the most pernickety was the very necessary work of presiding over the revision of the Society's laws and by-laws. Another was the addressing of special meetings in the country, but one could tease out all this to the crack of doom. In any considerable enterprise the important is important, but the unimportant may also be important.

In the latter part of my presidency, there arose the question of a new headquarters. Salisbury Square, Fleet Street, had been the Society's home since 1813, a home consisting at first of one small partly residential house, and later coming to occupy a whole side of the square and seeping over into adjacent premises. The building, at the time of its last internal reconstruction in 1911 must have been of some distinction, and it embodied a fine suite of interconnecting committee rooms which could be opened up as a hall for several hundred persons. This feature was incorporated into the new headquarters. In general, however, the building was antiquated and inconvenient, and it was decided to sell the freehold.

A new site was early acquired in Waterloo Road, a hundred yards south of the Old Vic. It was a bombed corner-site, but not at all easy for the accommodation of a modern building. Eventually, walls rose above the ground, offices and committee rooms appeared, and a chapel, the Chapel of the Living Water, of very original design, was made a prominent feature of the whole. The architect was Mr. Arthur Bailey, O.B.E., of Ansell and Bailey. The building was somewhat larger than our needs, since the specifications had to meet L.C.C./G.L.C. requirements. This has enabled the Society to make offices available for other like-minded bodies. This fine building was officially opened by H.M. The Queen on 24 October, 1966, Her Majesty spending over two hours meeting members of the Society from home and abroad.

The Lord Mayor had paid a formal farewell visit to the Society just before the move to the new headquarters, and on the occasion of the Society's Third Jubilee in 1948, Queen Elizabeth, later the Queen Mother, had attended a reception at Salisbury Square.

Much of the general supervision of the building project fell to others, since I was going through a period of poorish health. The General Secretary, the Dean of Windsor, formerly a missionary of the Society, and Mr. D. Williamson Milne were among those who carried a heavy load of special work and responsibility. I had the habit of going down to the site alone, when I could snatch an hour or so, to see how things were getting on. On one occasion there was a new gatekeeper on duty. He stopped me and said that only visitors authorised by the contractors could enter. I lacked the courage to say that I was the 'Boss' of the principals for whom the building was being erected, so I apologised meekly and fled.

* * *

> Sure he that made us with such large discourse
> Looking before and after, gave us not
> That capability and god-like reason
> To fust in us unus'd.

What, then, 'looking before and after' are my general impressions of the great enterprise of Christian mission?

By far the most important is this. All I have seen of this endeavour, chiefly and particularly overseas, has impressed me deeply with the converting and renewing power of the Christian faith. And, looking ahead, I also see that the field today is the world, east and west, north and south, and the reconstruction of religion in Europe or America is no less a task of mission than the evangelisation of New Guinea.

Beyond this, I prefer to quote by permission, from an address (unpublished) given at the Annual Meeting of the Conference of British Missionary Societies by my friend the Rev. R. K. Orchard, Secretary of the Conference. He defines three lines of development which lift missions right out of the sphere of the outmoded and antiquated, and reassert their essential place in the life of the Church and of the world. These are 'service to churches in Asia, Africa, Latin America, the Pacific, as the primary bearers of mission within their communities, to help them gain from and contribute to the universal Christian mission; service to the churches in Britain, as the primary bearers of the universal mission here; involvement in the struggle for human meaning and dignity, so that men may know Jesus Christ and come alive.' This is well said, but

> Let no man think that sudden in a minute
> All is accomplished and the work is done;—
> Though with thine earliest dawn thou shouldst begin it
> Scarce were it ended in thy setting sun.[9]

---

[9] F. W. H. Myers, *St. Paul,* Samuel Bagster and Sons.

CHAPTER VIII

Ecumania

TOWARDS the end of World War II a funny thing happened on the way to Frascati's. I was crossing Bedford Square for some refreshment at this well-known landmark of ancient London. I encountered a young clergyman whom I had met previously, Oliver Tomkins, a nice ecclesiastic and now Bishop of Bristol.

He said that in 1946 an international conference was to be held at Cambridge to discuss the Churches' responsibility towards peace and order. Would I attend? Being in a hurry to eat, I replied without thought that, if I were free, I would do so. It turned out later that I was free and therefore I went. Like most of us I have made some unfortunate errors but this was one of the worst. The effect was to disturb my existence for two full decades. I learned one lesson, namely to be very wary of clergymen in Bedford Square, where the London Diocesan Office is, particularly if they are on the way to becoming bishops.

I had not resumed a private journal, and I can only recall the event by memory and by summaries of a few incidents and conversations which I recorded.

It was a small conference of sixty persons from fifteen nations only, organised by the Commission on a Just and Durable Peace of the Federal Council of Churches of the U.S.A. at the request of the Provisional Committee of the World Council of Churches and the International Missionary Council. A substantial squad of North Americans with the rest of us made the occasion predominantly Western, and the Chairman was Mr. John Foster Dulles.

Dulles was one of a relatively small group of North Americans who had studied the intricacies of international affairs, during the years of isolationism. The United States approached World War II with twenty years of isolation from the League of Nations, and a deep suspicion of the Old World diplomacy, not least in Great Britain. Long before 1939 Dulles understood that this was not good enough, and the eccentric tacking and gybing of the European nations must be contemplated with something more than weary disdain. He saw that the nations were hurrying to a day when all the world would indeed be one stage, even if some bloody in-fighting had to be endured. It used to be said that Dulles was the mentor and tutor of Senator Vandenberg. I asked the latter if this were so and he said it was. He could not speak too highly of his understanding and foresight.

He was a man of faith. His father was a Presbyterian minister, and unlike some clergymen's sons, Dulles personally accepted the truth and meaning of the Christian revelation. From this he derived his association with the Church and his vigorous moral fervour. In his highest office, when he was Secretary of State, he never abated his basic convictions.

He was a complex character, but men of considerable capacities often are. He marshalled and mastered words with great skill and nicety and a Delphic quality haunted his oracular utterances which secured to him the best of various worlds although it did not always carry conviction. This was why many suspected him of bad faith, but they mistook the man. 'Brinkmanship' was a weapon of his armoury, but not bad faith. At times, he had only himself to blame if he was misunderstood for he could be difficult to understand. His leadership of the State Department was the personal forcefulness and initiative of a powerful, convinced and ingenious mind; he utilised rather than depended upon the advice of his officials. Whether this is sound in so tangled a field as foreign affairs is open to question.

At the Cambridge Conference I exchanged some words with him on the familiar theme that often our best intended actions failed to achieve our ends, and sometimes even obfuscated them. I quoted two of Shakespeare's rather bad lines:

> How far your eyes may pierce I cannot tell
> Striving to better, oft we mar what's well.

'Where did that come from?' asked Dulles. I replied, 'King Lear'. 'Lear,' said Dulles decisively, 'was mad'. And that was that. The words are not spoken by Lear himself, they are Albany's, but Dulles did not invite comment so I added none.

In the British view he oversimplified moral issues and equated Communism with the bad and the western 'way of life' (whatever that may be today) with the good. If theologians had discovered that the West at prayer was truly the Kingdom of God upon earth, it would have been no surprise to Dulles; he would have congratulated them. Some of his utterances do echo that doctrine of morality in history which one associates with Carlyle, or John Anthony Froude. One could always respect both his courage and his knowledge. Great men rarely create or educate their own successors; there are exceptions but Dulles was not one. He left no obvious torch-bearer. His achievement stands in his own name, and the worth of his name is assured. In my mind he will always stand out in strong contrast with certain others of the State Department whom I had been privileged to meet, for instance Sumner Welles and Cordell Hull.

The Conference convened in August 1946 at Girton College, Cambridge. It soon became evident that the North Americans were determined not to depart without leaving behind them an on-going body, the Commission of the Churches on International Affairs, commonly called the C.C.I.A.

I took small part in the debates. I was tired after the labours of the war so it seemed as well to let those who knew least speak first.

Professor Henry P. Van Dusen visited me one night in my room. He was President of the Union Theological Seminary in New York, one of the most distinguished theological colleges in Protestant Christendom. I had known him for some years and we had met in various places. He was one of the first promoters of the Committee to Defend America by Aiding the Allies, which a group of like-minded Americans set up at the very beginning of the war. His wife, Betty, was from Scotland, and on my visits to New York for official war business I used to stay in their delightful home. It was in his apartment or his clubs that I first met such well-known theologians as Reinhold Niebuhr, Paul Tillich and others, not to speak of distinguished Americans from other walks of life, including Walter Lippmann and Henry Luce, Sr.

Subsequent correspondence has shown that in an unguarded moment I said to Van Dusen that, after the war, if my services were required for the interests of the Church, I would try to arrange my affairs so as to make time available.

Henry Van Dusen told me what lay behind the proposed Commission, and added that it was to have an 'Executive Chairman' and would I occupy this post? The term 'Executive Chairman' is American and was not much used in England. Later the Commission abolished it, and I became just plain 'chairman'. For many years I worked on an honorary basis. At the same time, he handed me a paper which contained the aims of the Commission. I grunted and remarked that I would sleep on the aims; I had had no previous warning that I might be approached. Those who decided to invite me, made a bad decision, but carried it out skilfully. I doubt if I would have accepted the invitation, had it been mediated by anyone other than Henry Van Dusen, for whom I had great regard. The Commission's first and only president was Baron Frederik van Asbeck, a distinguished Dutch public figure and formerly the Dutch member of the Permanent Mandates Commission of the League. I had known him before the war, and he threw himself heart and soul into the work. After his resignation owing to failing health, this office was dropped.

The next day, I told Van Dusen that I would try and oblige. I was not sure that the organisation was as it should be, but that could be looked at. I suggested a few minor amendments to the aims which were accepted without controversy: in general they had been well-framed, and before the Conference dispersed the main deeds had been done. It took me a deal of work. There are some men who sustain an office and others whom the office sustains. I like to be among the former.

The Commission was founded on the basis of a charter, an inflated use of a term which was calculated to deter anyone disposed to offer services. At best it was a Parva Carta rather than a Magna Carta. It embodied the aims which included purposes such as the encouragement of human rights, the regulation of armaments, and advance towards self-government. It also contained very brief indications of the lines on which the Commission should work. It remarked rather sententiously that the Commission 'will draw spiritual sustenance from our Christian people'.

The Commission was set up in 1946 in anticipation of the establishment of the World Council of Churches. Between the wars the World Alliance for Promoting International Friendship through the Churches had done good work. After the war and the founding of the C.C.I.A. it faded away. It never had appealed to me, first because in Britain too many Christian pacifists rallied round it, and secondly because its pronouncements were either too vague or too pontifical. Much goodwill can be a bore; it is like too sweet a wine on the palate. You can't criticise it to your host, but it doesn't liven you. When once a World Council of Churches had been proposed, the interest of the European churches moved over to it and this was one factor in the fading-out of the Alliance.

All this was gradually straightened out and the Commission was established as a permanent agency of the World Council of Churches at its first Assembly in 1948, and shortly afterwards also by the Committee of the International Missionary Council. The original Charter was replaced by an amended version of aims, and suitable regulations. These dispositions, with occasional amendments, served the Commission well and remained operative until 1968 when a general revision was made. The essential point was that the Commission was virtually autonomous in the sense that it could make its own statements which could be repudiated by the parent bodies, although in practice this has never occurred.

The principal office of the Commission was in New York where there was easy access to the United Nations. The key officer, the Director, was the Rev. Dr. O. Frederick Nolde, a professor at the Lutheran Seminary in Philadelphia. He had long been concerned with international affairs, knew Dulles well, and was directly involved in the work of the American Churches for international justice and peace, and in the preparation of the Cambridge Conference, at which he had accepted appointment.

The partnership between Nolde and myself lasted for twenty-two years, until we both relinquished our duties at the Fourth Assembly of the World Council of Churches at Uppsala. By 1968 it was by far the longest such association in the history of the World Council. There are disadvantages in too long a partnership but in a new and delicate experiment of unknown scope and prospects, there are also great advantages. One of the characteristics of the Commission was its stability, for the other principal officers, the Rev. Dr. Richard Fagley at New York, the Rev. Dr. Elfan Rees and the Rev. Dominique Micheli who divided their time between Geneva and New York, and the Rev. Alan Booth of London, all served long sentences. I found the prospect of working with these learned and pious clergymen somewhat daunting, but they took it very nicely. Over the years, I came to know Nolde well, for we met on frequent occasions year after year, and exchanged our views by voluminous minutes or phone talks.

Nolde was a formidable figure by any standards, and in almost any profession or business he would have gone quickly to the top. Among his many qualities, two were from the first of incalculable value to the Commission, namely his single-minded devotion to the work, and the thoroughness with which he mastered his material. He rapidly won the respect of leading figures at the United Nations, and since he travelled extensively for the Commission, especially in the early years, he checked his views on the spot, and never allowed himself to be influenced by one-sided presentations. We made many journeys together, and, if the business and interests of the Churches were in any major way involved even indirectly in an international negotiation, we were almost always received, often at considerable length, by the Heads of the States concerned, the Prime Minister, or the Secretary of State. For our part, we were scrupulous to guard any confidences either explicit or implicit, in the nature of the discussion.

I was a greater trial to Nolde than he was to me. We differed widely in temperament and outlook. Nolde had an almost Germanic mind and what to me was an irritating, cumbrous way of expression, often on paper, sometimes in speech. The man was argumentative, on occasion with gestures which weakened the strength of his case. He could be dogmatic to the point of infallibility (which is not to say that he frequently was so). My difficulty was not to argue with equal detail or emphasis, but to decide whether it was worth doing so. I found it difficult to perceive the importance of the case, or that what the Churches, just one sector of public opinion, said was likely to carry influence. Nevertheless, the Nolde/Grubb partnership was commonly and appreciatively considered one of the features of the ecumenical scene. It will remain as one of the unforeseen and genial experiences of my somewhat disordered career.[1]

Nolde was fair-minded, penetrating and objective. This was vital to the Commission. In 1946 it seemed natural to appoint an Anglo-Saxon Chairman and Director, and since there were suitable men available there was no criticism. As the years went by the wounds of war healed, many Churches of Asia, Africa and Latin America joined the W.C.C., as well as the Orthodox Churches of the U.S.S.R. and her neighbours (the Greek Church was a founding member), and the Commission's composition came under repeated criticism. It looked on paper as if we were only concerned to advance the interests of the West. Nolde's objectivity, and the courage with which at times he criticised the policies of the State Department, and even of Dulles personally, decisively refuted any accusation of partiality. He was well-justified on one occasion, when at some committee of the World Council a cleric from Eastern Europe criticised him, in asking his challenger if ever *his* Church had criticised the Government.

In our many battles of words, we could be sure of one thing. We both had a sense of humour, each of his own particular savour but harmonising

---

[1] For a selection of material based on some of Dr. Nolde's major speeches, see O. Frederick Nolde, *The Churches and the Nations*, Fortress Press, 1970, with a Foreword by W. A. Visser't Hooft.

nicely. I learned much from this singular man. Having long since left Amazonia and moving around the world unarmed, I never came to shooting terms. Moreover, and by no means the last of these trifling observations, we had both seen something of life, and had had our own troubles and bereavements.

The Commission as it emerged from the First Assembly of the W.C.C. in 1948 consisted of forty persons. Mr. Dulles served as a Commissioner until he was appointed Secretary of State. The list further included such well-known names as Prof. Hromadka of Prague, the Bishop of Chichester (the Rt. Rev. George Bell), R. A. Butler, M.P. (later Lord Butler), Eric Fletcher, M.P. (later Lord Fletcher), Professor Arnold Toynbee, C.H., Dr. G. Heinemann (later, 1969, President of the German Federal Republic), Dr. S. Leimena, sometime Vice-President of the Indonesian Republic, Dr. Reinhold Niebuhr, Bishop Bromley Oxnam and the Hon. Francis B. Sayre of the U.S.A. There were inevitable changes by retirement and death. I do not omit from the lists of subsequent years such men as M. André Philip, Dr. Charles Malik, President of the General Assembly of the U.N., Fred Whitlam of Australia, Maurice Webb of South Africa, Dr. Francis Ibiam of Nigeria, Sir Walter Nash of New Zealand, Ulrich Scheuner of Germany, C. L. Patijn of the Netherlands — but this Homeric catalogue of human ships can sail on to the crack of doom if a catalogue does sail. It is meant to sell.

Something must be said about the World Council of Churches (W.C.C.). Such a body had often been discussed before the war, and it was constituted in Amsterdam in 1948 with 147 member-churches. When the enabling resolutions had been passed, Archbishop Geoffrey Fisher being in the Chair, there was much jubilation and all present sang the Doxology. I quoted to George Bell, as we were coming away, 'Time's current strong / Leaves us true to nothing long.'

But I have always been an optimist. The Second Assembly was in 1954 at Evanston (Chicago), and was conspicuous for the quality of the debating and of the reports. The third was at New Delhi in 1961, and three noteworthy events occurred. The Assembly admitted the Church of Russia and other Orthodox Churches as members; Churches in Africa likewise joined and the quality of the African representation was conspicuous; and the Assembly approved a merger, long under study, between the World Council of Churches and the International Missionary Council. The latter became the Commission on World Mission and Evangelism of the W.C.C. This move owed much to Dr. Norman Goodall, a distinguished British Congregationalist, who for years had steered the negotiating committee. The Fourth Assembly was at Uppsala in 1968, and the membership of the World Council then consisted of 235 Churches.

The World Council takes itself with the full gravity of a small-town alderman, and its new headquarters at Geneva are suitably impressive without being extravagant. It has six Presidents, co-equal but not co-eternal since they cannot be re-elected; they serve for a single term between two Assemblies. The effective governing body is the Central Committee, formerly of ninety, today of 120 members, which usually meets annually. It has a small Executive Committee now of twenty-five members who gather twice a year. These bodies do not necessarily meet in Geneva. In the last twenty years, they have met in Australia, North and South America, Nigeria, Hungary, the U.S.S.R., Rhodes, Crete, various other places in Europe, in India and in Argentina, to mention only a random selection.

I have been at nearly all these meetings, except when impeded by health. In the early years I was an elected member, on behalf of the Church of England, of both the Central and Executive Committees, and subsequently, as the Chairman of a Commission, I enjoyed and used the right of attendance and of speaking. I have also chaired one of the large debating sections of 200–300 members, at all the first three Assemblies, and am, so I am told, the only person to have done so and live.

An Assembly is a bafflingly complicated operation. The assortment of 126 nations at the United Nations makes the mind boggle. At a World Council Assembly, representation on committees and sections has to be balanced not merely in terms of nationality but also Church or confession. You can't just stick on the list, for luck, a Baptist or an Indian; you must consider what is the significance of an Indian Baptist.

There are useful tips to keep privately in mind. Clergy, although humble by definition, readily pick up a sensitive assertiveness. There may be some excuse for the Pope occasionally arrogating to himself the right to speak for all Christians, although it is an irritating habit. But all clergymen are prone to acquire self-importance. Whoever, in an ecclesiastical assembly, heard of an unimportant clergyman? If I did, I would say to my neighbour, 'I will now turn aside and see this great sight . . .' Again, high ideals and principles are very desirable. It is essential to profess them, even if the effort to possess them is too much for the nerves. In a large World Assembly there are people who do not believe much in much, but get on because others believe much in them.

In a debating body distrust the advocates of extremes. In the chair one must be not only firm but patient because it takes many words to produce one deed, and one mind, if it is a mind, suffices for a thousand hands. One must not assume that everyone understands Anglo-Saxon principles of debate, or has mastered the standing orders. Can a Russian, after fifty years of the regime, be expected to attach much meaning to an amendment to an amendment, or to discern that the object of moving one may be very different from what it seems? Most experienced debaters carry around a 'lamb for the sacrifice'; that is, their speech deliberately contains points which they are ready to drop or concede, in order to sail safely home with the rest of their freight and with all the appearance of generosity of mind.

Even with simultaneous interpretation, true understanding is not easy. Every occupation or profession has its own jargon and the churches, including the ecumenical movement, excel. I dislike an elaboration of language unless it is sustained by grandeur or urgency of thought. It is easy to quote Dr. Johnson's famous aphorism 'Clear your mind of cant'; the difficulty in the World Council is, that having done that, many good theologians do not express the residue in intelligible form. Delightfully refreshing truths are sometimes uttered. I record in my diary the words of one chairman, whose natural language was English, dismissing the Executive Committee with the remarkable dictum, 'When the new Executive meets, we shall find ourselves with fresh faces.' At one of the Assemblies, the Presiding Officer, at the final session, announced the result of the ballot for the new Board of six Presidents, and, after reading the names, said, 'Let us rise and sing the Doxology—Praise God from whom all blessings flow.' This finished me; I did rise but still cannot believe that *all* the blessings which God gives to men, or even to the Church, can be subsumed in and under the persons of six presidents of the World Council of Churches. Knowing them all personally I did not join in the singing.

To be in the chair at any large ecclesiastical body is boring but tricky. If the rules of order do not impose limits on speeches, find a frisky friend among the delegates, place him at the back of the hall, and arrange a code of signals, so that at the right moment he will jump up and say 'Mr. Chairman, must the speaker really elaborate his argument, the force of which we have already all grasped?'

Do not allow the public relations smile on your lips to be clouded by the baleful look in your eyes at breakfast. In sub-committees, if an ordinary member, sleep the sleep of the just, because even if the unjust do not do the same, at the end of the day, the chairman, the secretaries and the rapporteur will have their way. In hot weather, privily turn off the air-conditioning, and, if you are presiding, utilise the chairman's usual privilege to vary the order of agenda items. A controversial motion taken when everyone is sleepy in the tropics often gets through literally on the nod. Normally, do not accept a motion to extend the time of a session, since this may be very unfair to those who have other necessary engagements. Once I did so, late at night in a committee where no quorum had been established by rule. The Committee fell into the trap because when they could not agree, I told them I would stay in the chair until they had all gone to bed and then pass all my resolutions unanimously. If possible arrange a contentious debate so that it can be divided by a tea or coffee break.

Many interesting people foregather at World Council Assemblies and Committees. George Bell, Bishop of Chichester, was chairman of the Central Committee after Amsterdam. I had first met him before the war over his scheme for arranging the emigration of non-Aryans from Hitler's Germany to South America. Later, he was much interested in the Churches' Commission on International Affairs.[2] He was by no means easy to work with. He was a vigorous man of peace, and such men like to have their own way. If he did not secure it, he would go off on his own, ignore his colleagues, and navigate his own canoe, sometimes landing on the rocks. He would not scruple to take up the time of very busy people with a proposal which, it was obvious, would be soundly defeated in the end. He would similarly initiate schemes without discovering that others had worked on them, or without reference to their findings. For George Bell the value of a proposal rested not simply on its merits, but on the fact that he had thought of it. It often seemed to me that this truly great man over-argued his case. In 1939-45, that a war had to be won did not seem to worry him excessively; he was entitled to take up everyone's time in discussing with what arms it should be fought and what should be done when it was over. This did not in the least diminish his thorough detestation of all that Hitler stood for.

He was a distinguished Christian internationalist, deservedly loved on the Continent, in the Confessing Church of Germany, and in other such quarters. His human sympathy was not vague, collective and general, but

---

[2] There is a biography of him by Ronald C. D. Jasper, *George Bell: Bishop of Chichester*, Oxford University Press, 1967.

painstaking and individual. I owed much to him, but it would not have occurred to me to consult him on the mission of the Church; on Christian unity I would always listen to him with respect. His devotion, integrity, capacity for work and taste in the arts and culture generally were beyond criticism.

I knew some picturesque and powerful ecclesiastics in the World Council. But ecclesiastics can be oppressive *en masse*. Like manure they are pungent in a heap but beneficial when spread.

George Bell was succeeded as Chairman of the Central Committee by the President of the Lutheran Church in America, Franklin Clark Fry, who was very well known in North America and held many leading Church posts. He was a cleric of very subtle skill, smooth, experienced and at ease in the chair, felicitous and appropriately witty in his address. He mastered papers easily for he had a retentive memory and indefatigable application. He died comparatively early (aet. sixty-seven) just before the Uppsala Assembly in 1968.

The World Council of Churches is the work of many hands and countless prayers, but its chief architect is Dr. W. A. Visser 't Hooft, its General Secretary during the first two decades, and now Honorary President. I first met him in the 1930s. With some he inspired affection; with me respect. He was, and still remains, a man of exceptional drive, ability to penetrate immediately to the heart of a problem and analyse it in straightforward terms, and of thorough theological understanding. His judgment was salty, pithy and pungent. It was profitable to hear him speak and easy to keep awake. He had a short temper but took a long view. He was a man of vision, a builder of battlements, a user of talents, and an excellent administrator for he could refuse as easily as he could grant. He persuaded me to do many things which I would not have otherwise bothered about. He was cross when he was crossed; he did not easily admit he was wrong; and he did not often apologise. He was a superb defender of the indefensible. He rarely took part in any debate without making a striking, often an original contribution. His sympathies were far wider than many realised. I once met him by chance in a train on the Continent and he was reading *Coriolanus*; and he is the author of a fascinating and perceptive study of Rembrandt. He stands among the half-dozen or so ablest men I have known in any walk of life.

His public style and address were pleasing and convincing, if one were in the mood to be convinced. I am no good judge here, since I have a fixed prejudice against taking the speeches of Church leaders at their face value. Not the least of Visser 't Hooft's gifts was his effortless domination of the west European languages. Himself a Dutchman, he conversed with equal ease in German, French or English. I only once heard him mis-pronounce an English word dangerously. He spoke in a committee of some of the delicate issues which the World Council faced in its early relations with the Vatican. He remarked that in a certain negotiation the Council walked between two abbesses. This may have been true but what he meant was two abysses.

These are trifles. There are few men in the ecumenical movement whom I have more cordially admired.

Time would fail to tell of the other fascinating personalities. Chief among them were such men as Bishop Lilje of Hanover, Martin Niemöller, Bishop Dibelius of Berlin, Dr. Ernest Payne, C.H., of Britain (vice-chairman for many years of the Central Committee and now a president), Henry Smith Leiper, Sam Cavert, John Mackay, and many others of the U.S.A., the late D. T. Niles of Ceylon, Hendrik Kraemer of Holland, and Marc Boegner of Paris, Bishop Berggrav of Norway, M. M. Thomas of India, now chairman of the Central Committee, and others from Africa and Latin America, not to speak of old friends from the International Missionary Council.[3] But the listing of names is bound to be invidious. The new General Secretary today (1970) is Dr. Eugene Carson Blake.

A World Council of Churches is a noble ideal, and a partial achievement. I have not been an architect of it, except of the International Affairs Commission and then only in constant collaboration with abler men. But the ecumenical movement took much of my time, energy and attention, although it has not been a very satisfying experience. This is not a criticism of individuals, except of myself, since an organisation is greater than its members. Some of my dissatisfaction is due to an innate dislike of persons, the company of the pious, and of the bustle of hotels and canteens. Travel, which many like, lost its glamour for me after early experiences in Latin America and World War II.

As the World Council grew, it added the irritating anonymities of faceless bureaucracy to the annoying habits of backslapping democracy. Having had experience of large bureaucracies this had no appeal for me, and like William James I found myself against bigness, and for the

[3] There is a semi-official history of the Ecumenical movement up to 1948. See Ruth Rouse and Stephen Charles Neill, eds., *A History of the Ecumenical Movement, 1517–1948*, S.P.C.K. on behalf of the Ecumenical Institute, Chateau de Bossey, 1954. A sequel covering 1948–68 was published by the S.P.C.K. in 1969.

molecular almost invisible forces in society. But it was sadly obvious that there was no salvation that way. As the years went by the first fine careless rapture evaporated. It was rather like the young Wordsworth:

> Mighty were the auxiliars which then stood
> Upon our side, we who were strong in love!
> Bliss was it in that dawn to be alive,
> But to be young was very heaven!

The full title, often forgotten, of this well-known piece is *French Revolution, As it appeared to Enthusiasts at its Commencement*!

The World Council, and in particular the C.C.I.A., did take the laity seriously. It was difficult for the laity to reciprocate, because the Council's language was so involved, as the copious torrent of memoranda, the Amazon floods of the theological mind, poured into the ecumenical ocean at 60,000 tons or so per second—there is a trifle of exaggeration here. It is better to read a World Council document in French than in American. 'I love a man,' says Montaigne, 'that doth stoutly express himself amongst honest and worthy men, and whose words answer his thoughts. We should fortify and harden our hearing against the tenderness of the ceremonious sound of words', a curious and suggestive phrase. Happily, the language of ecumenical memoranda and the travels and contacts of conferences influence character but little. When Socrates was advised that an acquaintance had been in no whit improved by his travels, he commented, 'I believe it well, for he carried himself with him.' But a man had best do this anyway in ecumenical circles. At any rate, one has survived. I have often wished that the counsel of Roger Ascham, as quoted by Sir Ernest Gowers[4] could be taken to heart. 'He that will write well *in any tongue*, [my italics] must follow this counsel of Aristotle, to speak as the common people do, to think as wise men do, and so should every man understand him, and the judgment of wise men allow him.'

The laity are officially liked at the World Council, and there has been at least one layman among the Presidents from the beginning. At certain conferences, such as the Church and Society World Conference at Geneva in 1966, laymen and laywomen have been present in numbers. They tend to be professors, or professional men rather than active business men, but by no means exclusively. It is easier for professors to secure the time,

---

[4] *The Complete Plain Words* (Penguin, 1962), p. 261.

because of their vacations; presumably they must keep themselves out of mischief; they have mysterious periods known as sabbatical years; and they are paid to teach and can therefore talk. What they don't know is not knowledge, and because they need learn little they have much time to instruct and are suitable for conferences, particularly of the ignorant, let us say in this case, the laity. They need not believe in anything so long as others believe in them.

Since 1954, the World Council has had a Department of the Laity; one of the modern ideas of ecumenism is to rediscover them. A vast literature has arisen about these bizarre creatures. The principle is familiar, namely that when a species is on the verge of extinction, it attracts the experts. Some laity become more clerical than the clergy; and some clergy behave as though they had a prescriptive title to the vices of the laity. The clergy must be holy; the laity may be allowed a reasonable latitude. A layman in ecumenical circles is well-advised to keep his hands close to his chest, to give away little in debate, to conceal his full convictions, and to appear more innocent and ignorant than he really is. Never say you are ready to work or you will be driven crazy by the importunities of wild clergymen. A British layman can get along fairly well, because no other nation understands the British habit of understatement with an overtone of mild irony, and, also, because the Church of England, to which many English belong, although not 'one uncreated', is 'one incomprehensible', to borrow from the Athanasian Creed. An Anglican and an Englishman can pass as a curiosity instead of being scorned as a heretic.

In the last decade the World Council has suffered a sea-change. The Orthodox membership is now considerable and they are allocated a substantial block of seats in an Assembly, with corresponding representation on committees. I have been to many of their services and although I do not understand Russian or modern Greek, I have found them rather moving but very long. Russian church music and singing are heavenly. It seems strange that Russia has produced few great artists when her church singing is so beautiful. Russian Churchmen must be tough and can endure long services. The World Council ceased to wear a pan-Protestant air long ago.

At times I do not easily adapt to the habits and intercessions of other Churches. At the Uppsala Assembly in 1968 Morning Worship was once conducted after the manner of the Coptic Orthodox Church of Egypt, a very ancient Christian body. The Liturgy, carefully translated and printed in the Council's three official languages, English, French and German,[5] contained this formidable but, in part, appropriate, petition, 'Save us all from the excess of prices, plagues, earthquakes, drowning, fire, deportation by the Berber, the sword of the stranger, and the rising of heretics.' Would that the first clause in this prayer could find appropriate fulfilment!

Another change in the posture of the World Council has come through the *rapprochement* with the Roman Catholic Church. This Church was invited to send observers to Amsterdam; it declined. The invitation was repeated for Evanston (1954); it was declined. The matter was reopened for New Delhi and the Romans sent observers. Then followed Vatican II and the hospitality was reciprocated. At Uppsala about a hundred Roman Catholics were present in different capacities, many of them accredited pressmen. New ice was broken by arranging with 'Rome' for an official Catholic orator, an Italian Jesuit, to address the Assembly, which he did with genuine perceptiveness. Most committees at Uppsala had Catholic members or observers, and the permanent Faith and Order Commission persuaded the Assembly to elect Catholics to its governing body. There was a strong group of 'delegated observers' at Uppsala.

But neither this nor the visits of Anglican Archbishops to the Pope, nor the peregrinations of the latter, nor, indeed, the establishment of a standing top-level theological World Council/Roman Catholic Commission, implies that the Roman Catholic Church intends to join the World Council. Some Anglicans get wildly excited at the idea. It would encounter astringent criticism by some member Churches, and the susceptibilities of the Orthodox would have to be weighed. The prospect would raise a trampling host of questions, theological, historical and practical. Would the member-Churches accept the Pope as a super-president? It is doubtful. Would the Pope accept any other position? It is doubtful. Would the non-Roman delegates accept a permanent voting minority? Again, it is doubtful.[6] Such a development, which must be considered still distant, would require a radical *bouleversement* of the present World Council, and the elaboration of something new, strange and cumbrous, ponderous as an elephant, slippery as a serpent.

The Pope visited the Geneva Headquarters of the World Council in

---

[5] But you can speak in any other language if you provide interpretation into one of the official languages.

[6] Coxill and Grubb, *World Christian Handbook* gives the following world estimates: Protestant and Anglican, 316,286,081; Orthodox and Eastern, 122,100,770; Roman Catholic, 581,000,000.

June 1969 and said many of the right things. He quoted from the prayer of Jesus for unity (John 17) and referred to the need for 'interior conversion'. He spoke of the possibilities of a common Christian approach to the phenomenon of unbelief, of the tensions between the generations, and of relations with the non-Christian religions.

There is more at stake here than a *jeu des mots*. 'There is not, and there never was on this earth, a work of human policy so well deserving of examination as the Roman Catholic Church.' Such is the sentence of Macaulay's review of Von Ranke's *History of the Popes*. It is well to note the words 'human policy'. Not all non-Catholics, and today by no means all Catholics, would admit the divine origin of the whole astonishing corpus of institutions, doctrines, customs and disciplines which constitute the Roman Catholic Church. Yet the dream of one universal church, deriving from our Lord's own prayer for the unity of His people, explicit as many see it, in St. Paul's teaching of the oneness of the Church as the Body of Christ, still draws thousands by its magnetic power. There is a long way to go. Progress in Church unity seems in practice to derive, not primarily from renewed understanding among Christian people, or more faithful obedience to the will of God, but from fear of the triumphant ravishing strides of the secular in politics, economics, and almost the whole range of thought and life. Fear is a more potent cause of alliances than goodwill or even common belief, however sincerely held. 'When bad men combine the good must associate; else they will fall one by one, an unpitied sacrifice in a contemptible struggle.'[7] But the quotation can be misunderstood; some of the finest men I have known and whom I am proud to number among my friends are, of course, not 'bad men', but deeply thoughtful agnostics.

* * *

It is time to return to the Commission of the Churches on International Affairs. The brief report of the Cambridge Conference was too optimistic, especially in the analysis appearing under the much respected name of Dr. Henry Smith Leiper. He says that informed observers considered the Conference to be of more significance for world peace than the contemporary meeting of the diplomats in Paris. Dr. Leiper then deplores the difficulty of achieving the Commission's Aims without the active cooperation of the Roman Catholic Church, and conditions in 1946 were not

---

[7] Edmund Burke, *Thoughts on the Cause of the Present Discontents*, 1770.

appropriate for that. He stresses the fact that the officers of the new Commission had the advantage of personal contacts already established with 'those in official life who bear direct responsibility for the making of policy'. But such contacts are not difficult to secure. He attaches much importance to the United Nations, rightly reports that churchmen gathered at Cambridge took the threats of the atomic age very seriously and dwells on the contribution of the Churches to reconciliation. He concludes: 'There was no blinking the ultimate tragic possibilities of the international impasse. The best—and perhaps the only—cure for it is a wide acceptance by the churches of such opportunities as are opened to them for full use of the new Commission of the Churches on International Affairs.'

There is a curious mixture here of sense and unreality. The weakness of the C.C.I.A. is not recognised. It is inherent in the weaknesses of the Churches which in many countries, taking the very widest interpretation of the words 'Christian Church' or 'Christian Community', are precariously small in members and tragically divided. Nothing would make the C.C.I.A. more effective than a great increase in the size of the Churches of Asia, Africa and Latin America.

In practice the Commission has been embarrassed because it has been unable to speak for more than a fraction of those concerned, just as it has been gravely hampered by the sheer inability to get a sound analysis or well-argued policy advice from local Christians and Churches, simply because there are not enough of them to produce leaders capable of thinking in these terms, and doing it rapidly and representatively. Since Dr. Leiper wrote his words, the Russian and other Churches of Eastern Europe have joined the World Council and have representatives on the Commission. Conversely, since 1949 China has been a 'closed land'. To all this it can be quite properly replied that one of the purposes of the Commission is precisely to help secure rights and freedoms for minorities. This is not included in so many words in the Charter but it may be justly inferred from it, not least because the position of minorities is a tiresome and recurring cause of international friction.

The Churches are often weakest in areas of potential conflict. The Near and Middle East is a good example. When ancient and modern Churches are added together there, the total Christian distribution is very small. All know the historical reasons for this. Christian people talk about the 'World Church' being the new fact of our time. The Church is usually there, that is, there does exist a *présence ecclesiastique*, but sometimes this talk is little more than whistling to keep up courage.

The C.C.I.A. has made a valiant effort to relate the ecumenical to the international. The task is simple to state but hard to tackle. When all reservations have been made, it does remain true that the spread of the Christian faith in the world and its embodiment in local and regional institutions called Churches is a fact, and an ecumenical reality. The members of these Churches owe a double loyalty to God and to Caesar. Here we trench upon a subject which has occupied theologians, statesmen and philosophers across the centuries. How is the man who aspires to be a citizen of that 'heavenly city which has truth for its king, love for its law and eternity for its measure' (St. Augustine) to come to terms with a world of sovereign states, governed by ambition and power, but nevertheless the generators of such peace and order, justice and community as make life tolerable?

The perennial challenge has taken on new aspects precisely because ideally conceived the Church is ecumenical, and the political order international. Both exist in only the most immature forms. The ecumenical 'order' is an aggregation of Churches, often quarrelling and disguising ambitions of power under professions of meekness. The political order has its centres of debate and sometimes action, as at the United Nations, but States treasure as much of their sovereignty as they can, and share their strength only when their existence is threatened. The C.C.I.A. has had to work in this muddled area, seeking by practical experiment, by trial and error, to bring ecumenical understanding to bear on international order. The task is hardly yet begun. No one who has listened, for example, to Greek Christians arguing about Enosis, can easily assume that the faith and membership of the Church modify or assuage political passions. And why should they, when in so many instances the Church itself has been the bearer and defender of nationhood?

It was hard for someone of my temperament to feel at home in the C.C.I.A., but I did my best. My colleagues were, one and all, brilliant men, well-educated, well-read, and well-*ecclesiasticised*. They were clergymen and they knew about the Christian religion. I had had a vivid and personal experience of Christ but theology was repulsive and frightening: it was something to keep clear of. Nothing in my previous experience had furnished me any preparation for the C.C.I.A. In my early years, I had lived largely alone, doing a peculiar line of research, relying almost entirely on my initiative, neither desiring the company of others nor seeking their counsel—very stupidly, but there you are. Then came the war and I was propelled into one of the large wartime departments and presently found myself in control of considerable operations, involving thousands of people. War was war, and one had to decide quickly and clearly. There was no time to rush off to the other side of a building and run to earth the Minister or the Director-General. I made up my mind, put on my uniform for Home Guard and waited for what was coming to me.

The C.C.I.A. was neither fish, flesh, fowl, nor good red herring. It started in a very small way, namely with Fred Nolde and myself, plus minimal office assistance. Neither of us took any pay—I did so some ten years later for, had I not done so, I would have had to give up the Commission and devote more time to business. At Cambridge Dulles asked me how many secretaries or executives would be needed when the Commission really got into its stride. I replied 'six', but this was not based on any analysis but on a realistic sense of what the World Council and the International Missionary Council might be persuaded to pay for. At the time of our maximum activity, say from the early 1950s to the mid-1960s, we had for the most part just this number. This was very different from working with scores of assistants. We had clever men, and I—well I had not only never been to a university, but had spent my early career in wandering through forests with my baggage on my back. And in the war, it was hopeless to find time for serious reading; an odd Trollope was the height of achievement.

My colleagues understood all this. We did not talk about it much because we were sensible; indeed, if it was mentioned I was the culprit because of my inferiority complex in theological company. It was even harder to divest myself of the wartime habit (or Americans might say that it belonged to the British imperialistic tradition) of giving orders, but, once again, wars have to be won. My solution was to revert to the other extreme, namely to abandon an argument for the sake of peace, or, more often, because the point at issue did not warrant a major exercise in exhausting polysyllabic volubility. I felt that in war I was a success and in peace a failure.

The first appointment made after Dr. Nolde and I had got going was of the Rev. Dr. R. Fagley, a Yale man, in 1951. He became Executive Secretary of the Commission. Fagley was both efficient in business and very competent as a thinker and writer. For many years his memoranda on questions ranging from race to aid and development or self-Determination were essential material for our annual meetings. He was a pioneer in the Churches' study of the population explosion and family planning, and his fascinating writings on these topics reached a wide and influential public. He was well known at international conferences, not merely Church ones, where these topics were discussed, and maintained an exchange of ideas with leading Roman Catholics.

The Rev. Dr. Elfan Rees was allocated to the Commission by the Department of Inter-Church Aid and Service to Refugees of the World Council. He knew everyone from the High Commissioner for Refugees of the United Nations downwards. Welsh by origin, he was an Oxford man and believed in the United Nations and in the Congregational Church of which he was a minister. Like many of his countrymen he was eloquent. The Rev. Alan Booth was Secretary to the London office of the Commission, the chairman's office. He was from Eire, a former General Secretary of the Student Christian Movement, with clear, sentimental, Irish blue eyes, a good brain and a slightly difficult literary style, a quality which he shared with Dr. Fagley. The Rev. Dominique Micheli was a Swiss minister of the Reformed Church, and of a distinguished Swiss family of long history and Italian origin. He was a pleasingly accurate employer of the English and other languages, exact and careful in all his writing, a most necessary qualification in international work. These men were all Christians, for they were clergymen, and they were of liberal, civilised and progressive outlook. They well understood Mazzini's words, 'If you would withdraw yourselves from beneath the arbitrary rule and tyranny of men, you must adore God.'

A real difficulty soon arose. The Commission became popular with the Central and Executive committees of the World Council. Year after year, flattering speeches were made about it which I tried to counteract by presenting the worst reports which could be construed as having some relation to truth. In spite of this, there was some green-eyed jealousy of the Commission, on the part of the secretaries of divisions and departments of the World Council. At one period there was a deal of sparring between officers of the Commission and welter- and heavyweights of the World Council. On the whole, all behaved well although now and then one would be greeted in Geneva with a sharpened and steely look capable of opening an oyster at fifty paces.

The policy of the Commission was elaborated in various ways. The officers met often. While the General Assembly of the United Nations was in session, there would usually be three or four of the C.C.I.A. team available in New York. The travels of the chairman and the director, the regular meetings of the Commission's own Executive, and of the committees of the World Council of Churches provided frequent *rencontres*, where a delicate course or the formulation of a statement would be as nicely and minutely dissected as in that speech of the younger Pitt's known as 'Pitt's Buts and Ifs'. There was the usual correspondence, cabling and phoning. Only a fraction of the Commission's paper and statements saw the light in its own name. Many were for the guidance of the officers, or for communication to Commissioners, or to the Commission's many registered correspondents all over the world. Others were prepared for the Executive or Central Committees of the World Council, and if adopted, stood in their name, and, if so ordered, were communicated to governments by the Commission on their behalf.

Some of my colleagues had more faith in statements than I could muster. The Commission frequently received very appreciative replies from governments. A government naturally treats an international, or in this case an ecumenical, body of standing, with respect. No government wants more slanging matches on its hands than is strictly necessary for self-respect. In the war, when on the other side of the fence, I soon learned the art of destroying criticism by appreciatively deflecting it. Once an aggrieved citizen of public standing in the North of England wrote to the wartime Minister of Information a long and reasoned letter objecting to the expenditure of the taxpayer's money on overseas information and political warfare, and threatening to write to his M.P. He had had a letter on the same lines published in a well-known newspaper and he enclosed a copy. I immediately wrote to a friend even better known in the North, enclosing a reply to the published letter and inviting him to sign it and send to the same editor. The editor published it. I wrote simultaneously to the aggrieved citizen and suggested that I should go down to see him before the matter went any further. He replied very cordially saying that it was unnecessary; his views had been entirely changed by the forcible and spontaneous contribution from a distinguished gentleman of independent mind whom he knew and who had answered him to his complete satisfaction in the same journal. It was nice to think that the little question had been disposed of so ingenuously and sincerely.

From the very first some had suspected the C.C.I.A. of being the Church meddling in politics. Those who disapprove the Church's position on a public question describe it so; those who approve say that it is taking a much-needed stand. The Church itself, when it is strong or established as in England, may well have views on political questions; where it is weak it must watch its step. Dryden got the point—

> But when the chosen People grew more strong
> The rightful course at length became the wrong.

In other words, in politics, what the Church advocates as a small minority it may well modify when it acquires public influence. What is wrong to the weak is right to the strong. But even Machiavelli argues that 'where there are good arms there should be good laws'.

The C.C.I.A. had to tread carefully, but its patron, the World Council of Churches, welcomed a body ready to speak out loud and bold and take the consequences. They did so because they realised that the Commission was competent, detached from the ambitions of particular nationalisms, and, so far as sinners can be, reasonably objective. As the years went by a slightly different line of criticism found expression. This was that the Commission was generally too political in overall tone; it might be hard to pick holes in what it said, but what it said was not spiritual; it lacked theological depth, it was derived from fair but political reasoning. The Commission was not a study group, although the total corpus of its study work, particularly on religious liberty and also on aid and development, not to speak of local situations, is impressive. We tried to involve theologians, and now and then weighty theological papers were presented and discussed. But we were not a theological Commission and could not function as such. As a layman I was presumably debarred from theological understanding. For decades I had had a good knowledge of the Bible, but I fully appreciated that theology had acquired a momentum, almost an existence, of its own, and had long since passed the point of take-off. Indeed this was bound to be, for it is difficult even for theologians to keep their feet on the ground and have their heads in the air simultaneously.

What occupied the Commission's attention? Only the merest indication can be given here and indeed the detail would be boring. The officers of the Commission issued, every year, a printed report of fifty to sixty pages, giving an account of their stewardship. As one turns over the pages summarising twenty-two years' work, the variety of topics is baffling. They contain a resumé of the jobs tackled by local (national) commissions and committees of the Churches which maintained formal relations with the C.C.I.A. There have been twenty to twenty-five officially representative cooperative Church bodies with which the Commission has maintained relations.

The Commission early obtained recognition and registration at the U.N. Department of Public Information, and at the U.N. Economic and Social Council. There are many non-governmental organisations so registered; competent observers have agreed that the Commission has handled its responsibilities with exceptional skill. At an early stage Elfan Rees was elected chairman of the Conference of non-governmental organisations. The Commission is similarly registered in appropriate status with most of the leading Specialised Agencies such as UNESCO, and the Food and Agriculture Organisation (F.A.O.) and I.L.O. All this, along with necessary appearances at ecumenical bodies, has required the C.C.I.A. to be represented at forty to fifty ecumenical or international meetings every year, a considerable drain on time and strength.

The Commission's work is often classified under six main headings. These are International Peace and Security, Human Rights and Religious Liberty, Advancement of Dependent Peoples, Economic and Social Development, Refugees and Migration, and the Development of International Institutions. It is possible to assemble most of the practical issues in these groupings. The headings vary across the years, but the general pattern is surprisingly consistent. The very first report after the formal constitution at the Amsterdam Assembly in 1948 deals with matters which afterwards became either ominously or helpfully familiar, such as the H-bomb, technical assistance to underdeveloped countries, Southern Africa, non-self-governing Territories, Indonesia, the racial question and a host of others. The later reports carry the story on and record the Commission's work in the field of peace and justice in many different aspects, including outer space, Vietnam, the population 'explosion', the world food crisis, development and international trade, the Sudan, many Middle Eastern problems, and the future of the United Nations itself.

Two of the major topics merit a word of comment. From the very beginning, before Amsterdam, Dr. Frederick Nolde gave Human Rights and Religious Liberty his special attention. He followed closely every phase from the earliest discussions which resulted in the proclamation in 1948 of the Universal Declaration of Human Rights, arguing the issues involved, in season and out, with members of delegations and of the Secretariat at the United Nations. He was well-equipped since it had long been a field to which he had given the closest attention. Every turn of the debate received his precise and critical judgment, and in particular the well-known Article 18 of the Universal Declaration, 'Everyone has the right to freedom of thought, conscience and religion; this right includes the freedom to change his religion or belief, and freedom, either alone or in community with others and in public or private, to manifest his religion or belief in teaching, practice, worship and observance.'

The Universal Declaration was adopted at the Paris meeting of the U.N. General Assembly on 10 December, 1948. A few months previously, namely on 4 September, 1948 the First (Amsterdam) Assembly of the World Council of Churches (followed by the Committee of the International Missionary Council a few days later) had made its own declaration on religious liberty. This brief and comprehensive statement was largely Nolde's work. The next step in the international protection of human rights was long delayed, and it was not until December 1966 that the General Assembly of the United Nations adopted the text of the two International Covenants on Human Rights, one on civil and political rights and the other on economic, social and cultural rights. The Commission had to follow all this closely making representations on matters within its special purview. Nolde maintained his mastery over the subject; in the latter years assistance in the laborious task of preparing drafts and influencing opinions and votes was shared by others, particularly M. Dominique Micheli.

The Commission's Report for 1947–9 states drily, 'Judgments from impartial sources credit the C.C.I.A. with making a substantial contribution to the drafting and adoption of the Universal Declaration of Human Rights, especially with respect to the provision for religious freedom and the rights related thereto.' In the perspective of the years this is an understatement. When the full history of the C.C.I.A., or that of the World Council of Churches, comes to be written, this 'substantial contribution' will be the most significant of the many monuments which could be erected to Nolde's work and achievement.

The end of the road is not yet reached. The Universal Declaration is what it claims to be, a declaration; it is not a legal instrument ratified or adopted by any nation. Some modern states have written into their constitutions references to the Declaration as constituting a proper standard. But if they then suspend their constitution, as does happen, then everyone is back to square one. The two covenants provide for special committees of good offices and reporting, but even if they are ratified the sanctions against violations are very limited. In this respect the European Convention on Human Rights goes much further. It is easier to secure agreement in a regional area where the traditions and backgrounds are both similar and familiar.

The Universal Declaration may eventually modulate the constitutional outlook of the nations more deeply, and, above all, may exercise an almost unconscious influence on the thinking of forward-looking and liberal men. This is much to be desired, but fundamental changes in men's attitudes to the claims of the State and the rights of the community and the individual are not defined and secured overnight. They may challenge the essential assumptions and foundations of political, cultural and religious systems. Although the Churches are constantly engaged in the struggle for the fuller definition and application of human rights, they only represent one current of concern and approach. Moreover only some two centuries have passed since wars of religion within Christendom have ceased and up till lately there has been much unpleasantness in countries like Spain, Colombia and Ulster. The consenting movement of many minds, the prior assumptions about the nature of human rights, the ancient notion, so often discredited today, of the law of nature — natural law — all condition the thinking of men and the policies of states. On all this Christians have their own views, but in the achievement of a tolerable order of right they must work with many others of different outlooks.

The C.C.I.A. has never been content to leave the matter wrapped up in documents. Nolde and I together visited many capitals to discuss violations or threats to human rights and freedoms. I raised the question repeatedly with those who were framing the constitutions of the new African States, or with ministers of countries like the Sudan, where the position became very distressing, and with authorities where difficulties had arisen in Southern Europe or Latin America.

I also took a special interest in religious liberty in Roman Catholic countries. For several years I chaired, as indeed I had largely created, the Evangelical Council for Spain, at the special request of Spanish Evangelical leaders. This was when Evangelical pastors and workers were being imprisoned on flimsy pretexts, infinite difficulties were put in the way of marriages between Protestants, and many church buildings and meeting-places were closed. It would have been difficult for a Spaniard to chair the Council then. I had a certain standing and since many of the properties were still held by foreign holding bodies I kept in close touch with several embassies in Madrid and with the Papal Nuncio.

Even so my movements were evidently watched for I was once visited in my hotel in Barcelona by an inquisitive government official. I observed that he was himself acting under orders and personally uneasy. I asked for his *carnet* which he produced, and stepped across the room, picking up the telephone and saying I was going to call the British Consul. He produced some trumpery excuse and disappeared with the speed of a saint finding himself accidentally in a night club.

The Council itself managed to bring together representatives of pretty well all the Evangelical bodies in Spain, and it was in those difficult years that a special Commission on Religious Liberty was set up under Sr. J. Cardona G., a man admirably fitted for this delicate task. After Vatican II things improved, although the situation is (1970) by no means altogether satisfactory.

In Latin America, Colombia was a difficult case. The disturbances were largely of economic and social origin, but Evangelicals were gravely molested and even killed in riots which in certain cases seem, beyond doubt, to have been stimulated by priests. I visited the country more than once, and discussed the situation thoroughly not only with the Evangelical leaders, but with the Cardinal-Archbishop of Bogotá, the Papal Nuncio (with whom I discussed partly in Italian, partly in Spanish and — not to be outdone — partly in Latin), and with the clergy in CELAM, the Episcopal Conference for all Latin America, which has its headquarters in Bogotá. The gravity of the Colombian scene may be judged from the estimate, held in sober quarters today, that some 300,000 persons were killed in the years of the 'Violence'; in some parts of the country conditions are still far from stable or satisfactory.

International peace and security have always been a principal concern of the C.C.I.A. Not one of the Commission's annual reports fails to deal with them. Here again, Fred Nolde rendered yeoman service and other members of the Commission have worked like war-horses. The C.C.I.A. was among the earliest bodies to press, vigorously and behind the scenes, for the establishment of a U.N. Peace Observer Commission. This was set up, but its full potentialities have never been used. The C.C.I.A. prepared scores of memoranda, resolutions, background papers and minutes, and at all its meetings some aspect has been in the forefront of debate. Church delegates from both Eastern and Western Europe, the U.S.A., and elsewhere held protracted discussions in Geneva on disarmament and the limited test-ban and these were addressed by the leading personalities engaged in the political negotiations.

The general approach of the World Council of Churches and of the Commission has changed with the passage of time. Early on, much talking and writing was devoted to argument with Christian pacifists, and with the 'Historic Peace Churches' such as the Quakers and the Mennonites. I found this unrealistic and boring, but sat through it with the appearance of earnest concern. The all-out pacifist conviction is a minority current in the Christian Church taken as a whole, but minorities often have a conspicuous gift for taking up everyone's time. People say that minorities are eventually right and must be heard with corresponding deference. I do not believe this. Anyway, to be right at the wrong time is almost as useless as to be wrong at any time. Minorities are sometimes right and successful, sometimes right and unsuccessful, and quite often wrong and inconsiderate, especially when they become majorities. However, I have often been in a minority and well-whipped and none the wiser.

This phase of our thinking was accompanied by another familiar debate, namely that about the 'just war', what it was, and if the conception still held water or had ceased to do so first with the passing of the Middle Ages, and, second, with the indiscriminate nature of modern weapons. This was serious, for it involved the validity of the limited or tactical use of atomic weapons. These are subjects which only lend themselves to public debate with difficulty. It is to the Commission's credit, and that of the World Council of Churches, that the debate was maintained continuously, and at a high level. An honest critic will, I think, admit that the later papal encyclical 'Pacem in Terris' owes a lot to the thinking and work of the Commission.

The next stage came with the realisation of the state of play, namely that the great power blocs were moving into the nuclear 'balance of terror', an unstable and precarious absence of actual hostilities, a kind of paralysis of power, which at least was, and is, better than a clash of powers. This stage has lasted; the 'nuclear holocaust' has not lit up the skies and blasted the earth. The fatal trigger has been fingered, as it was in the Cuban crisis, but it has not been pulled. One consequence of this uneasy 'peace' has been the multiplication of local conflicts. Still, the great power blocs have used the respite to attempt further agreements, sometimes with success, sometimes without, on such crucial matters as weapon testing, the peaceful uses of atomic energy, the spread of nuclear weapons and the peaceful exploration of outer space. The Commission has been concerned with all this, and it is for this reason that it calls down on itself the criticism of being a political rather than a spiritual body.

In 1967 the Ecumenical Review devoted the whole of an issue to subjects of international concern, in recognition of the twentieth anniversary of the C.C.I.A.[8] This contains a brief and succinct summary by Dr. Nolde of his long experience in the Christian effort for peace and justice. He makes several main points. Oversimplification is dangerous, and those who act on behalf of the Churches must be competent and command the respect of government and intergovernmental leaders. Church conferences are useful, but a Christian contribution to peace requires day-to-day work, and the Churches must provide the staff and resources. International crises are not timed to suit ecumenical huddles. Resolutions are educationally necessary, but to carry influence they must be explained and pressed home at the point where decisions are taken and to the men who take them. The Churches must accord far more extensive, intelligent and above all, prayerful support to those on whom the heavy burden of this work rests. Finally, there is urgent need, and today there is a greater possibility, of coordination with the Roman Catholic Church, on these awesome and anxious questions which, if mishandled, can destroy the life of the world.

Since much of the C.C.I.A.'s work was focussed on, or at, the United Nations, I add a few words in a tone of hope and optimism. I do not see any decisive difference between the peace-keeping task of the U.N. and that of the League. Peace still rests on the balance of power, and to maintain this in Europe was always a British policy since the War of the Spanish Succession. Today it must be a balance between the U.S.A. and the U.S.S.R., for China is in the sabre-rattling stage and her vast population may be a liability rather than an asset, weighing her down. Both the great powers ignore the United Nations when it suits them, particularly when there is a crisis within their own sphere of influence. The U.S.S.R. in Hungary in 1956 and in Czechoslovakia in 1968 took little notice of American or United Nations words. The Americans had their way in the Cuba crisis, and in Santo Domingo where the camouflage was provided by the Organisation of American States.

The United Nations should have been able to deal with all this more easily than the League since it has a special peace-keeping organ, the Security Council. But the Council itself has become increasingly impotent and irrelevant because of the enlargement of its membership, the use of the veto and its inability to impose solutions. You cannot

[8] *The Ecumenical Review*, Vol. XIX, No. 2 (April, 1967).

keep peace without commanding force, or the threat of it and known readiness to use it, especially between great powers. This now familiar position has become all the more dangerous first because of the nuclear age, and secondly because of the prolonged failure to solve such inflammable confrontations as between Israel and the Arab States. It is not surprising that in Britain, busily contracting her overseas commitments, there are strong misgivings about the United Nations and, in spite of fingers stretched out towards the Common Market, a depressing degree of sheer insularity.

Long ago De Tocqueville foresaw that Russia and the United States would divide the world. He was right, and this position is likely to continue for years to come. No great power is going to surrender a significant part of its own power, in other words its own sovereignty, to the United Nations as a peace-maker. This is not to deny that the U.N. has done good work in such fields as nuclear tests, proliferation, the peaceful uses of outer space and similar questions. But so far as superseding the era of great power competition, antagonism or balance, it has failed, and the great powers rule the roost.

All great nations bear a part of the responsibility, Britain in her great past and France, and certainly the U.S.A. and the U.S.S.R. It has always been fatal to suppose that in the world as it is the U.N. can relieve the great powers of their peace-keeping burden; and the enlargement of the organisation to the 126 member-states of today has simply made business more difficult without preventing the great powers from going their way. The U.N. has a natural fascination for goodwill bodies like the Churches and for men of high idealism. If it did not exist one would have to create something like it. But its efficacy and reputation have suffered through over-rapid growth, over-optimistic hopes, superficial convictions that getting-together solves power problems, and heady and thoughtless adulation. If the Charter cannot be revised—and this seems a formidable task—then let the U.N. continue as an expressive illusion, and an organisation useful in minor affairs.

Paradoxically, a balance of power between two super-powers does not mean peace, but only, with luck, the avoidance of world war. It may actually create the conditions favourable to lesser conflicts, simply because none dare unleash the final holocaust; the lightweights occupy the ring because the heavyweights do not, happily, square up. This may lead to situations of great risk as in Vietnam or the Arab–Israel War. I shall be howled down for admitting it, but there is something to be said for quite minor conflicts, which stop a long way short of the horrors of, say, the Nigerian war—but no wars are so cruel as civil wars. There is something inherently pugnacious about some individuals and states at a certain degree of development, which the pacifists have not so far done much to mitigate.

Peace rests on desperately precarious foundations. Listen to Hobbes, in *The Leviathan* 'Warre', he says, 'consisteth not in Battell only, or the art of fighting; but in a tract of time wherein the will to control by battle is sufficiently known ... the nature of Warre consisteth not in actual fighting; but in known disposition thereto, during all the time there is no assurance to the contrary. All other time is PEACE.'

Alongside this, one can put an even greater and older authority: 'The work of righteousness shall be peace; and the effect of righteousness quietness and assurance for ever.' (Isaiah 32:7)

Peace then is the result of justice; of the timely redress of grievances; of economic satisfaction; of good faith; of social change; of many other qualities and goals which the nations are far from agreeing on. Ideally, peace is natural in a society of men and nations who decide to seek and to do the Will of God, for in His Will is our peace. But we do not live in a world where ideals are easily achieved. Equally, it is not true that the causes of war cannot be removed, or that war is inevitable.

Men cannot take peace for granted; indeed peace itself, as much as prosperity and comfort, blinds our eyes to the conditions of peace. Peace is not an insurance for selfishness. We know this, but when the dark clouds gather, it may be too late to stay the storm.

I confess to pessimism. I do not know if we are moving into the end of history, or to the time of the Parousia, the Second Coming of Christ. The Second Epistle of Peter was written largely to remind Christians to be alert, to watch and to make no false assumptions of earthly security. This may be the pessimism of advancing years, and I do not forget that there is much that is fine and progressive in man's achievement, although there is also a tendency to confuse evolution with progress. Yet one has to ask whether England, at least, is not in a strict sense becoming ungovernable. The challenge of liberty, or sheer permissiveness, to authority is only valid when it produces its own positive discipline. There is an impatience abroad, an increasing revolt against the values of the good life, almost a dissolution of the bonds of society with nothing to take their place.

Meanwhile, although the world holocaust has so far been averted, the

Lord Fisher of Lambeth unveiling a portrait of the author at C.M.S. headquarters

The author with Billy Graham and Sir Cyril Black

H.M. the Queen opening the new C.M.S. headquarters in 1966

The Board of Hooker, Craigmyle Ltd.: (*left to right*) R. Biles, Esq., Major J. Bell, Dr. M. Hooker, Lord Craigmyle, J. Sizmur, Esq., K.G.G., Air-Comm. J. Manning

amount of unrest, distress and actual fighting is disquieting, whether it be in Korea or Indonesia or Vietnam or Nigeria or anywhere else. The human tragedy is grievous and men's consciences are numbed and dumbed. The tumult and the fighting may be over for a breathing space, but through the mask of fire, there comes the sobbing of litanies and the last cries of despair. The dark canvas of man's life is woven in colours sad and angry, shot through with scarlet and black.

* * *

My advisers say I am too critical of the World Council of Churches. It may be, but the Council need not be sensitive or thin-skinned. I have been much criticised myself and have made many enemies. I rarely win or lose a quarrel: one arranges, one compromises, one dissimulates. A World Council of Churches is a good idea; even more, it has been an encouraging achievement, reflecting lasting credit on brows which need no laurels from me. I think highly of men like Martin Niemöller, Hans Lilje, Marc Boegner, Ernest Payne, Bishop Dibelius, M. M. Thomas of India and a host of others, and above all Visser 't Hooft; and I do not speak of those long dead — 'passed to their reward' is the correct religious phrase. Whether the Council will continue to attract the prayers of Christians and the support of the Churches is impossible to say; there is no reason to assume the contrary. The World Council might sink through its own weight, decay through the decline of Christianity, be wrecked in a sea of troubles through ill-advised policies, or simply become secularised and merely humanistic. If so, then something young and vigorous, something endued with hope and vision, something which is the focus of the prayers and aspirations of many millions will have perished from the earth.

I have been urged to explain why I have given time to this work. If someone whom I esteem invites me to do a job, I try and do it if I have the time, provided it is this side of gross perversity. If, which is rare with me, I have misjudged the claims and precise nature of the task, I continue to discharge it if still required. It is said that a man works best when he likes his job; this is only true of some. There is no credit in doing what you like, and only limited satisfaction in liking what you do.

I cannot add anything to the generous words of Dr. Visser 't Hooft,[9]

---

[9] The Commission of the Churches on International Affairs, *Report, 1968–9*, p. 5.

speaking of the urgent need, after World War II, for the Churches to concern themselves intelligently and seriously with international affairs, and referring to Dr. Nolde and myself. After summarising the task to be pursued he says:

> This could only be done if men could be found who had clear Christian convictions themselves and who had also a sufficient knowledge of international affairs to be taken seriously by the statesmen and the international civil servants. Did such men exist? And if they could be found would they be willing to undertake this unprecedented task? It was indeed fortunate that two such men were found and that they were willing to take the risk involved in this new adventure. They were very different. A very English Englishman and a very American American. But both able to open their eyes to problems of worldwide dimension and willing to listen to men of all sorts of nations and races. A layman and a theologian, but both eager to bring something of God's design into the disorder of men.

* * *

I was not very much satisfied with the work of the Churches, whether the World Council of Churches or the British Council of Churches, in international peace and justice, severely limited as it was by financial stringency. I kept in touch with those at Chatham House and in other quarters who were studying the lie of the land. In 1956 four men met privately to discuss chiefly the alleged distinction between the tactical and strategic use of atomic weapons. They were Admiral Sir A. Buzzard, lately Director of Naval Intelligence, Professor P. M. S. Blackett,[10] the distinguished scientist, Mr. Richard Goold-Adams and Mr. Denis Healey, later Minister of Defence. Eventually they had a pamphlet produced, *On limiting atomic war*.

Anthony Buzzard attended an international consultation at Bossey. The Chateau de Bossey is a conference centre near Celigny, on the north-western side of Lake Leman, belonging to the World Council of Churches. Buzzard was anxious that something should be done in Britain to carry the discussion further, and in July 1956, Dr. George Bell, then Bishop of Chichester, wrote to me to introduce him. I saw Buzzard

---

[10] Later Lord Blackett, C.H., F.R.S.

and listened very carefully to his words. His approach was new to me and I said little, but pondered much.

Later Buzzard and I met Healey and Goold-Adams and I agreed to consider seriously the holding of a small conference. I was impressed by the account which Colonel Leghorn of the U.S.A. had given me of the volume and thoroughness of the work being done on the tactical atomic weapon question by such men as Kissinger, Wolfers and Nitze, all of whom and many others of their colleagues, I came to know later.

The Brighton Conference met in January 1957 in a hotel. No organised or recognised body convened it. Buzzard, Healey, Goold-Adams and I simply wrote to the people we knew on a list we had compiled of names in the services, Churches, politics, universities and press, not only in Britain but in the U.S.A. and the Commonwealth. The Conference met with sixty to seventy persons present. We had little faith, because the subject had attracted lively attention and in the event we could have rallied up many more. I was press-ganged into taking the Chair. Healey shared the speaking with others and the quality of the *assistance* was impressive. The Rev. Alan Booth, who had done a lot of the preparation, and the Rev. David Edwards[11] acted as secretaries. With the exception of a few critics, the occasion was considered a success.

I was summing up at the end when an unexpected incident occurred. Lord Salter rose and asked what was to happen when we dispersed. Was it all to vanish into air, into thin air, and 'leave not a wrack behind'? I replied that this depended on the conference. A permanent institution might be erected, but not by mere vote right then. If we willed the end, we must will the means. We would need a Brighton Conference Association, with a few hundred pounds at its disposal, so that the sources of adequate finance in the United States and Britain could be explored, a director found, a proper council convened, and articles of association prepared and adopted. I added that as it was Sunday no one would object to a collection and I would be happy to receive cheques or cash there and then.

All this was done, but it took time. The Ford Foundation proved interested, and the new institute was set up with an international outlook and membership. Alastair Buchan[12] eventually agreed to become the first director. The title was to be the Institute for the Study of International Security, afterwards dropped in favour of the Institute for

---

[11] Later Dean of King's College, Cambridge and now Rector of St. Margaret's Westminster.
[12] Now Alastair Buchan, C.B.E., Commandant of the Royal College of Defence Studies.

Strategic Studies. The Ford Foundation offered an initial grant of $150,000 over three years, and on 20 November, 1958 the Institute was formally incorporated under British law. Unfortunately for long periods during these discussions I was myself abroad in Africa and Latin America. They were handled with conspicuous competence by Goold-Adams, Healey, Buzzard, and in particular Alan Booth and Buchan himself. Nevertheless I strove to bring to the Institute something of my long experiences of voluntary organisations. But Alastair Buchan exaggerated when he remarked that I could have got the Hell Fire Club registered as a non-profit-making charity!

The Council elected me as chairman, Goold-Adams as vice-chairman and Lord Salter as hon. treasurer. It was a distinguished body with persons of standing from the services, the political parties, journalism, the law, the Church and scientists of repute. It elected an executive committee which, in addition to those who had planned the Brighton Conference, included Professor Blackett, Mr. Donald Tyerman, editor of *The Economist* and Professor Michael Howard.

Alastair Buchan had already done much work. Money had to be raised, following the lead given by Ford. After a short delay premises were found in one of the most central and suitable sites in London, namely the Royal Society of Arts' handsome building at 18 Adam Street. I served as chairman until 1963; the office of president was accepted by Lord Attlee who held it until his death in 1967 and has been succeeded by Mr. Lester Pearson.

In 1963, the Institute was reorganised to take on a more genuinely international dress. The Council had for some time been convinced of the rightness of this and the move was strongly supported by the Ford Foundation. I resigned the chairmanship and was succeeded by Richard Goold-Adams who had done such sterling work for the cause; and I 'went upstairs' as a vice-president. The Council ceased to be British in its composition and became representative, not only of the NATO area but of the whole free world. Indeed the membership in 1970 embraced no less than thirty-three countries.

The Institute has gone from strength to strength. Alastair Buchan proved a fortunate choice; indeed, there are touches of genius and of prophetic insight about his work. He left in 1969 to become Commandant of the Imperial Staff College renamed in 1970 the Royal College of Defence Studies, only the second civilian to be so appointed. His grasp of the vast range of the subject matter was masterly, and his ability to win respect from the highest authorities and to engage their interest, whether in Britain, the Continent, the Commonwealth or the U.S.A. was invaluable. In Britain, particularly, this was not easy; an Institute for Strategic Studies deals with delicate material. It is not the policy of the Institute to press for access to 'classified' data, a quest which would anyhow be abortive, but the establishment of mutual confidence is essential.

I owe much to Alastair Buchan and also to other colleagues in the Institute. We worked well together, and this is essential in the first stages of a new enterprise. Many a good ship, in the old days, came to grief shortly after leaving harbour: a long voyage requires a good skipper and officers from the start and a comradeship which can stand a few buffetings. The passage of time and the reorganisation of 1963 necessarily meant a change in the 'feel' of the enterprise, and some old friends fell out of the running. But the annual conference provides good opportunities to renew contacts and to adjust one's perspective. The monthly publication *Survival* and the books published by or under the auspices of the Institute are indispensable to anyone seeking to keep up with this crucial subject of life and death for the nations. There were those who felt that the Institute did not give enough attention to the 'moral issues'. It may be so, but the real task was to clarify and deepen an understanding of the situation. A man is well advised to take a firm grip on himself when the discussion turns to 'moral issues'.

* * *

The C.C.I.A. came of age in 1967 after twenty-one years of useful life, and the Central Committee of the World Council of Churches had decided to hold a consultation at The Hague to look at the future prospects, since it was known that Nolde and myself would shortly retire. This convened in April 1967 with an attendance of sixty to seventy persons from most major areas of the world, but not the People's Republic of China, and the weather was cold, dispiriting and blustery. The clergy and professional religionists were present in numbers, and the level of behaviour was accordingly suitable. Only about one-third of those present had been previously associated with C.C.I.A. activities.

The members of the consultation were delighted to have in their hands and transfer to their minds a mass of documentation dealing with both the organisation of the Commission and the international issues with which it had striven to deal. Dr. Eugene C. Blake opened the meeting with a very appropriate speech in which he laid down the three aspects which needed particular study: the review of the record of the C.C.I.A.; the theological justification for such work; and the future organisation if there were to be a future. These were remitted to working parties. Dr. Blake remarked that he was 'personally happy' that we had all gathered together; this was nice of him; *de gustibus non disputandum est.*

The consultation report produced some good practical suggestions. It is an ecclesiastical report in its approach, and its outlook is of the Church churchy. This was inevitable. It does not really enter into the dilemmas which worry a Christian man, or a man of positive constructive and secular outlook, when he has to take or recommend vital political decisions. It discusses the use of 'statements' but has very little to say about other ways in which the Church through its members can exercise influence in the tortuous fields of diplomacy and international relations. One notable omission, hinted at in the course of debate, is that it does not contain a 'philosophy of the minority'. It does not analyse the political psychology or demands, hopeful or hopeless, of minorities, their justification for existence, their ultimate worth or their nuisance value. This is odd, because the Christian churches are usually minorities, and Christians, even in nominal figures, are only about one-third of the world's population. And it must be repeated that minorities, their status and claims, are often the cause of international friction.

It was not the Conference's job to draft a new constitution for the C.C.I.A. That has been done and was adopted by the Uppsala Assembly of the W.C.C. Whether it is a good constitution depends on whether you like the Church and the W.C.C. In the past the C.C.I.A. has managed its own policy and affairs; in future it will be more closely subject to the W.C.C. This will please many, including its enemies. The Director of the Commission will reside in Geneva; the W.C.C. has its headquarters there, and it suits Christians to be agreeably and neutrally protected from the power-struggle of the world. Geneva is only now and then a good place at which to make contacts with Heads of States and Foreign Secretaries. But it is a good place in which to do so with the present General Secretary of the W.C.C., who will increasingly dominate the Commission. And it is, one supposes, desirable that every new conflict among the nations should produce a world safer for the clergy.

I do not grudge the time which I have given to the ecumenical

movement. What is the point of doing that when it is too late? I think I would have been happier in the interior of South America. In the ecumenical movement one meets too many clever men, and too few brave ones; and too much action but too little prayer. This is often the case in gatherings or organisations of religious and intellectual folk.

* * *

Finally, there is one business commitment worth mentioning, being concerned, as I have been all my life, with the nourishment of the voluntary element in society. Hooker Craigmyle and Co. have established themselves in a period of less than a dozen years as the leading British firm of fund-raising consultants specialising in schools, Oxbridge colleges, universities, cathedrals and other non-profit-making bodies, and for these objects the Company has since 1959 helped to raise over forty million pounds.

It is essential to a proper understanding of the Company to grasp their fundamental tenet that professional fund-raising consultants cannot displace volunteers but can reinforce them and make their efforts more productive. It is difficult in these days to find men and women of high calibre who will undertake voluntary posts in Church organisations and similar bodies. By providing full-time executives and experts drawn from wide experience, a professional fund-raising firm can make it very much easier for leading business and professional people to play their part in charitable work, since the professionals can see that the work of the volunteers is limited to those tasks which can only be done by an honorary worker. More and more in recent years, leading business and professional men who have been asked to lead fund-raising campaigns have made their acceptance dependant on the employment of a professional firm. This partnership between the full-time professional and the part-time volunteer seems a natural and a healthy development.

Lord Craigmyle, the chairman, is a prominent Roman Catholic, active in many religious, educational and charitable fields.

Dr. Michael Hooker, the managing director, was the only executive director when I joined the Board.

Since I was extensively involved in their field of interest, it was inevitable that our paths should cross. After Michael Hooker and I had met on various occasions, his Board authorised him to invite me to become a director of the Company. He explained engagingly over lunch that since the other directors were all under forty, they felt the need for an 'elder statesman', particularly one who already knew the background to their work. I accepted the invitation and have been with them ever since.

CHAPTER IX

A Man in Church

WILLIAM TEMPLE's remark (p. 137) that he hoped I would give time to the Church of England weighed with me. To expect a welcome was too much, but it did seem as if the Church might not wholly reject active help. Other friends urged me to take some interest in Church government, and among these were Canon Max Warren and Sir Stafford Cripps.

The prospects were depressing, and I might well have done nothing, had it not been that Archbishop Garbett of York made a simultaneous attack. I had first met him when he attended the Tambaram (Madras) meeting of the International Missionary Council in 1938, where his chaplain was the present (1970) Bishop of Chester, Gerald Ellison. Garbett was chairman of a group on Church and State relations, religious liberty and the like, and the late S. A. Morrison of Cairo was secretary. He was impressed both by contributions I made to the debate, and some minor efforts to help Morrison in making drafting sense of a very rambling international discussion. I also assisted the interpretation in several languages. At one session Garbett was annoyed with a North American delegate who befogged his remarks by the obscurity of his exhalations, and he said, 'Please tell Mr. Grubb in the coffee-break what you want to say, and when we re-assemble, say it.' I wrote out what the man was trying to say long before the coffee-break, since I was thirsty, handed it to him and disappeared to read my novel. I afterwards learned that his speech had been a great success.

After the war, until his death, Garbett used to consult me regularly on speeches he wished to make on international questions, in the House of Lords or elsewhere, and frequently I supplied him with complete drafts at his request. He was much senior to me and in every way far abler, but one of the minor services which the laity can occasionally and privily perform is to help keep bishops—one must not say 'on the straight and narrow' — but at least out of immoderate errors of judgment on non-theological concerns.

At about the same time, I also became acquainted with a young clergyman of the name of Coggan. I record in my diary that he had it in him to be a future archbishop if the Christian church could manage to last out in this country for a little longer. This instinct was justified since some twenty years later, in 1961, he was appointed Archbishop of York. No mean scholar himself, he devoted many years to theological education in Canada and later as Principal of the London College of Divinity. When the United Bible Societies were formed by the cooperation of most of the Bible Societies of the world, it was fitting that he should become their second president following Bishop Berggrav of Norway. To know him has been one of the many privileges that have rewarded my later activities in the Church.

The National Assembly of the Church of England did not strike a responsive chord. It conjured up a picture, inaccurate as such imaginings are, of infertile aridity, the endless legal complications of the Establishment, cumbrous and toilsome organisation like an anaconda which cannot unscramble itself, the law's delays and the niceties of ecclesiastical causes. My critical and jaundiced mind could produce no alleviating considerations. A debating body of some 750 persons meeting for about a week, three times a year, takes up much more than three weeks, if one is enticed into committees and commissions, to say nothing of the hours needed to master the torrents of reports, and help draft bills or measures.

Moved by a profoundly self-righteous sense of duty I stood in the London diocese for membership of the House of Laity in the election of 1945. I lost the election, which is easy in London. There was no reason why I should have won it, I was little-known, I had given no attention to church government, there had been a war on, and my printed election address was bad.

I do not cherish defeat and I do not like an enterprise unless I can see an eventual way to a place near the top. This is partly due to egoism, pure and undefiled, and partly to the conviction that it is much easier to get things done if one has power, not to order but to influence. I remarked to a friend, in strict confidence, that I would press on, and was determined before I had finished, to be chairman of the House of Laity, the principal post which a voluntary layman can hold at Church House. Shortly afterwards, there was a by-election in London which I won. The House has thrice elected me to the chair, an honour which I have little deserved. The first time was towards the very end of Lord Selborne's chairmanship, since to the regret of all, he gave up the post in 1959 owing to deafness. The second and third times were for full five-year periods ending in the autumn of 1970, when the Assembly itself committed hara-kiri, and was succeeded by the General Synod of the Church of England.

I served in this office longer than any of my predecessors except the second Earl of Selborne who became chairman after the Enabling Act (1919) had set up the Church Assembly.

The House of Laity in particular and the Church Assembly itself derived immense benefit from the expertise and interest of men of parliamentary experience, and the sound sense of professional and business men of standing. The Palmer family, in particular the second and third Earls of Selborne, stand out for their concern and devotion. Lord Hugh Cecil was a member throughout the inter-war years, conspicuous for his interest and devotion to ecclesiastical affairs. Brigadier Miller was twice vice-chairman of the House of Laity. I think also of some who served in the important office of chairman of the Central Board of Finance, such as Sir Arthur ffiorde, Sir Eric Gore Browne, and Sir Edmund Compton. Others discharged a multiplicity of duties, such men as Sir Robert Martin, well-known for his public service in the Midlands, or Mr. Chancellor Wigglesworth, who handled so skilfully a long succession of legal questions in the House of Laity, in particular in the many sessions devoted to the revision of Canon Law. Sir (later Lord) Eric Fletcher, sometime Deputy-Speaker of the Commons, joined the Assembly in 1962. There have been many ladies who have rendered indispensable service. Among them is the late Caroline Bridgeman, the only woman to have served as vice-chairman of the House, and others such as Viscountess Falmouth, Lady Bennett, Miss Sybil Thesinger, Mrs. Rawlinson and Miss C. M. Ady. It would be easy to add to the list to the point of boredom.

A warning is needed similar to that in other chapters. A thorough and considered critique or appreciation of the Assembly and its work is not attempted here. This needs a more skilful pen, and the stance of an observer more spirited, but less committed to the drama on this stage. Some views which might be relevant to a serious study are briefly expressed in a paperback published in 1964.[1]

I do not know how the debating practice and atmosphere of the

---

[1] *A Layman Looks at the Church*, Hodder and Stoughton.

Church Assembly compare with those of Parliament. A crucial debate in a full Assembly can be a dramatic occasion. This is true of a really significant debate in the House of Laity sitting separately as it has frequently done in the last decade. There is no real comparison with the House of Commons, a political body whose members receive a salary, a body which sits the year round except for vacations, and, above all, a body in which the party system, and usually therefore the voting, is well-entrenched on lines which are clearly known in advance and where there is the discipline of the whip. Every debating assembly has its own ethos, and comparisons mislead. This is even more obvious if such experience as I have had in international debating bodies is also regarded.

In the Church Assembly there were no parties in the hard-line sense. There were groups of members, clergy and laity, who shared well-recognised outlooks, Anglo-Catholic, High Church, Protestant and others; there was even the Non-Party Group. Such groups held meetings to discuss the agenda and some occasionally issued voting advice. Whips and strict party discipline would be out of place. There were members who rose, and one knew before they opened their lips, on which side of a question they would speak. The spirit of the Assembly was good; occasionally there was tension or stone-walling, and in the House of Laity it was sometimes hard not to show annoyance. Contrary to what may be thought, the bishops do not speak much, perhaps because, in a hierarchical system, they have the last word. Zeus settled his problems with a nod, and where power resides gestures, or even words, need be but sparingly deployed.

Speeches must not be read, although licence is extended to a speaker who must fill (not pad) his speeches with figures or difficult facts. In the House of Laity I used to extend licence to a member making a maiden speech. By definition the clergy are competent speakers, although a sermon is, or ought to be, of a different kidney from a debating speech. The laity, other than Members of Parliament and barristers, are not usually trained speakers, although many acquire the art by instinct, interest or practice.

The relations between the three Houses, Bishops, Clergy and Laity were good. The latter two Houses were about equal in numbers; in the full assembly the clergy did not monopolise the speaking, except somewhat in debates which peculiarly affected their standing and service, and consequently their self-interest. The rules of order for the conduct of a debate were reasonably broadly drawn. There were a few essential ones which the chairman had to keep in his mind without referring to the book. If a debate degenerates into a series of interventions on 'points of order' from the floor, it usually implies one or more of three things: tempers are frayed or exhausted; those who fear the main question will be lost eke out time so that the adjournment arrives 'without question put'; or the motion meets the desires of hardly anyone except its mover and seconder.

Sometimes debates, even in the full Assembly, reach a nadir of boredom, and the members (including myself) seem like hippos in an African swamp, but this is true of most debating bodies which usually have their 'off' days. Then the yellow jack is hoisted, that is, people leave the chamber; and business having gone by default there, it is recovered by the caterers in the tea-rooms.

Many years ago, I was coming away at the end of Church Assembly week when I met Garbett in the lobby. I said 'Thank goodness: that's over; the captains and the kings depart.' 'Do you look at it like that?' he said, and I awaited a rebuke. 'I prefer Gray to Kipling; I say to myself "the lowing herd winds slowly o'er the lea!"' This struck me as a felicitous quotation by an archbishop.

I cannot explain why I held office for so long in the House of Laity. I never lobbied for any personal support. When first elected to membership I knew nothing of Church affairs, although a son of a vicarage; I read a lot. In very early days, I was in a large committee and made a few remarks which irritated an archdeacon at the other end of the room. He said sarcastically, 'And what havoc would not the great Hensley Henson have made of Mr. Grubb's views!' The room was large, the Venerable spoke low, and I could not distinctly hear. The chairman invited me to reply further, so I observed in complete good faith that I had long known Mr. Leslie Henson (the famous comedian of those days) but that it had never occurred to me to discuss an ecclesiastical question with him. The secretary did not record the matter.

This appalling ignorance was steadily remedied by assiduous reading and seeking advice; it is surprising how the higher clergy open up over a good lunch. I never became a fluent orator, and nearly all my speeches in the Assembly have been brief, devoid of popular appeal, and winning scant attention. 'Th' applause of list'ning senates to command' has proved beyond me, and I have envied Halifax, the 'Trimmer' who, according to Dryden[2] was

---

[2] *Absalom and Achitophel.*

> Endued by nature and by learning taught
> To move assemblies, who but only tried
> The worse a while, then chose the better side
> Nor chose alone, but turned the balance too,
> So much the weight of one brave man can do.

In the House of Laity I rarely intervened in the substance of the debate, although I not infrequently reminded the House of what the issues were, and endeavoured to explain clearly and fairly, what were the respective positions to which weight must be given. I lean too readily to leniency and to an incurable penchant for seeing the absurd side of serious matters. Members of the House of Laity who ought to have been shot at sight by a Sergeant-at-Arms have escaped with a caution.

In early days in one of the Latin American republics, if you went to watch a football match, there were stewards who felt you round the hips as you passed through the turnstile. Only the referee was allowed to carry sidearms. This precaution has never been necessary in the House of Laity in my time.

Few things are more boring than a tale of committees and commissions but, poor dears, they merit a passing word. They pile up in Church House like leaves in Vallombrosa, almost as much, in proportion, as in the Palace of Westminster. A large Assembly must have committees to examine a proposal, recommend action, prepare drafts and revise legislation, or simply to report on some 'odd' issue. Ordinarily, a committee should recommend action, since inaction settles naturally on most people; sometimes it is a convenient device for diverting unwise precipitancy, and securing a pause not for somnolence but consideration. For it may be hard to distinguish at first sight between the unreasonable and the unseasonable, between the impracticable and the badly timed.

At Church House someone is sure to say, 'Let us have a small committee, we must keep it small.' This is a popular cry since all desire to economise in the use of the Church's manpower. The motives of those who thus plead vary. Ordinarily, the main motive will be that just described; sometimes a few vigorous characters will demand a small committee, so that being on it, they can more easily sway it. If this be suspected, the committee's report may be challenged when it is laid for debate. Often the plea for a small committee fails, not because it is a bad idea, but because there are many interests which demand representation, and it may be better to satisfy them at the start than antagonise them at the end. Many people, if consulted, acquiesce in weak arguments, but if ignored oppose sound ones.

The Chairman of the House of Laity has had to deal with objections and complaints, usually in the form of correspondence between sessions. If the objector was serious it was my custom to invite him to see me, should he be in London, although it is not easy to fit such interviews into the business day. Sometimes it is as well to adopt diversionary tactics. In a long debate in the House of Laity a gentleman came up in the lunch interval and asked whether he could speak; he had not sent up his name but he felt that the debate was going off the rails. I asked him what his important points were, and perceived that they were important to him. So I said that as a special favour I would call him as soon as the House reassembled. I knew the debate would last the afternoon, and by the time the vote was taken the important remarks would be forgotten. The timing of a speech may be as influential as its substance.

Standing Boards and Councils discharged the permanent work of the Assembly. The functions of the Central Board of Finance, along with the Church Funds Investment Trust are obvious. Others were the Boards of Social Responsibility, and of Education; the Advisory Council for the Church's Ministry, and the Missionary and Ecumenical Council. These were the principal ones, and traditionally they were chaired by a bishop; the Missionary and Ecumenical Council, a comparatively new body born out of previously existing councils, has been chaired by laymen from its establishment, at present by the Earl of March and formerly by myself. In general, much of this has been carried over into the regime of the General Synod.

These interests have been represented at the Standing Committee of the Assembly, along with elected members, bishops, clergy and laity. The Standing Committee was not a Cabinet, nor is the Church a democracy. The chairmen of the main boards have lots of other things to do; probably they will not reside in London; their contacts with the secretaries of the boards may vary greatly according to the temperaments concerned. The Standing Committee exercised a general supervision but its powers were limited. It prepared the agenda for the Assembly, and it made its own observations on agenda questions. It dealt with many appointments which were within its power, or on which it tendered advice to the archbishops, and with many matters of general policy.

Almost everything can be said against this system, except that it did not work, and many alternative systems can be imagined provided they do not have to do so. The machine has worked, but even when well-lubricated it has creaked. It was cumbrous but the Church of England is a loosely articulated and gangling body, seized with sudden attacks of arthritis, and decision at the centre is not easy to translate into action at the circumference.

There are several good ways by which a commission or committee can lose its main recommendations when its chairman presents them to a large debating assembly. He can argue that his proposals are the only solution: the English dislike this because they know they know better. Or, he can argue that all his recommendations must be taken or refused as a package; the English dislike this because it is rarely to their liking. Line upon line, precept upon precept, here a little and there a little, is the English way of reform. He can claim to have taken all the best advice available; obviously this puts off many clever people since experts are so numerous today that no one consults them all. Finally, he can ask that his report be given a special and urgent priority, but all men know that this plea may simply be an attempt to stifle discussion.

A key figure at headquarters (Church House) has been the Secretary of the Assembly, Sir John Guillum Scott who served it from 1948 until its demise in 1970. The Church owes Sir John an accumulated debt of esteem and appreciation. He has managed a delicately inter-connected range of bafflingly assorted responsibilities, and he has done so with aplomb and general acceptance, frequently without the authority normally indispensable for such duties. Relations with the Church Commissioners, with Lambeth Palace, with the Ecclesiastical Committee of Parliament and with many other bodies have perforce engaged his time. A horde of eager people have sought his advice, like the dignitaries met in the outer apartments of a Moslem sheikh. Conflicts of interests and of personalities in Church House have had to be mollified and settled. Innumerable committees and the meetings of the Assembly itself needed, and always received, Sir John's personal attention.

At the apex is the Archbishop of Canterbury in his capacity as Chairman of the Assembly. During my short time there have been two Archbishops in office, Lord Fisher and Dr. Michael Ramsey. The post of Archbishop of Canterbury is arduous. It is no longer a seat of decorative ostentation and ample emoluments; it involves very hard work, much of it in public, many high official duties including presiding over a wide variety of bodies from Convocation to the Church Commissioners, much attention to the internal workings of the Church, much

Presiding in the House of Laity at the Church Assembly

With the C.M.S. Treasurer, Sir Kingsley Tubbs, and the Archbishop of Canterbury at K.G.G.'s C.M.S. farewell, 1969

With Lady Grubb

Outside their home, Moot Farm

After receiving the K.C.M.G. for services to the Church, with Lady Grubb and his sister, Miss. V. M. Grubb

public speaking, and in general the duties from which leadership is never exempt. The office has both its dignified and its efficient aspects, to adopt the terminology of Bagehot, and before all else both its spiritual and pastoral duties. The Archbishops, both of Canterbury and York, also have their own diocesan responsibilities, as bishops of their dioceses. The staff at Lambeth Palace is ludicrously small, not so much in the number of secretaries and chaplains, as in persons of judgment available to be consulted on matters of public and urgent moment. The contrast with the resources available to the chairman of a large business, or to a Secretary of State, let alone to the Prime Minister is alarming and depressing.

I have known both Archbishop Lord Fisher of Lambeth and Dr. Ramsey reasonably well, and record my gratitude equally to both of them, very different as they are. In ways peculiar to their special gifts and outlooks they have both encouraged and helped me to play a part in the central affairs of the Church and my chairmanship of the House of Laity overlapped their respective terms of office. Lord Fisher is greatly my senior in age; Dr. Ramsey a few years my junior.

It is common knowledge that Geoffrey Fisher first rose at the public schools, and as Headmaster of Repton at the age of twenty-seven he is said to have been the country's youngest. Later he was Bishop of Chester and then of London before succeeding William Temple at Canterbury. He preserved both his school-masterly and his masterly bearing and grasp to the end. He gave every appearance of enjoying such onerous tasks as the Church Assembly and all its business. He was rarely at a loss in the chair, and his rulings were prompt, clear and decisive. He readily controlled an awkward crisis; he could easily have settled an earthquake; he commanded where he would not reason. He did sometimes give the impression that the laity as much as the clergy were the paid servants of the Church and therefore bound to accept his behests. This is a small thing; Fisher would have risen quickly if tempestuously to the top in any profession or business. He communicated his mind without havering or ambiguity, and this is all-important when one must decide or drown. The forthrightness or (as I once heard it described wittily but most unfairly) the forthwrongness of his public statements was criticised, often by the same folk who grumbled that the Church gave no leadership. When I held office in the Assembly, I never had occasion to complain of lack of consultation on matters which concerned the House of Laity.

At first, I was uncertain whether I would easily appreciate the mind of Dr. Ramsey, but in practice this soon solved itself. Shy myself, and forced into a dim limelight through a crazy concomitance of circumstances, it was easy to sympathise with the corresponding trait in him. His remarkable appearance, a fascinating mixture of the professional and the ecclesiastical, with a marked impression of the venerability of age which his years denied, was both engrossing and puzzling, until one appreciated his homely humour as well as deep spirituality, two qualities which ride well in tandem, each enriching the other. Dr. Ramsey does not easily amass popularity, and the somewhat artificial cadence which accompanies his public speaking, puts off many who do not appreciate his depth. He has a rare spiritual touch, a combination of simplicity, humility and Christian love, which is very moving, but which it requires time to explore and appreciate for it is not devoid of much shrewdness. His theological writing is deceptively direct and easy; it is only on second reading that one perceives its depth and strength. He has grappled manfully with duties that cannot be always agreeable, and in his chairmanship of the Church Assembly and its Standing Committee, he has acquired an increasing sureness of touch and instinct to deal with the awkward moment by an avoiding action, a word of decision, or a calculated aside in the true tradition of the best English wit.

I have no knowledge of the Convocations of Canterbury and York. Each of these ancient bodies consists of two Houses, an Upper House of Bishops, and a Lower House of Clergy of whom a good part are not elected but are there by right of rank or dignity, as is proper in a hierarchical order. Constitutionally, they have been the authority in the Church in matters spiritual, such as the trickily technical business of Canon Law, the revision of the Prayer Book, or questions of intercommunion or reunion such as the Anglican-Methodist scheme. They are not legislative bodies in the sense that on their sole authority they prepare measures to be laid before Parliament, eventually to receive the royal assent. During my time the Convocations regularly invited the views of the laity on such questions as the above, and the House of Laity spent many hours in separate session debating them.

The complications of church government are disconcerting. They remind a man of the Schleswig-Holstein question. Palmerston said that only three people had ever understood it. One was Albert and he was dead. The second was a German professor: he had accordingly gone mad. The third was himself and he had long since forgotten all about it. There are many good Anglican Christians and true, who long and pray for

Church reform, even a new life and liberty movement, and for the fuller liberation of the national Church for the reconstruction of true religion through modern and wider evangelisation, but who lose heart over the complications and obstacles. In the parishes, among the people of our land, it is the secularism of society, the indifference rather than hostility, that baffles the clergy and render their task a rough and tough challenge to the most courageous, dedicated and spiritual men, whether High Church or Low. At the centre, the sheer complexity of the rules of the game and the time taken to promote a major reform by legislation 'exhaust the energies of strongest souls, and numb the elastic powers'.

Centrally, the Church of England only functions with expedition and force when three seats of direction, decision or supply are in easy relationship. These are the Archbishop of Canterbury and Lambeth Palace; the Church Commissioners at No. 1 Millbank; and the General Synod at Church House. These are at the angles of an equilateral triangle with the Archbishop at the apex, the Commissioners at one of the base angles, and the Synod at the other. They represent the spiritual, the administrative and financial, and the legislative processes of the Church. For the Church to work well at the centre, currents of common conviction and understanding must pass speedily and constantly, as it were, along the sides.

Of the archbishop something has been said. The Church Commissioners on which I have served in varying capacities for many years, control the main financial resources. The First Church Estates Commissioner who is, by statute, chairman of their General Purposes and Assets Committees, is, in effect the managing director of the business. This responsible post was held with conspicuous competence for many years by Lord Silsoe (formerly Sir Malcolm Trustram Eve) and has recently passed to Sir Ronald Harris, K.C.V.O., C.B. The Archbishop of Canterbury, the Chief or General Secretary of the Assembly (or Synod), and the First Church Estates Commissioner must understand one another's language and, so far as may be, anticipate one another's thoughts. There is still much to be done to bring 'Church House', that is the General Synod which has succeeded the Assembly, into closer relations with the Commissioners.

The primary function of the Assembly has been legislation. It dealt with much else, such as the reports of its own boards, those of special commissions and committees (which often lead to legislation), private members motions and questions, and its own supply including the assessment of the diocesan quota. A National Assembly must perforce be engaged in legislation. Many do not understand this, and think gaily that concern with law is inimical to the proclamation of the Gospel. But a large, loosely organised body like the Church of England, particularly since it is an Established Church, cannot conduct its affairs, reform its ministry or alter its worship, without firm legislative authority commanding the assent of the whole Church. Mere aspirations lead to anarchy, simple resolutions to ambiguity. Bishops have so wide a discretion in their dioceses, that a solid body of law is required to maintain common standards, both in conserving the values of the past, and meeting, if possible anticipating, the claims of the future. Legislation is tedious and need not be described here. The Church of England is centuries old, and whole lists of ancient statutes, long spent, lie piled up in the path of the reformer and must be repealed. When men discover this they get angry with the past, which is like kicking a pyramid of Egypt. They do not reflect that they are perforce the product of it; this may be unfortunate for the present but cannot be helped.

Men forget, too, that until the Convocations set up the Assembly, and it was given legislative powers, Church Law could only be amended by Bill in Parliament.[3] This led to an intolerable and stultifying log-jam, for a simple reason which has grown with the passage of years, namely the shortage of parliamentary time. At present a Synodal (formerly Church Assembly) measure goes eventually to the Ecclesiastical Committee of Parliament. This Committee lays the measure together with its report on it before both Houses forthwith, and a resolution is passed in each House to present the measure for the Royal Assent which gives it the force of an Act of Parliament. The resolution can be debated but the measure cannot be amended by Parliament but only referred back.

In the years 1880 to 1913 217 Church Bills were introduced into the Commons, thirty-three were passed, 183 dropped for lack of time, and one turned down. It is not surprising that the Church Assembly had to devote the first three decades of its existence to bringing up-to-date much out-moded law. Only in the 1950s could it plan legislation designed to effect positive and new advances. To list all the measures of the last two decades would be an abuse of patience, but some at least merit a brief word.

[3] In this and the next four paragraphs I am much indebted to a special communication from Sir John Guillum Scott.

To start with supply or money. Under a Measure of 1951 the Commissioners took over certain benefice endowments in return for money capital and the guarantee of interest on it at a rate fixed at the time of transfer. The endowments taken were added to the Commissioners total portfolio which by skilful investment has produced additional income to the great benefit of the clergy. The Commissioners have used part of this surplus income to make block grants to dioceses for increasing clergy stipends. Some years later, in 1959, the Central Board of Finance was empowered to create the Church Investment Fund. This ranks as a trustee investment and dioceses, parishes and many Church societies have enjoyed the benefit of a unit trust through its agency. Non-contributory pensions for the clergy had been established in 1954 and seven years later the laws governing clergy pensions were consolidated and brought up-to-date.

The 1960s witnessed other reforms. The Ecclesiastical Jurisdiction Measure amended the law on Ecclesiastical Courts. It created special courts to deal with matters of doctrine, ritual and ceremonial and removed from the Judicial Committee of the Privy Council the final appeal. The law about cathedrals was amended and updated, and under the Cathedrals Measure all cathedrals have been provided with new statutes. The revision of Canon Law was completed during the decade and various small measures were passed to give legal force to certain Canons. The general object was to bring the Canons into line with modern needs and practices. This somewhat tedious subject occupied many separate sessions of the House of Laity. It was necessary, but did not invariably attract the wildest enthusiasm.

For the ordinary churchgoer the results of the Prayer Book (Alternative and Other Services) Measure have been of much greater concern. The extreme rigidity of the Act of Uniformity of 1662 prevented, in theory, any deviation from the Book of Common Prayer; in practice this was nowhere followed *au pied de la lettre*. The subject was approached with caution, for the fact that the Revised Prayer Book of 1927-8 had never been experimentally tried in the parishes contributed to its defeat by the Commons. Accordingly, the measure authorised forms of service alternative to those of the Book of Common Prayer, and quite new services for occasions for which the Book made no provision, for experimental use. This question also occupied the House of Laity and required special open conferences from time to time between the bishops, clergy and laity of the Assembly. In practice, the Service which gave rise to much the most debate, that of Holy Communion, seems to have been used most widely and possibly to have gained most acceptance.

Other matters of moment came before the Assembly in its final years. Two reports containing recommendations for drastic changes in the status and tenure of the clergy, and much constructive criticism of the parochial system attracted a nice mixture of concern and approval. One was Mr. Leslie Paul's *The Deployment and Payment of the Clergy*, and the other was *Partners in Ministry* by a Commission under Canon Fenton Morley. If the recommendations of these reports are eventually passed into law, the face of the Church of England will be lifted and its features enlivened and adapted to a more contemporary style of work and address. Some do not like the thought.

The subject of Church and State, involving the Establishment of the Church of England, is perennial and long before they die all sorts of people in the Church Assembly (or Synod), and many others who write to the Church press or *The Times*, become authorities on it. It has been the object of earnest study and recommendation by appointed bodies, but the Assembly usually failed to act on their more drastic proposals. It is not unusual for the members of Royal Commissions to find the fruit of their devoted labours shelved, unread, unhonoured and unsung: it is the unavoidable price of such procedures. This was particularly apt to happen in the Assembly when the report insisted on emphasising that unless its proposals were adopted, the Church would disintegrate forthwith. The present Commission on Church and State, under the Master of Selwyn College, Cambridge (and Vice-Chancellor of the University), Professor Owen Chadwick, reported late in 1970. It is easier to collect information than to profit from it, and a report or measure on so vital a subject accepted or passed only by a small majority, may prove to be a Pyrrhic victory, or Dead Sea fruit, or whatever. As the Spanish proverb goes, '*El vencido, vencido, y el Vencedor perdido.*[4] I return to the subject later (pp. 217–9).

This brief and dull review must not omit the steps by which the Assembly quietly dug its grave and lay down in it. Subsequent diggers for light and truth, finding its skull, now emptied of so many brains, can at least exclaim 'Alas! Poor Yorick'. Or, to put it another way, 'Some pious drops the closing eye requires.' It gave way to the General Synod of the Church from which much is expected and more hoped.

Mr. George Goyder made one of the earliest proposals for a general

[4] 'The conquered, conquered; and the conqueror, lost.'

synod over fifteen years ago, in a forceful speech. The arguments are various. The Assembly was an elephantine body for these crowded times, with over 700 members. Its gestation was painful, its labour long and successful delivery in the balance till the end. The position of the faithful laity has changed since the Enabling Act. They are fewer in the land, but the House of Laity included a wide range (although not wide enough) and among them are many persons of intelligence and devotion. Amid today's distractions, only those with deep convictions will clear the time for this work. The laity, therefore, should have a more responsible place both generally in the Church and in church government. They will not do their duty unless they learn their lessons. There is justification for the governing of the Church by a synod of all the people of God, bishops, clergy and laity sitting together, and it is the usual practice in churches of the Anglican Communion. Such arguments are, however, dismissed by some with the objection that the English situation is peculiar; it certainly is. The Church, like slavery in the Southern States, is England's 'peculiar institution'. England, as often, is the odd man out and very odd at that.

A general synod of the Church was decreed after much Assembly debate, and inaugurated late in 1970. The Church Assembly as elected in 1965 was due to lapse then and elections had in any case to be held. My chairmanship of the House of Laity ended, because the House did. I did not stand for membership of the new Synod and thus closed my career in Church government, presumably to the satisfaction of my enemies, and, hopefully, to the regret of my friends.

The new Synod has 545 members. They are the diocesan bishops; and clergy and laity in equal numbers. The idea is that they will almost always sit together; if there are too many separate sittings of the Houses the conception of a synod will be defaced. When I gave evidence to the Synodical Government Commission sitting under Lord Hodson, someone asked if I advocated a separate House of Laity. I replied No, unless the clergy wanted a House of their own. They did (in the form of the Convocations) so the laity had one too.

The habit of cosy and close clerical association dies hard. Most professions have their exclusive associations, and, as the clergy repeat *ad nauseam*, the Convocations are the oldest debating assemblies in the land. The older the riper is a very English view, but the next stage after ripeness is rot. Age does not wither nor custom stale their infinite satiety. The Convocations will exist side by side with the Synod, and matters of doctrine and worship may be referred to them, but the General Synod possesses the full spiritual authority as well as the functions of the Convocations. Conviction that the Convocations are indispensable in the constitution of Church and State is slowly losing its grip of the clerical mind. Time does make ancient good uncouth, and God fulfils Himself in many ways lest one good custom should corrupt the church.

Synodical government attempts to make Church interests livelier and more intriguing to the average Churchman in the parishes, but the Church is hardly intended to mediate the excitement of an Ian Fleming novel. Parochial Church Councils remain. More responsibility will rest on Deanery Synods: the Deanery is our old friend which even in a large city masqueraded under the title of Rural Deanery with a Rural Dean, but so often the Church forgets that four-fifths of England's working population is employed and concerned with industry. The Deanery Synods elect representatives direct to the General Synod. Steps have been taken to organise diocesan synods.

No one can be sure in advance that reforms will succeed: elation and gloom should both be avoided. Organisations alone do not implant faith; but public religion will perish without adequate organisation.

The General Synod of the Church of England was inaugurated on 4 November, 1970. The solemn service of Holy Communion in Westminster Abbey was ushered in by decorative processions, including the groups of synod representatives, bishops, clergy and laity from every diocese, and civil and official dignatories. The most moving moment was when the Queen advanced alone from her seat at the west end of the Choir to receive the Holy Communion. At the end of the long service she was led to the sacrarium by the Lord Chancellor and, after brief formalities, declared the General Synod duly constituted.

The Houses of Clergy and Laity then met separately to elect their chairmen and officers. In the afternoon the Queen and the Duke of Edinburgh attended the opening of the Synod in Church House, and Her Majesty briefly addressed it. Greetings were conveyed by the Heads of other Churches. Later the first business session was convened.

The official programme of the day says that the opening of the first session 'starts a new era in the government of the Church', and expresses the hope that the 'renewal of church government may serve the renewal of the Church'. One must, indeed, endorse this wholly laudable sentiment for much thought and work have gone into the creation of synodical government. A change of Church government, it must be repeated, will not of itself revive the appeal and power of the Gospel, but if it proves a good change, it may provide new opportunities if the Church and its members are spiritually alert to seize them.

The most difficult question for tomorrow may be the Establishment. There are two parties, the Church and the State, and the present relationship does not exist elsewhere in the Anglican Communion. Since two parties are in the game the recommendations of one will hardly be automatically accepted by the other. The Church's commission on Church and State reported late in 1970, but even if the Synod accepts all or some of its recommendations, it does not follow that Parliament will. Parliament might insist on making its own enquiry.

The Establishment represents a relationship which has grown up over the centuries and was drastically altered and given a new dress at the Reformation. The Sovereign is the Supreme Governor of the Church of England. She (or he) is crowned at an elaborate, impressive but quaintly antique ceremony, performed by the Archbishop of Canterbury in Westminster Abbey. Other public occasions, of which a recent example was the state funeral of Sir Winston Churchill, find their highest expression in the stately yet moderate ritual of the Church. The bishops and certain other ecclesiastics are appointed by the Crown on the recommendation of the Prime Minister who, in turn, is equipped with special facilities for privately seeking the advice of those concerned in the Church and other spheres. Parliament has a final control over Church legislation, and although it cannot amend a Church measure, it can refuse to forward it for the Royal Assent. The Book of Common Prayer is, in its main rubrics and regulations, a part of the law of the land, except in so far as Alternative Services (see p. 213) have been sanctioned. In the field of ecclesiastical jurisdiction, the relations between Church and State have already been altered (see p. 218). Only under special conditions can a clergyman refuse baptism, marriage, or burial in the church of the parish. There are other lesser points at which the tenets or practices of the Church involve the interests of the State or require the sanction of civil authority.

The Establishment does not mean that the State subsidises the Church. The Church Commissioners do not receive a penny from taxation. They are a merger of two bodies, Queen Anne's Bounty, established in 1704, when Queen Anne restored certain taxes to the Church in order to assist poor clergy, and the Ecclesiastical Commission, set up over a century later, also with a very small fund, to make additional provision for the cure of souls in parishes. All the rest is the fruit of the Commissioners' stewardship.

The form and fashion of the Church of England may be substantially changed by the Pastoral Measure of 1968 which repeals the accumulated legislation of many decades. Each diocese will have a pastoral committee to make recommendations to the bishop. Two or more parishes may be united to form a new one, and boundaries, whether of parish, deanery, archdeaconry or diocese may be altered by due process. The whole or part of the endowment income of a benefice, viz. for this purpose, the area over which a clergyman exercises oversight, may be transferred to the diocesan stipends fund. 'Team', or 'group' ministries may be set up; and a new parish may be formed without a consecrated parish church, provided the bishop licenses a building for public worship. The central administration of this far-reaching measure will be in the hands of the Church Commissioners.

Redundant churches are the object of special consideration, having in mind that a church no longer needed for public worship may have great historical or architectural merits. Recently the Government agreed to contribute a matching £200,000 to a fund for the preservation of redundant churches of special historic or architectural merit. Similarly, local authorities often contribute to special appeals for the repair of cathedrals.

It is said that the disestablishment of the Church would mean its disendowment which, in practice, would be the confiscation or diversion of much of the funds held or handled by the Church Commissioners. But this is by no means certain, and, if disestablishment is decided to be for the spiritual good of the Church and people of England, the cause must be paramount and the cost accepted.

Some want total disestablishment. The Church, they say, must be footloose to fulfil its mission; at present it is a slave of the past and of outmoded laws, its hands are tied; it cannot even appoint its chief pastors. Others would leave things as they are on the ground that the system works, and in so delicate and historic a field an attempt to better would result in worse. There are many who think the idea of Establishment is good, albeit peculiar; it is embedded in our history; and, as is the English way, it would be better to modify it to meet modern conditions than blow it up or poison it as a useful experiment in biological warfare. After listening for many years to great argument by doctor and by saint 'about it and about', I am sure modification is desirable and will be eventually found feasible.

Many ancient landmarks have gone, as they have from other areas of our national life. No longer is Christianity co-extensive with men's common loyalties and outlook; no longer can it be assumed that Members of Parliament are communicant members of the Church. Regular church attendance is very small; the Bible is hardly to be found, still less read, in most new households. However, elements in the Free Churches which were very critical of the mere idea of Establishment seem to have modified their position. There is talk of an establishment of religion, a rather meaningless phrase since we are here dealing with institutions. An establishment of churches might be 'on'.

It would be wearisome to deploy my own views: I merely give one illustration. I dislike the present system of episcopal appointment, administered though it is, as I have good reason to know, with the utmost care and concern for the good of the diocese as well as of the Church as a whole. In every diocese there should be a body of clergy and faithful laity, whose counsel it would be obligatory to seek but not to adopt, without excluding other sources of advice, before recommending to the Crown. The 'Vacancy in Sees' Committee, a recent innovation, is indeed now grappling with this. I would leave the remainder of the process of episcopal appointment unaltered for an experimental period. In time, advice thus tendered would acquire weighty influence.

I leave all this to comment on other points. The House of Laity was criticised for not being representative even of the faithful laity of the Church. Both bishops and clergy made this criticism; it did not become either. The House was, at least, elected; among some 350 members ten could be coopted, and this right was for years not fully used. Diocesan bishops were in the Assembly by right of office; they do not run the gamut of election, and this is as it should be; and they are paid. A goodish number of the House of Clergy, that is 'dignitaries' of consequence, were there by right; and they are paid as full-time clergymen. The laity are not paid (except those employed by a diocese) and give their time freely, and, as I well know, often to the detriment of their affairs. I hold no high opinion of persons who, from seats of privilege, publicly make inconsiderate judgments; their animus is only equalled by their impertinence.

Criticism of the House can properly come from its own members, and often does. Some members were diocesan secretaries or otherwise gainfully employed in the work of the Church or its societies. Others were the wives or widows of clergymen, or otherwise actively connected with, but not paid by, the Church except by way of pension. A fairish proportion were retired, including members of the Services. The number of Members of Parliament declined over the years, owing to the pressure on an M.P.'s time. The House was more representative of the professions than of business or the many grades in industry from the shop floor upwards. This is hard to change, so long as the Synod makes such large demands on a man's time. The chairman of the Laity was in an exceptional position and it was rightly expected that he give his attention liberally to his responsibilities. Had I not been able steadily to diminish other and more lucrative commitments, I could not have done justice to the office. This is partly because I am slow in the uptake and require time to master reports and distinguish thoughts from sentiments. In spite of all, the Church has been well served by the House of Laity. In its last decade the House was called on to play a much more active part in Assembly affairs. Attendance has sometimes been thin, but in the absence of Whips, it is not easy to keep a fullish house. As for the debating, there are bores, but where not? Swans sing before they die; I wish that some orators would die before they speak. They are not many and in a *Church* body they provide practice in the Christian virtue of patience and long (or long-) suffering. I once grumbled about all this to a Member of the Commons who was also in the House of Laity, and who held high office in politics. He replied, 'You exaggerate. There are as accomplished speakers in the House of Laity as there are in the Commons, and these put difficult arguments with truly exemplary brevity. Cheer up!'

Right and close relations between the clergy and the laity are important. I do not speak of bishops because, although most devoted and able, they are enigmatic, and it is well to regard them with caution. If a man has a serious discussion with a bishop, it should not be *à deux* but with a witness, say, one's solicitor, accountant, or psychiatrist, in attendance.

Relations at Church House between the clergy and the laity are easily upset by ill-judged or by untimely speeches, of which the full import is not always perceived. But all are the *laos*, the people of God, and it is a Christian duty, albeit at times unpalatable, to understand one another, and go the second mile to do so. The task of a clergyman can be heart-rendingly disheartening; the pay is small in spite of the valiant skill of the Church Commissioners; and the clergy need encouragement and should be given it both with tact and force. Their status has changed. The parson is no longer automatically the leader even of a rural community. His own attainments, particularly his training, may be inferior compared to some of his 'flock': very little thought has been given to retraining, as it is recognised in industry. He is isolated, the bearer of a message which he commends by his life, words and works, but which is often received with the polite indifference which the Athenians accorded to St. Paul on his first visit to their famous city.

The position of the clergy will be substantially affected if the main recommendations of the report *Partners in Ministry* (see p. 214) are eventually applied. I only comment on one question, that is, the parson's 'freehold'. Those unfamiliar with these abstrusities may misunderstand the term. It means that a clergyman once instituted in a 'living', cannot be bunged out of it during 'the term of his natural', saving for heresy or open sin. He may grow old while still young, or indifferent when he should be devoted, but nothing can be done. The system has its defenders: the parson is poorly paid; his freehold is his precious possession; he needs time to know his people; individual independence is much to be valued in a collective and 'anonymous' society. Whenever I hear these worthy words, I also hear a voice from Macbeth:

> And you all know, security
> is mortals' chiefest enemy.

Partners In Ministry suggests two forms of tenure. One is the appointment for a term of years with the possibility of renewal by mutual consent; the other is appointment without a term of years but subject to review.

The state and prospects of the ministry in the Church of England give cause for furious thought. For many years the intake of ordinands was reasonable; lately it has fallen suddenly and seriously. During these years the Church has contracted, benefices have been united, livings held in plurality, churches closed, 'team ministries' developed. The distribution of the clergy has never been tackled on a nation-wide basis, nor could it be under the present diocesan system. The Church has still a rural emphasis in an urban society, but every year the Church is putting up modern buildings in new areas. The average age of the clergy is increasing, and younger men, called to serve their fellows christianly, see other vocations in which they feel they can do so better.

Graver even than this is the quality of the ordinands: I am struck in the theological colleges with two things, the sincerity of the young men, and their immaturity. The situation is dangerous. As at 31 December, 1967 there were 15,548 clergymen holding full-time appointments, by no means all in parochial work. The number of ordinations in 1967 stood at 496, the lowest for a decade. The 1968 report of the Advisory Council for the Church's Ministry stated frankly, 'If the number of ordinations continues to decline, then the Church will probably be driven to look for new forms of ministry, i.e. of self-supporting ministry.'

Retired men get ordained, after training; this helps, but does not solve. The emphasis in the Church of England has traditionally been on a full-time ministry. Some other churches of the Anglican Communion rely considerably on men who, although ordained, work at their business in the world, the so-called 'tent-making ministry'.

I do not see any sufficient theological or practical reason to forbid the ordination of women to the priesthood, but this is not a popular view. They are admitted to the higher ranks of almost every other profession and vocation. It is hard to believe that they would swamp the ministry — they might vamp it. Neither alternative has been the experience of the Congregational Church where ordination has been open to women for decades. The same argument was used when women were admitted to Parliament, but there are still men there. On this matter, St. Paul was pig-headed.

The Assembly was not successful in discussing what should be the heart of the Church's mission, namely evangelisation. Today this is called evangelism, thus putting it among the '-isms', but evangelisation is a task and a process rather than a condition or system. After World War II, a Commission under the Bishop of Rochester (Dr. Chavasse) produced a report *Towards the Conversion of England* which was received by the Assembly, and which aroused much general interest. Its practical effect was small. Recently the archbishops set up a Council on Evangelism the results of whose work have not yet (1970) been published. A legislative body like the Church Assembly is not well-adapted either to inspire or to tackle 'The Conversion of England'. A real spirit of evangelisation must be widely diffused and personally felt: it is a witness at the circumference rather than a function of the centre. While studying and utilising the best methods of communication, it depends on the vigour and depth of spiritual life and conviction in the Church, and must start in the individual, in the parish and the theological colleges. The Church of England is not alone in its failure to grapple with this, the outstanding challenge to religion in our time. Other Churches are equally stuck and just as anxious. Such approaches as the Billy Graham crusades have been widely welcomed in the Church, but not lastingly effective among the people. Anyhow, the possibilities of a single—or two or three—campaign(s) by an Evangelist and his team, however well-conducted, are today limited.

This raises wider questions. How deeply are the clergy and laity of the Church convinced of the essential and unique claims of Christ and their relevance to modern man and community? If there were a true revival of Christian faith and a movement of the Holy Spirit among the people of England, is the Church equipped to understand and nourish it? Many would answer in the negative, and I am among them. Perhaps the Church must die for the Gospel to live, that is the Church of England as we know it today. There are forms of expression of the Word and Sacraments which would largely dispense with the regular use of our church buildings and great cathedrals. These latter will remain centres for special occasions as monuments of history and reminders of the Christian roots of our past. The present diocesan organisation may disappear; already men talk of creating much smaller dioceses. Some form of local worship seems indispensable. And Christians must fight for conversion and for the revival of private piety, Bible reading and prayer, the meeting of the small group, the occasional mass gathering, and the means of formulating and applying the public and social outlook of the Church.

Many maintain that the tide of indifference will not turn if the Churches do not heal their own divisions. This does not imply unreflecting support of every scheme of intercommunion or reunion. Ecumenical enthusiasts both bore and weary; in so delicate a field more is accomplished by shrewdness than by fervour and the fixing of dates for all-round reunion is to be warily regarded. Equally, one suspects that some arguments against reunion schemes are thought up rather than out. They represent little more than a series of defence points, each built, like an eighteenth-century fortress in the Low Countries, as an example of how to stay put for a pause of relief rather than a spur to further reconnaissance and advance. A union of all would not of itself re-Christianise our society; it would help. A task so immense is not solved by adding on divisions to make an army, but by the depth, and desire of faith and prayer, by love of Christ and devotion to others, and by harmony of purpose and affection among all who name the name of the Lord, irrespective of denomination. 'By this shall men know you are my disciples, if you love one another'.

I have not enjoyed work at Church House. In a mission body like the Church Missionary Society, there is more of purpose, and the feeling of 'we few, we happy few, we band of brothers'. In ecumenical work (owing to the cost of large international gatherings) one need not meet the *cognoscenti* too often. In Church government one constantly encounters people of great piety and virtue; few things are more trying to the nerves. Meeting is at best wearisome, and meeting the good exhausting.

Several friends who have kindly read some of this material in draft have remarked 'But you don't say what your motives are. You don't explain what makes you "tick".' I cannot answer this one, beyond the hints already dropped in this narrative. Apart from conversion and the perennial but fading appeal of my dream, I have never had any visions or even any inborn sense of obligation. Life brings its opportunities and challenges and one accepts them. Once having decided, I do what I dislike with as much or as little efficiency as what I like. A man must earn his living and provide for his family; beyond that, such work as is here described, arid as it must seem, does at least keep a man from sporting 'with Amaryllis in the shade', that is getting into trouble with the girls: there isn't time.

* * *

During these years I did other things, some of which I have briefly referred to. For years, I was chairman of twenty to thirty voluntary causes and committees, omitting minor affairs and temporary exertions. Some of these involved cartloads of work and responsibility. Apart from ordinary correspondence, interviews and meetings, I was lucky if I got away with under thirty pages of minutes, memoranda and reports per diem, and often it was more. On turning up at a board, I often found that I was the only person who had read all the papers and knew my mind, which was never much to know.

It would be plain silly to refer to all these enterprises. One of my early appointments was as President of the two Colleges of Education, as the modern title goes, at Cheltenham, St. Paul's and St. Mary's. They have well over a century of life behind them and have turned out a long succession of trained teachers, men and women. I chaired the Colleges' Council, and negotiated with the Department of Education and Science —then the Ministry of Education—the scheme which governed their existence up till recently. At home in Highgate, I was churchwarden of Christ Church, Crouch End, in those days of six to seven hundred members, and I served for many years on the Council of the North London Y.M.C.A. in Hornsey, one of the largest residential Y.M.C.A.s in the country.

I had early been interested in the laity, being of the species. The use of the laity overseas was of concern to the Survey Application Trust (see pp. 91–92) and in 1931 I followed up some of the writing of the Rev. Roland Allen[5] with a paper entitled *The Need for Non-professional Missionaries*. But one should not be a prophet out of due time; it may be better to hold one's peace until the stones cry out. Thirty-one years later the World Council of Churches' Commission on World Mission and Evangelism published a study by Dr. Paul Löffler.[6] Dr. Löffler after noting this goes on:

[Sir Kenneth Grubb] was also the first to take action by establishing a small scale business exchange and appointment bureau in London. Through contacts with Christian businessmen in various capitals overseas he was regularly advised on vacancies in local establishments of British firms. In Britain Sir Kenneth passed on the information to training centres and other places where Christians with appropriate qualifications were available. In this way it was possible to place many keen Christians in key posts overseas.

I do not recall where Dr. Löffler obtained this information: if from one of my friends (or enemies) it was correct; if from me it was, incredibly, no less so.

In World War II, Dr. J. H. Oldham, C.B.E., who died in 1969 at the age of ninety-four, established the Christian Frontier Council under the chairmanship of Sir Walter Moberly. The idea was that the Church failed to influence the institutions of society because it addressed them from outside. The fruitful approach was not the official pronouncements of Church bodies, but the work and witness of laymen and laywomen with their stalls in the market-place or sweating in the engine room. They alone could interpret industry and professions from the inside and, with the help of theologians and divines, work towards discovering the relevance of the Gospel: they were on the *frontier* between the Church and the World.

The group was small and during the war most of its members were Under-Secretaries in the war departments, or engaged in Parliament or

---

[5] See also David M. Paton, ed. *The Ministry of the Spirit*, Lutterworth Press for the Survey Application Trust, 1968.

[6] Paul Löffler, *The Layman Abroad in the Mission of the Church: A Decade of Discussion and Experiment* (Edinburgh House Press for the W.C.C. Commission on World Mission and Evangelism, 1962), p. 27.

public life, but we struggled to meet every six weeks or so. Dr. Oldham, and later Dr. Kathleen Bliss, edited and published *The Christian Newsletter*, a sheet of distinction, every word of which carried weight. After the war, the character of the Frontier Council changed, if only because the associations of the members did. I held office in it for some years, and continued my membership until 1969. I also got interested in the publication side, and eventually the Survey Application Trust acquired what had started as *The Christian Newsletter*, and we expanded it into a quarterly. Sir John Lawrence edited it, as he had done its predecessor, with conspicuous flair and success. Under him *Frontier* has been a distinguished and sustained achievement of spiritual and intellectual depth.

A reference is due to Christian Teamwork. This originated in discussions between the Rev. Bruce Reed, an Australian clergyman in London and myself, and was organised in 1957. Its primary object was to investigate how people in business, the professions and other walks of life can draw upon the resources of God in understanding and implementing His purposes for them in a technological society. By 1962, five years later, it had begun to reach policy conclusions in a largely unexplored field. From the beginning the movement had had close contacts with some large industrial enterprises and it developed a practical and intimate liaison with the Centre for Applied Social Research, one of the staff groups within the Tavistock Institute of Human Relations. Backed by a strong body of Trustees latterly chaired by Sir Maurice Parsons, it expanded both its thinking and its contacts. Its courses, along the lines developed by the Centre have had much influence among those who have attended them, whether from industry, education, social service or the Churches. In 1969 the Grubb Institute of Behavioural Studies was formed to carry forward this work through consultancy, research and courses in human behaviour. The Christian Teamwork Trust remained as a fostering and fund-raising body. I was embarrassed by the new choice of name but it was universally desired, so I subsided quietly like a spent hurricane. No one can pretend that the name Grubb adds beauty to an idea or euphony to a title.

Finally, but by no means least, something must be said about the Royal Foundation of St. Katharine in Ratcliffe. On the retirement of Sir Walter Moberly in 1957, I was invited to assume the chairmanship of the Court of the Foundation. The Hospital of St. Katharine by the Tower of London was founded in 1148 on land hard by the Tower of London, roughly the present St. Katharine's Dock. It was to help the poor, provide for the sick and accommodate strangers. Over a century later it was restyled the Royal

Hospital of St. Katharine, received a new Charter from Aleanore (Eleanor) wife of Henry III, and became a Royal Peculiar. This charter established that 'every Queen succeeding us shall possess in perpetuity' the patronage, and Queen Elizabeth the Queen Mother is the present Patron.

From the beginning St. Katharine's has been administered by a Chapter consisting of Master, brothers and sisters. Later a Court was established under a lay chairman, with the duties generally of cooperating with the Master, financing the work of the Foundation, dealing with the tenants of its farmland in Kent, and making recommendations to the Patron within the scope of the Ordinances. The Patron is the supreme authority and she alone can decide changes in the Ordinances, formerly called the Charter.

The Foundation has been through many vicissitudes: its functions have changed; and it has long since ceased to be a hospital. By the time of Henry VIII it had become prosperous and, although scheduled for dissolution, it just escaped. Later it passed through troublous days. It became a refuge for foreigners from the Continent which, since they were often those persecuted for conscience sake, was a Christian service. But, as time went by, this practice was abused and by the end of the eighteenth century, it was an overcrowded slum of some 3,000 people. Since the precinct was largely self-contained and immune from the civil and church authorities, it was a refuge for scallywags being independent of both the City and the Bishop of London.

Early in the nineteenth century, following the passing of a hotly disputed private Act of Parliament, the inhabitants of the precinct were evicted, and St. Katharine's Dock was built. The Master, brothers and sisters, moved to Regent's Park and new buildings and a chapel were built there. Divorced from its historic setting, it rapidly declined. In 1914, and again after World War II, it was completely reorganised. Before 1914 it ran schools in Regent's Park and between the wars it was responsible for maternity and child welfare work in Poplar on behalf of the local authority. This came to an end with the passing of the National Health Act in 1948.

The upshot was that the Foundation quit Regent's Park and later returned to East London, namely to its present site in Butcher Row, Stepney, just off Cable Street. Father St. John Groser became Master in 1956 and developed the work to meet the needs. These included his long-standing interest in the conditions of London's docks and dockers, his close collaboration with the churches in the East End and with the Borough of Stepney (now part of Tower Hamlets), his concern for housing, and for assistance to the aged and the sick. His mastership lasted till 1962 and definitely re-established the Foundation, after the lapse of many years, as a centre of living Christian work and witness in East London. He was followed by Father Henry Cooper, and in 1968 the Court, with the authority of the Patron, negotiated an agreement with the Community of the Resurrection, to occupy the premises and further develop the work to meet modern demands. The Community moved their London House from Holland Park to Butcher Row and the Sisters of the Community Chapter are now members of the Deaconess Order of St. Andrew's.

This latest reform required a slight further amendment of the Ordinances to which the Patron consented. Generally, the system of government through a Master, brothers and sisters at the Foundation, and a Court under a lay chairman (with the Patron's representatives as regular members), and a Treasurer, Mr. W. Hill-Wood, C.B.E., has worked very smoothly. This has been due in the first place to the Masters concerned, but also to the constant interest of the Patron, the long service of Mr. H. J. Wasbrough, M.V.O., as Clerk of the Court, and the assiduity of his successor, Mr. G. M. U. Young.

CHAPTER X

So What?

WHEN questioned, Jesus answered, ' "Love the Lord your God with all your heart, with all your soul, with all your mind." That is the greatest commandment. It comes first. The second is like it: "Love your neighbour as yourself." ' (Matthew 22: 37–39.)[1] And again, 'If a man says "I love God", while hating his brother, he is a liar. If he does not love the brother whom he has seen, it cannot be that he loves God whom he has not seen.' (I John 4: 20.)

Looking back over the years, here is a real difficulty. Loving is different from liking, but the latter is a great help to the former. I rarely like people. I have a very few friends and a vast number of acquaintances and contacts whom one politely calls friends. It seems much easier to love those whom one decides to like, and if there are only a few whom one likes, it is hard to find many 'neighbours' whom one can love. This leads to a further difficulty. One cannot love God unless one loves one's neighbour and brother. It appears comparatively easy to love God, although it is more difficult in civilisation than in the wilds. I have never found it hard to do what seems to be God's will at any juncture, but clearly I do not love God in the sense of which Jesus spoke since I so rarely love my neighbour.

With rare exceptions, I have seen no beckoning hand, felt no challenge, been moved by no vocation, inspired by no anticipated joy or hope of achievement. One day has followed another. I read my Bible and say my prayers. I go to work knowing exactly what I intend to do and how long to devote to each chore, correspondence, interview, committee, or brief journey. I rarely think of what I am doing: I have done that beforehand: while I am doing it, I think of the next thing. I have decided even major proposals, likely to occupy much of my time for years, swiftly and usually without subsequent regret. These are the powers of a limited mind. Too much conscience, too much thinking—or what passes as such makes cowards of us all, and 'the native hue of resolution is sicklied o'er by the

[1] All quotes from the New Testament in this chapter are from the New English Bible.

pale cast of thought'. A world of Hamlets would be a world of hesitation and Christianity is a religion of decision and faith.

Much of this is due to another defect of character, namely that I have little spontaneous instinct or emotion, or rather I suppress it. If I like anyone, it is not primarily because he appeals to me, but because I decide to like him. I rarely decide to hate since that is clearly un-Christian, but I frequently fail to like. Almost without reflection, I approach relationships with a neighbour or colleague with a reserve and suspicion which I usually conceal. This may be derived from early days in the interior of South America, in an environment where unless you looked after your own interests jealously you soon went under.

It makes no difference to me whether I like, or love, a man whom I work with. All I need to know is whether he is efficient, and who has the right and ability and the power to give orders. Nor does it make any perceptible difference whether I like a task or no. All that matters is whether I am qualified and it is right for me to do it. I could never accomplish any great thing, for great accomplishments are born from strong passions.

So much for youth and middle years, now for maturity and old age.

We are taught at school to repeat 'the best is yet to be / The last of life for which the first was made'. At least Rabbi Ben Ezra, and presumably Browning, thought so. But is it true?

It seems strange that English literature, with all its wealth and variety, contains few descriptions by the very old of their inmost thoughts. There are moving and imaginative reconstructions; perhaps the best known today is in the *Indian Summer of a Forsyte*. The aged tend to be silent. The desire for achievement, ambition itself, energy, the driving wish to be in on the argument and the deed, fade. 'Let them have it their way, let the geese be swans, and the swans geese', is a natural reaction. The flames of desire burn low, the ashes sink in the hearth. Winston Churchill relates a touching incident about the Duke of Marlborough in his last retirement, watching from the palace of Blenheim, the farther walls rise slowly from the ground, stone by stone. 'It is the truth that only a single remark of his [the Duke's] about himself has survived. One day he paced with failing steps the state rooms of his palace, and stood long and intently contemplating his portrait by Kneller. Then he turned away with the words, "That was once a man." '[2]

It is the most trite of commonplaces that life is fleeting and short, and

[2] Winston S. Churchill, *Marlborough: His Life and Times* (Sphere Books, 1967), Vol. IV, p. 539.

its end irresistible and universal. There are those who contemplate the prospect without melancholy or inner questioning. There are, perhaps, few men of action who would not prefer to die in combat or adventure, rather than eke out spent energies without blame but without contentment. Those who find contentment to the last in the society of friends who survive with them through fresh moments of thought, faith and prayer, are, one supposes, exceptions. I am not among them. I hold the faith, but with constancy rather than contentment. Existence can be 'cherished, strengthen'd and fed without the aid of joy'.

When the pressures on time and the demand on energy have lessened somewhat, I have found much satisfaction in travelling to see the riches of yesterday, particularly in Spain, Italy and Greece. From youth, I have known something of these countries and many others, but their culture and history from the earliest Minoan or Etruscan days to the Renaissance and later has fascinated me to the point of devotion, as it has thousands of others. In this sense I am a true European. Journeys made with my wife, with my friend Mr. M. G. Talbot Rice and with a few others constantly come back to me in pensive mood, with the gleam of an indestructible treasure. I have studied but little history, just enough to know what I like and like what I know. The contemplation of sheer beauty, in nature and in art, is a relief from the discipline of work and responsibility. Art offers satisfaction; and the critique of satisfaction is one of the unsolved and major challenges of the age of progress. But it is not so easy. Philosophers may deplore that thinkers must die; artists no doubt regret that the living must think. Each must hope that 'something from our hands have power, to live, and act and serve the future hour'.

I do not perceive a pattern in history. I have read Guicciardini, Toynbee and Spengler, H. A. L. Fisher, Trevelyan, Grote, and others of Europe's great historians, not to mention the classical ones. The picture they present, the very canvas on which they paint it, is mostly too vast for my interpretation, and defies my limited power of criticism. One is tempted to perceive little significance in individual life because one cannot feel any sense of attainment or influence for the good. To some extent this is a matter of moods, and power of expression. A distinguished historian present at a dinner party in London where I was being quizzed about my behaviour and reactions during the weeks of solitude in Amazonia commented, 'I could not have lived it through'; to which I replied 'Neither can I describe it'. If I could ask one gift from the gods, it would be the pen of a ready writer.

It is very easy to exaggerate moods, and to give the impression that an outlook or impulse which grips the mind is thereby characteristic of a man's total or general attitude. This must be avoided. The Bible and Pascal have much to say on the grandeur and misery of man's lot. It is hard to escape from either of these moods. Man, in his grandeur, plants his feet on the moon, and tells of what stuff planets and suns are made. It is false to decry his greatness, the splendour of his achievements, the endless thrust of his progress. He is the heir of the ages, the explorer of the universe, the master of the air, the silent peaks, the homely valleys, and even sometimes the wind on the heath. The ceaseless flow of the rivers, the world of nature and the wings that sweep the sea, the moon-silver'd roll of the ocean, the glory of art, the triumphs of science, the dignity of palace and city are all his.

'You never enjoy the world aright till the sea itself floweth in your veins, till you are clothed with the heavens and crowned with the stars... till you love men so as to desire their happiness, with a zeal equal to the zeal of your own; till you delight in God for being good to all; you never enjoy the world'. So Traherne in *Centuries of Meditation*, and in an even better known passage: 'The corn was orient and immortal wheat, which shall never be reaped nor was ever sown. I thought it had stood from everlasting to everlasting. The dust and stones of the street were as precious as gold, the streets were mine. The temple was mine, the people was mine... all the world was mine; and I only the spectator and enjoyer of it.'

So it was also with the young Wordsworth imbued with the sense of a presence whose dwelling was 'the light of setting suns, and the round ocean and the living air, and the blue sky, and in the mind of man'.

But man's misery is poignant. The brief candle is soon out and 'the glories of our blood and state are shadows not substantial things'. 'Life's but a walking shadow, a poor player that struts and frets his hour upon the stage and then is heard no more.' Or, at best, our days are passed as a tale that is told, and 'our little life is rounded by a sleep'. Cities are destroyed in a minute of war, freedoms seized and murdered by tyrants. Sin and death, discontent and malaise, even elementary poverty and hunger haunt the world in the day of its plenty. There is misgiving, doubt, jealousy and hardness in the core of man's heart, and his fear and pain blight the glory of time. The brave face hides the inner ache and the wounded pride, be it of race or power; and there is a day of the Lord upon every haughty triumph. Precious moments of visionary insight are lost for ever in the waste of years, drifting into the mist of the past along with the sweetness of childhood, the beauty and joy of youth, the deed of love done unknown. All that is left is the ashes, the regret and the melancholy. 'Brightness falls from the air', from out of the night comes death the most holy, even to the young and fair, leaving for a frail memorial only the tender grace of a day that is gone. Such is the pathos of life and death, the long embrace or the hand stretched out in vain, the moment of tragedy or the pain of unrequited devotion.

> Is there no life, but these alone?
> Madman or slave, must man be one?[3]

For many, such moods divide between them most of the splendours and many of the troubles of life. To indulge either to excess would be almost unnatural; to share both in due proportions is a large part of man's lot. In experience little or nothing is as good as we hope, or as bad as we fear.

For behind and within such questings is the great question, unanswered and probably destined to remain so, 'What is man?' Or must we always say, contemplating past experience, 'That was once a man?' What lends to Don Quixote some of his fascination is that he was ready with an answer, crazy although it was, 'Your worship' (said the labourer) 'is not Baldwin or Abindarraez, but that worthy gentleman Master Quixada.'

'*I know who I am*', replied Don Quixote, 'and I know, too, that I am capable of being not only the characters I have named, but all the Twelve Peers of France and all the Nine Worthies as well, for my exploits are far greater than all the deeds they have done, all together and each by himself.'[4] Such is the triumphant answer of fantasy, but we live in a hard, real world, where the dawn is grey and the night dark, where hatred is stronger than affection and power than love.

Happy Don Quixote! In his madness, he solved his problem to his satisfaction. But to some of us it is not so easy, perhaps because we are so distressingly sane. The ancient landmarks are every day being removed, and many, not only the thoughtful but the simple, are puzzled about the old problem of man and his place in the universe. The triumphs of science, the dissection of personality by the psychologists, the search of the skies by astronomers and astronauts, the splitting of the atom by the physicists,

---

[3] Matthew Arnold, *A Summer Night*.
[4] Trans. by J. M. Cohen (Penguin Classics, 1950), p. 54.

the predictions of the computer by the mathematicians and the technicians, have destroyed old conceptions of man's place. This is nothing new. I have stood, long ago and often, in the vast confusion of the tropical forest, miles from my nearest neighbour, and in that solitude and baffling proliferation of living growth, I have realised that nature cannot ask the ultimate questions or understand itself; it cannot ask them either of itself, or of God. Only man can ask the questions about himself. All the wealth of modern discovery and achievement neither deprives him of that power nor finally adds decisively to the explanation of why he can use it.

Man can do so because he is 'made in the image of God'. He is free to respond to God's grace and love; alone among living beings he can perceive that he needs God, and his need is deliverance, or salvation from himself. This perception is the highest hall-mark of his humanity. I quote from Alec R. Vidler.[5] 'Bishop Westcott put it thus: "No view of the human state is so inexpressibly sad as that which leaves out the Fall. The existence of evil in its many forms, as self-will and suffering and vice and crime, cannot be gainsaid; and, if this evil belongs to the essence of man as created, then there can be no prospect of relief here or hereafter."' The point was made more piquantly by G. K. Chesterton when he said, 'If I wish to dissuade a man from drinking his tenth whisky and soda, I slap him on the back and say, "Be a man!" No one who would wish to dissuade a crocodile from eating its tenth explorer would slap it on the back and say, "Be a crocodile!"' I have found this true to experience; if a crocodile, or alligator, shows a disposition to eat only its first explorer, it is best to shoot it forthwith, between the eyes, and not attempt to slap it on the back. The tail is good eating, and you can, so to speak, get your own back with satisfaction.

Christian belief does not blink a superficial eye at sin. It accepts it, but it also accepts that the nature of man is such that he can be personally related to God, in a manner wholly different from the rest of creation. This constitutes him a man. Theologically, this is probably all wrong. It is better to say that God takes the initiative and personally relates or reveals Himself to man, making Himself known to him, offering His friendship, even spiritually dwelling in him. The historical evidence and consummation of this is in the incarnation, life, death and resurrection of Jesus Christ and the coming of the Holy Spirit. 'The Word became flesh; he came to dwell among us, and we saw his glory, such as befits the

---

[5] Alec R. Vidler, *Christian Belief* (S.C.M. Press, 1950), pp. 32–33.

Father's only Son, full of grace and Truth' (John 1: 14). And again, speaking of Christ, St. Paul writes, 'The divine nature was his from the first; yet he did not think to snatch at equality with God, but made himself nothing, assuming the nature of a slave.' (Phillippians 2: 6–7). It became possible for man to realise his full potentialities as a son of God, not through his discovery of God, but through God's revelation of Himself.

Any belief, or non-belief, presupposes not one but many assumptions which cannot be proved. This is so obvious that it would hardly be necessary to say it, were it not that we live in an age when that only is truth which can be demonstrated by an equation or an experiment. The Bible itself, the greatest of the religious works which have come down to us, does not attempt to explain the universe even to the limited extent that it was known. But in its accounts of the earliest wanderings of the Hebrew people, it calls for a decision. 'Choose you this day whom you will serve.' (Joshua 24: 15).

It is not easy for laymen to write on these questions, unless they belong to the small band of specialised religionists such as Baron von Hügel, Clement Webb, J. H. Oldham and a few others. I once attended in Britain, by special invitation, a small conference mainly of clergy and I ventured on some remarks of a theological character. They were intended to be based on the Bible, and I had always understood the Bible to be concerned with theology. In the lunch interval I overheard one nice cleric say to another, 'It is a pity that the laity express themselves on these matters: it makes one wonder whether proper discipline is maintained in the Church.' It is not.

I have for long not been satisfied with the extreme Evangelical or Protestant emphasis often concentrated on the individual. 'I am the Way; I am the Truth and I am Life; no one comes to the Father except by me' (John 14: 6) is a great saying of our Lord's but is not the whole Gospel. There is a consummation of all things in Christ. 'The whole universe has been created through him and for him. And he exists before everything, and all things are held together in him.' (Colossians 1: 16–17). The phrase 'the end of history' is often used in discussing this consummation: sometimes it seems uncertain whether the speaker uses 'end' to mean the termination and final conclusion, or rather the object or purpose. A 'Grand Assize' of all the living and the dead is a dramatic but a rather meaningless conception to our limited minds. Equally I see no reason to accept the state of things as they are as implying that they can suffer no radical or total change. Mankind is to be judged, and the possibility stands of falling away from God into a final egotism, a tragic and self-destroying antagonism to or alienation from personal fellowship with Him. A transformed social order, to use a contemporary phrase, or the 'communion of saints', to use a credal one, must surely depend on a harmony which at present passes our grasp.

The pilgrimage and goal of the individual, the joy of the consummation of the redeemed society, the peace and love, and the unsullied light of the Divine Presence, are nowhere more nobly portrayed than in the supreme poetry of Dante's *Paradiso*, unless it be in the splendid and moving symbolism of the New Jerusalem come down from heaven as a bride adorned for her husband.

I have accustomed myself to think of eternal life not as an altogether new existence, but as existence in a new age. 'Eternal' as simply meaning 'everlasting' is a conception which 'puzzles the will, and makes us rather bear those ills we have, than fly to others that we know not of'. All life is one and continuous simply because it is life, and death the crossing of an equator into fairer climes. 'Death is a low mist which cannot blot the brightness it may veil' as Shelley has it. But this is not the whole truth. Death is the door of 'eternal life', but it is also the moment of radical change. It is right to ask rhetorically, 'What is our failure here but a triumph's evidence of the fullness of days?' It is right to exclaim 'Held, we fall to rise; and baffled to fight better; sleep, to wake'. It is right to believe that 'eternity fulfils the conception of an hour'. All this is good healthy Browning, and pretty fair Bible, but it is not the whole story. The climax of the story is the Resurrection of Christ, without which all our faith is vain.

Death is real and earnest. Many people grow up without seeing a corpse. They have not fought a deadly war, whether in Flanders, or in North Africa or in Vietnam. They have not comforted men dying of fever, or starvation in the wilds, unsuccoured and unbefriended. They have not dug the bodies from the ruins of an air-raid. I think those who have, often inwardly revolt against the wastage of death, the passing of the strength of youth or the wisdom of age. It all seems extravagant and unnecessary. Yet many men would rather burn out than rust away. Christ himself felt this aversion to death bitterly, dramatically and strangely.

This is surely because death is a real demarcation line. Beyond that line there is a larger life to be explored but in a sense that we cannot portray in human terms; to us it is one of those convictions 'that break through language and escape'. The 'immortality of the soul' is a phrase not used in the Bible: perhaps the nearest to it is in II Timothy 1: 10: 'Our Saviour Jesus Christ ... has broken the power of death and brought life and immortality to life through the Gospel.' The 'soul' seems an impoverished way of speaking of a personality which realises its full meaning because of uninterrupted communion with God in the mystical fellowship of saints. It is true, on the one hand, as Emily Brontë says, 'There is not room for death, nor atom that his might could render void,' but it is also true, as St. Paul says, that death has yet to be conquered. 'The last enemy to be abolished is death.' (I Corinthians 15: 26) Death both links and distinguishes between the life of this age, and of the next age which we do not know, but Christians believe that 'we shall know him as He is'.

Many people are concerned about the recognition of their friends and loved ones. After World War I this led to a revival of interest in spiritualism. There was little of this in the more secular atmosphere of the post World War II years, and a welcome decline in the sentimental inscriptions which used to be put up on gravestones. The subject is as much shrouded in mystery as other aspects of the age to come. Dante has a beautiful passage in which his own arrival in Paradise is celebrated by the rejoicing multitude. Virgil, the good pagan, could but say 'Through all the circles of the world of woe am I come hither'; Dante is greeted with the acclamation 'Behold one who will multiply our love'.[6] We move again in the realm of speculation in which, however, it remains true that man has been created in the image of God, and in God's presence his sinful defacement of that image will be finally restored. 'Things beyond our seeing, things beyond our hearing, things beyond our imagining [are] all prepared by God for those who love Him.' (I Corinthians 2: 9).

This needs to be said because enquiries have shown that a disquieting number of those who profess and call themselves Christians are almost wholly agnostic about the life of the age to come, at most admitting a wistful hopefulness.

Faith and instinct mingle here. Not all have the latter, and it is hard to cite it as proof of anything. Some possess it and it was said of Columbus that 'the instinct of an unknown continent burned in his blood'. I have often been led on through unknown wastes of forest and marsh by a similar instinct, that beyond the vast dark tangle, there stretched the sunlit plain. And it was so. But there are adventures not to be explored in this life and aspirations not to be fulfilled.

[6] *Purgatorio*, Canto VIII; *Paradiso*, Canto V.

It is hard to improve on the quaint words of Sir Thomas Browne:

> To be content with death may be better than to desire it, a miserable life may make us wish for death, but a virtuous one to rest in it: which is the advantage of those resolved Christians, who looking on death not only as a sting, but the period and end of sin, the horizon and isthmus between this life and a better, and the death of this world but as the nativity of another, do contentedly submit unto the common necessity, and envy not Enoch or Elias.[7]

Not seldom, God mingles the everlasting vision with the vesper-light of a long day passing away in peace. Yet much must remain hidden about that hour when the old order of time has changed, when hill and valley shall be no more, nor crag nor chasm, nor yet the great unvintaged ocean, but there shall break forth the glow of a new morning, and all things shall be renewed in the light of Him who has created them, whose creatures they are. Such is the guerdon of those whose evening is gladdened by the dawn of another sun, making one unbroken day of time and eternity. 'Eternal be the sleep unless to waken so.'

---

[7] *Letter to a Friend.*

Index

R. = River

Act of Uniformity 213
Aden 127
Ady, C. M. 203
Africa 33, 34, 143, 146, 154–6, 174, 196
Africa, South 21, 23, 185
Africa, West 19, 154–5
Aguaruna Indians 37, 48
Aguascalientes 68
Aguirre 31
Allen, Roland 91–92, 99, 225
Alliance for Progress 89
Almada 28
Amazon, R., sources 29–30, 60; length 29–30; civilisation of 36–41, 45; tributaries 29–32, 43–45; Booth Co. 31–32, 45; seasons and climate 33–37; health 35–36, 40, 43–44; Upper Amazon 47–49, 63. *See also* Amazonia.
Amazonia, travels in 29–51; game and fishing 34–37; rubber 37–41; Indian wars 40–41, 45–46; Indians, languages and habits 27–28, 41–43; rapids and gorges 46–49. *See also* Indians.
America, Central 54, 57
America, South 26–90. *See also* names of republics, Amazonia, America, Latin.
America, Latin, rubber boom 37–41; Vargas 56; revolutions 53–54, 56, 81–85; prison life 53; research in 27, 41, 54–75; dictatorships 56–57; travel, by railway 57–58, 64–65; by road 57, 64–66; by mule 59–64; by plane 64, 112–13; on foot 37–44, 62–64; Machu Picchu 60–61; Andes 53–67; banditry 70–73; religion 67–76, 83–87; population 76–80; Negroes 80; economy 80–82; U.S.A. influence 87–90; industrialisation 77–78, 81; politics 56–57, 81–83; international relations 87–90; War Information in 103–17. *See also* Amazonia, Indians, individual republics.
Amerindians, *see* Indians
Amsterdam Assembly 169, 172, 186
Anchieta 84
Andes 29, 34, 46–47, 57–67, 78–79, 95, 142
Angel, Salto del 31
Anglican-Methodist unity 210
Ankara 127
Ansell and Bailey 161
Antofagasta and Bolivia Railway 57
Apristas 57
Aquinas 97
Arab-Israel War 191
Araguarí, R. 40
Araguaya, R. 32
Araujo, J. G. 44
Arbenz 88

INDEX

Argentina 29, 50, 57, 67, 73–75, 78–79, 82, 84, 89–90, 105–7, 134
Argentine Club 135
Aristophanes 97
Aristotle 175
Armenia 61
Arnold, Matthew (quoted) 233
Arnold, M. L. (Mrs. Fordham) 134
Arrow, John 119
Arundel, Nancy Mary 54
Ascham, Roger 175
Ashton, Sir Leigh 127
Astrakhan 129–30
Asunción 73
Atahualpa 63
Athanasian Creed 176
Attlee, Lord 15, 197
Australia 23, 154
Azaña 93
Azariah, Bishop 101
Aziria 127
Aztecs 78

Bagehot, Walter 209
Baghdad 127, 129
Bahia, state of 69
Bailey, Arthur 161
Ballard Point 25
Balsas 64
Banditry, see Cangaça, Cangaceiros
Bamford, Sir Eric 111, 117
Barcellos 36
Barcelona 188
Barranquilla 36
Barth, Karl 97
Belém (Pará) 28, 30, 33, 37–40, 106
Bell, Dr. George, see Chichester, Bishop of
Belo Horizonte 77
Bennett, Lady 203
Berenson 97
Berggrav, Bishop 174, 202
Berne 125
Betjeman, Sir John 22
Bible 17, 26, 42, 55, 85, 96–99, 184, 218, 235

Bible Society 149, 202, 223
Bingham, Hiram 60
Blackett, P. M. S. (Lord Blackett) 194, 196
Blake, E. C. 174, 198
Bliss, Dr. K. 226
Boccaccio 97
Boegner, M. 174, 193
Bogotá 36, 61, 84–85, 88
Bolívar, Simon 56
Bolivia 34, 49–50, 53, 58, 62, 65–67, 75, 79–80, 82, 106
Bonny 20
Bonompak 61
Booth, Alan 151, 167, 182, 195
Booth, General 100
Booth Steamship Co. 31–32, 44
Bossey, Château de 194
Boswell 97
Bournemouth 21, 146
Braden, Spruille 90
Bradlaugh, Charles 17
Braga, Erasmo 49–50
Brasilia 68, 77
Brazil 28–29, 38, 56–57, 66–67, 78, 80–83, 105, 106, 112, 113; conditions in interior 26–51, 68–76; rubber 37–41; Indians 40–46, 74–76; politics 56; north-east 68–72; droughts 69–70; banditry 66, 70–72; religion 83–87; Jesuit reductions 74–76. See also Amazon, R., Amazonia.
Brendan Bracken (Lord Bracken) 110–11, 114, 117–18, 122–3
Bridgeman, Viscountess 203
Bridges, Sir E. (Lord Bridges) 116
Britanski Soyuznik, see *British Ally*
Brighton Conference 195–6
British Ally 130
British Community Council in Buenos Aires 111
British Council 106, 120
British Council of Churches 139, 145, 151, 159, 194
British Information Services (New York) 118, 121

Brontë, Charlotte (quoted) 123, 237
Brooks, Gen. Sir Dallas 114
Brotherhood of Freedom 12
Browne, Sir Thomas (quoted) 238
Browning, Robert (quoted) 230, 236
Browning, Webster 49–50
Buchan, Alastair 195–7
Buenos Aires 31, 49–51, 73, 75, 78, 85, 87
Burgess, Guy 109
Burke, Edmund (quoted) 22, 153, 177
Butler, R. A. (later Lord Butler) 169
Buxton 17, 18
Buzzard, Sir Anthony 194–6

Cable St. 227
Caboclo 39
Cahir 16, 17
Cairo 102–3, 127, 201
Cajamarca 63
Cali 61
Calla Calla, pass of 63
Calvin 97
Camara, Mgr. Helder 82
Camaraí, R. 34
Cambridge 142
Cambridge Conference 163–6
Campbell, Sir Gerald 121
Campeche 61
Canada 23, 202
Canal Zone (Panama) 88
Canford School 21
Cangaça (banditry) 70–71
Cangaceiros (bandits) 70–71
Canning, C. B. 21
Canning Club 135
Canning House 134–5
Canon Law 203, 213
Canterbury, Archbishop of (Dr. M. Ramsey) 208–11, 217
Canterbury, Convocation of 210
Caracas 77
Cardona, J. 188
Carey, William 100
Carlyle, Thomas 98, 164
Carnegie Institute 62

Caroní, R. 31
Carpentier, Georges 20
Carr-Saunders, Sir Alec 151
Cash, Rt. Rev. Wilson 142
Casiquiare Canal 31, 36
Caspian Sea 130
Castro, Fidel 83, 89
Castroism 57, 82
Cat and Fiddle Inn 17
Cathedrals Measure 213
Cauahib Indians 43
Cauca, R. 61
Caucho, *see* rubber
Cavert, Sam 174
Cayenne 40
Cecil, Lord Hugh 203
CELAM 84, 188
Ceará, State of 39, 70–72
Celigny 194
Central America 67, 78, 112, 154
Central Board of Finance 207, 213
Central Cordillera 61, 63
Central Office of Information 132
Central Railway of Peru 57
Cerro de Pasco 29
Cervantes, Miguel de 97, 233
Ceylon 23, 38
Chachapoyas 63
Chaco, Paraguayan 26
Chaco War 90
Chadwick, Owen 214
Chamberlain, Neville 115
Chandos, Viscount 123
Chatham House, *see* Royal Institute of International Affairs
Cheltenham Colleges of Education 224
Chester, Bishop of (Dr. Ellison) 201
Chesterton, G. K. 234
Chiapas 61
Chibchas 78
Chicha 66–67
Chichen Itzá 61
Chichester, Bishop of (Dr. George Bell) 139–40, 169, 172–3, 194
Chichester, Earl of 136

INDEX

Chile 49, 57, 78, 85, 105, 112
China 27, 90, 141, 179, 190, 197
Chiquimula 62, 112
Christ Church, Crouch End 224
Christian Aid 150
Christian Frontier Council 225–6
Christian Newsletter 226
Christian Teamwork 226
Chungking 124
Church and Society Conference 175
Church Assembly 153, 160; House of Laity 202–15, 219–20; debating practices 203–6; committees and boards 207–8; Standing Committee 207–10; officers 208–10; archbishops 201–2, 208–10; functioning of Assembly 210–15; Central Board of Finance 207, 213; Synod, General 215–17; bishops 211–12, 219–20; Convocations 208, 212, 215–16; Measures of Assembly 212–15; Church and State 214–18; Establishment 214–19. See also Church Commissioners, Church of England.
Church Commissioners 208, 211, 217–218, 220
Church Funds Investment Trust 207, 213
Church Missionary Society 15, 19, 131; Presidency 136–7, 155–61; M. A. C. Warren 142–5; Society's origin 149, 157–8; influence of William Temple 136–7; J. V. Taylor 144–6; finance 146; family connection 19–20, 146–7; post-war problems 149–50, 158–60; reorganisation 158–60; Society and the Independence era 147–54; travels on behalf of 154–6; Society and the Laity 157–9; committees 158–60; new Headquarters 160–1
Church of England 26, 98, 201–24; archbishops 202, 208–10; ecumenical outlook 172, 176, 207; bishops, clergy and laity 215–16, 219–20; Prayer Book 213, 217; legislation 212–14, 221; reforms of 214–23; General Synod 215–17; evangelism 222–4; position of clergy 221–2; future 223–4. See also Church Assembly, Church Missionary Society.
Church of England Zenana Missionary Society 147
Church of South India 153
Churchill, Sir Winston 57, 115–18, 122, 131–2, 143, 217, 230
Cicero, Padre 70–72
Civil Service Commissioners 104
Claver, San Pedro 84
Clark, S. J. W. 90
Clonmel 16
C.M.S. Bookshops 152
C.M.S. *Newsletter* 144
Coca 62
Cochabamba 65–67, 77
Cochrane, Thomas 90, 95
Collins, James 38
Colombia 36, 61, 64, 78, 80, 83, 89, 187–8
Commercial Relations Division of the Ministry of Information 125
Commission of the Churches on International Affairs (C.C.I.A.) 163–9, 178–90; Cambridge Conference 163–7; officers 165–8; Nolde's work 185–90; membership 169; criticism of 182–4; organisation 166–9, 182; statements by 182–5; relations with the World Council of Churches 166–7; work at the United Nations 185–91; concern with human rights and religious liberty 185–8; concern with Spain and Colombia 187–8; peace and justice 188–93; Visser 't Hooft's views 193–4; Hague Conference 197–8
Commission on a Just and Durable Peace 140, 163
Commission on Church and State 214
Commission on World Mission and Evangelism 169, 225

INDEX

Common Prayer, Book of, *see* Church Assembly
Community of the Resurrection 228
Compton, Sir Edmund 203
Comte, Auguste 34
Conference of British Missionary Societies 139, 151, 162
Congregational Church 170, 182
Coningsby 100
Convocations 208, 212, 215-16
Cooper, Duff (Lord Norwich) 114-16
Cooper, Henry 228
Copán 62, 112
Coptic Orthodox Church 176
Corcovado 77
Cordillera de Merida 64
Coriolanus 173
Corumbá 75
Costa Rica 79, 113
Cotacachi 65
Craigmyle, Lord 199
Crete 127
Crichton-Stuart, Margaret Adelaide 17, 19-22. *See also* Grubb, Sir Kenneth.
Cripps, Sir Stafford 201
Cromwell 16
Cross, Robert 38
Crowther, Bishop 154
Cruikshank, Robin 117-18
Cuba 67, 89-90, 189-90. *See also* Castro, Fidel
Cuelap 63
Cuernavaca 85
Curtin 131
Cuzco 60, 78
Czechoslovakia 83, 190

Daily Herald 117
Dante, Alighieri 104, 145, 236-7
Davidson, Lady (Baroness Northchurch) 134
Davidson, Lord (Viscount) 104, 111, 133
Davis, Elmer 132
Demosthenes 94

De Tocqueville 191
Diable, Île du (Devil's Island) 40
Diaz, José Porfirio 68
Dibelius, Bishop 174, 193
Disraeli 99-100
Divina Commedia 97, 104, 236-7
Dominican Republic 67, 88-89, 190
Dryden, John (quoted) 184, 205-6
Dulles, John Foster 140, 163-5, 168-169, 181

Ecclesiastical Commission 217
Ecclesiastical Committee of Parliament 208, 212
Ecclesiastical Jurisdiction Measure 212
Economic and Social Council 185
Ecuador 48, 59, 64-65, 67, 79
Ecumenical Movement, *see* World Council of Churches, International Missionary Council, Commission of the Churches on International Affairs
Ecumenical Review 190
Eddy, Sir Montagu 104, 111
Edinburgh Conference of 1910 101, 137
Edinburgh Conference on Faith and Order 139
Edwards, David 195
Egypt 129, 176
Eire 182
Ellison, Gerald, *see* Chester, Bishop of
El Salvador 106, 113
Enabling Act 215
Encarnación 73
Enosis 180
Erroll, Lord 134
Establishment 214-20
Ethiopia 90
European Convention on Human Rights 187
Evangelical Council for Spain 187-8
Evangelism 222-3
Evanston Assembly 151, 169

Fagley, Richard 167, 181-2
Falmouth, Viscountess 203
Farrer-Brown, Leslie 151
Fernando de los Rios 94
fforde, Sir Arthur 203
Field, J. C. 49-50
Fisher, Archbishop (Lord Fisher of Lambeth) 169, 208-9
Fisher, H. A. L. 231
Fisher, Leslie 158
Flamengo, Parque de 77
Fletcher, Lord Eric 169, 203
Food and Agriculture Organisation 185
Ford Foundation 195-6
Foreign Office 103-4, 107-11, 121, 124, 132
Freehold, parson's 221
French 127
Frontier 92, 131, 226
Froude, J. A. 164
Fry, Franklin Clark 173
Fund-raising 199

Gairdner, Temple 136
Galba, Emperor 122
Gandhi 125
Garbett, Archbishop 201-2, 205
Garvin, J. L. 122
Geneva 51, 167, 170, 175, 182, 188, 198
German Lutheran Church 73, 85, 105
Germans 73, 78, 85, 87, 105, 110, 127, 132
Gibbon 22, 97
Gladstone 17
Godber, Lord 104, 111
Goethe 94, 97
Gomez, Juan Vicente 56
Gogol 130
Goodall, Norman 169
Goold-Adams, R. 194-6
Gore Brown, Sir Eric 203
Gowers, Sir Ernest 175
Goyder, George 214-15
Graham, Billy 222

Granada 79
Greece 97, 127, 180, 231
Greek Church 180
Green, G. H. 134
Grenfell of Labrador, Sir Wilfrid 137
Grindley, Hugh 113
Groser, St. J. 227
Grote 231
Grubb, George 23-24
Grubb, Harold 21
Grubb, Harry Percy 17-19, 23-24
Grubb, Henry 16, 27
Grubb Institute of Behavioural Studies 226
Grubb, Margaret Adelaide 17-19, 22
Grubb, Norman 15, 21, 25
Grubb, Sarah 16
Grubb, Sir Kenneth, early life 15-25; ancestors and forebears 15-18; parents 18-23; education 20-23; conversion and religion 23-25; in World War I 24; literary tastes 22-23, 97-98; missionary work 26-28, 41-46; in South America 26-76; marriage 28-29, 54-55; in Amazonia 26-51; linguistic work 27-28, 41; solitude 35, 41-42, 95; 'death' of 49-51; theological outlook 52-53, 96-100; revolutionary activity 53-54; research work 27, 41, 55-93; in prison 53-54; travels in the Andes 57-67; in Mexico and Central America 61-62, 67-68; in northeast Brazil 68-73; in south Brazil 73-76; in the Jesuit 'reductions' 74-76; with the Survey Application Trust 91-93; attitude to social ethics 93-96; to pacifism 93, 166; to Spanish Civil War 90, 93; interest in international affairs 93-95; knowledge of the Bible 96-97; concern with the Church 98-100; with Christian unity 98-99; health 100-102; in Ministry of Information 103-33; in ecumenical movement 163-94; Commission of the

INDEX

Churches on International Affairs 163–9, 178, 194, 197–9; Institute of Strategic Studies 194–7; with Messrs. Hooker Craigmyle 199–200; in the Church Assembly 201–224; views on the Establishment 217–19; on evangelism 222–3; personal reflections 229–38
Grubb, Violet 16, 17, 27, 158
Grubb, W. Barbrooke 26–27, 137
Grubbe 16
Guaqui 58
Guaraní Indians 75, 78, 84
Guatemala 62, 67, 79, 83, 88, 106, 112
Guedalla, Philip 113
Guevara, Ernesto ('Che') 82
'Guiana Shield' 31
Gulbenkian Foundation 134
Gumbel, E. 158
Guyana 44

Hailey, Lord 151
Haiti 67, 79, 88, 106
Haji Baba 128
Harris, Sir Ronald 211
Healey, D. 194–6
Heart of Amazonia Mission 54
Heinemann, Gustav 169
Helena 100
Hemel Hempstead 134
Henson, Rt. Rev. Hensley 205
Henson, Leslie 205
Heracleitus 145
Herodotus 97
Hevea Brasiliensis 38. *See also* Rubber.
Highgate 19, 54, 94, 224
Hildebrand, S. S. 44
Hill-Wood, W. W. 228
Hispanic Council 133–4
Historic Peace Churches 189
Hitler 90
Hoare, Sir Samuel, *see* Lord Templewood
Hoare-Laval Pact 90
Hobbes 97, 192
Hodson, H. V. 151

Hodson, Lord 215
Holden, E. R. 28
Homer 19, 97
Honduras 62, 112–13
Hong Kong 154
Hooker, Michael 199
Hooker Craigmyle and Co. 199–200
Hooker, Sir James 38
Hooker, Richard 97
Hoover, President 50
Horn, Cape 54
Howard, Michael 196
Hromadka, Prof. 169
Huallaga, R. 47, 58
Hügel, Baron von 235
Hull, Cordell 164
Human rights 185–8
Humboldt 31
Hurdsfield 17, 18

Ibiam, Francis 169
Iguazu (Iguaçu) Falls 19, 69, 73–74
Iliad 19
Imbabura, Lake 65
Imperial Staff College, *see* Royal College of Defence Studies
Inca Empire 60, 63, 78
Independence 155–6
India 19, 23, 38, 92, 129, 140
India, Government of 38, 125
Indians (Amerindians) 26–49, 53–68; of the Chaco 26; of Amazonia 26–49; Maquiritarés 31; travels with 33, 43–46, 48–49; habits 42–46; treatment of 40–41; languages 27–28, 41; Aguarunas 37, 48; Parentintins (Cauahibs) 43; Jauaperys 44; in Manaus 44–45; Sirionós 53; in Peru 48–49, 58–64; Quechuas 48, 60, 62, 66; Incas, *see* Quechuas; Mayas 61–62, 78–79; Zapotecs 61; Guaranís 75, 78, 84
Indian Protection Service 34, 44
Institute for Strategic Studies 195–197
Institute of Race Relations 151

Inter-Church Aid and Service to Refugees 182
International Labour Office 185
International Missionary Council 101, 139, 146, 159–60, 163, 169, 174, 181, 186, 201
International Review of Missions 140
International security 188–93
Ipixuna, R. 43
Iquitos 29–30, 32, 37, 106
Iran 127–9
Iran, diocese of 154
Irazú, volcano of 113
Ireland 16, 17
Israel 191
Istanbul 125, 127
Italians 79, 87, 127
Italy 97, 129, 182, 231
Ithaca 139

Jaen 96
James, William 174
Japurá, R. 47
Jauapery Indians 44
Jauapery, R. 34, 44
Java 38
Jerusalem 97
Jerusalem Assembly 101, 139
Jesuit 'reductions' 74–76, 84
Jivaro Indians 37, 103
Johnson, Bishop James 19
Johnson, Samuel 171
Johnson, Spencer 25
Juàzeiro 71–72
Juruá, R. 30, 32, 40

Kaieteur Falls 31
Kant 42
Kenya 155
Kerr, Sir A. Clark (Lord Inverchapel) 130
Keswick Convention 23
Kew 38
Keyham 24
Kirkpatrick, Sir Ivone 132
Kirkwood, Kenneth 151

Kissinger 195
Kneller 230
Knight, Eileen Sylvia 28–29
Kon-tiki 48
Koran 128
Kraemer, H. 174
Kuibyshev 129

Labouchere, Henry 17
La Guaira Falls 74
La Libertad 113
La Maquina 60–61
Lambeth Conference 145
Lambeth Palace 208–9, 211
Lambton, Ann 127
Lampeão 70–71
Lancaster University 125
Lang, Archbishop 126
La Paz 49–50, 53
Largo Caballero 93
Las Casas, Bartolomé de 84
Lawrence, Sir John 129, 226
League of Nations 103, 132, 163, 190
Lebanese 79, 127
Leeper, Sir Rex 114
Leghorn, Col. 195
Leguía, Augusto B. 50
Leimebamba 63
Leimena, S. 169
Leiper, H. S. 174, 178–9
Leishmania 64
Leixões 28
Lilje, Bishop Hans 174, 193
Lima 49–50, 62, 106
Lincoln, Abraham 56
Lindsay Commission 139
Lippman, Walter 165
Lisbon 125
Liverpool 28
Liverpool Journal of Commerce 122
Liverpool University 133
Lloyd, Geoffrey 114
Locke 97
Lockhart, Sir R. Bruce 114
Löffler, Paul 225
London College of Divinity 202

INDEX

London Diocesan Office 163
Lowdham 17
Lowestoft 20
Luce, Henry 165
Lusiadas 96
Luke, Baron 111
Luso-Brazilian Council 133-4
Lutherans, 173
Lutheran Seminary 167

Macadam, Sir Ivison 103
Macallum, Sir William 111, 113
Macaulay (quoted) 177
Macclesfield 17, 18
Machiavelli 94, 184
Machu Picchu 60-61
Mackay, John A. 174
Mackintosh, Hugh 118
Maclean, Donald 109
McLeish, Alexander 92
Macmillan, Lord 114
Macú Indians 42
Madeira, R. 30, 35, 42-44, 50
Madras Conference, see Tambaram
Mãe da Cachoeira 69
Magdalena, R. 36, 61
Magellan, Strait of 44
Maicy, R. 43
Makarios, St. 37
Malaya 154
Malik, Charles 169
Mamoré, R. 34
Managua 112
Manaus (Manaos) 28, 32-33, 37-38, 44-45
Mance, Sir H. 158
Manchester 20
Manco Capac 60
Manseriche, Pongo de 29, 47-49
Maquiritaré Indians 31
Marañon, R. 29, 37, 47-48, 63-64, 69, 96
March, Earl of 207
Marett, Sir Robert 105-6, 112, 117, 125
Marlborough College 21, 22, 24, 145

Marlborough, Duke of 230
Marmellos, R. 35, 43
Maroa 31
Martin, Hugh 126
Martin, Sir Robert 203
Marxism 57, 82, 89, 95, 97, 164
Maryknoll Fathers 84
Mason, Philip 151
Mato Grosso 34, 38, 78
Mayas 61-62, 78-79, 112
Mazzini 182
Meiggs, Henry 57
Mein Kampf 94
Mendl, Sir Charles 110
Mennonites 189
Mercurio, El 49
'Messianism' 70
Mexican Revolution 67-68, 80
Mexico 38, 54, 57, 61, 67-68, 78-79, 105, 112
Mexico, Archbishop of 67
Mexico City 61, 78, 85
Micheli, Dominique 167, 182
Middle East 120, 127-9, 179
Miller, Brig. 203
Millington-Drake, Sir E. 113, **134**
Milne, D. Williamson 161
Milton (quoted) 160
Ministry of Information 103-33, 183; preparation for 103-7; early days 107-9; relations with Foreign Office 107-11; Latin American Section 104-14; overseas organisation 117-121; Commercial Relations Division 125; Ministers 114-17, 122-3; Overseas Controllership 117-33; Middle East 127-9; U.S.S.R. 129-131; end of 133
Misiones, Department of 74-75
Missionary and Ecumenical Council of the Church Assembly 141, 207
Missions 147-50; family associations 15, 19, 146-7; Keswick Convention 23-24; in S. America 26-51, 83-87; Worldwide Evangelisation Crusade 21, 27, 52; linguistic work for 27;

Missions (*cont.*)
  travel for 52–76, 154–6; research 91–93. *See also* Church Missionary Society, Roman Catholic Church.
Mitla 61
Moberly, Sir Walter 225–6
Momotombo, volcano of 112–13
Monckton, Sir Walter (Viscount Monckton) 127, 129
Monroe, Miss (Mrs. Neame) 128
Monroe Doctrine 87
Montaigne 175
Monte Albán 61
Montevideo 50, 87, 134
Monzó, Julio Navarro 49–50
Morley, Fenton 214, 221
Morrison, S. A. 102, 201
Mott, John R. 99, 101, 137–40
Moyobamba 58–59, 62–63
Morris, Harold 43–44
Morgan, Aubrey 118
Moscow 129
Mura Indians 42
Mussolini 90

Nación, La 49
Nash, Sir Walter 169
National Assembly of the Church of England, *see* Church Assembly
National Christian Council of India 139
NATO 196
Nazis (in South America) 73, 105
Neblina, Cerro de 30
Negrín 93
Negro, R. 29–32, 34, 36, 42, 44, 47
New Delhi Assembly 169
New Orleans 113
New York 106, 167, 182
New Zealand 23, 154
Niagara 19, 74
Nicaragua 88–89, 112, 124
Nicolson, Sir Harold 121–2
Niebuhr, Reinhold 165, 169
Niemöller, Martin 174, 193
Nigeria 19, 152, 154–5, 193

Niger Mission 154
Niles, D. T. 174
Nitze, Paul 195
Nixon, Richard 16
Nobrega 84
Nolde, O. Frederick 167–9, 181, 185–190, 194, 197
Northamptonshire 16
Norway 129
Norwood, Sir Cyril 21
Nuffield Foundation 151

Observer 122
Office of Strategic Studies 118, 132
Office of War Information 118, 132
Oldham, J. H. 100, 225–6, 235
Old Harry 23, 25
Oliveira, João Mendes de 72
Ollantaytambo 61
Onitsha 152
Orchard, R. K. 162
Organisation of American States 88, 190
Orinoco, R. 30–31, 36–37, 42, 78
Orthodox Churches 168–9, 176
Otavalo 65
Otto, N. A. 38
Overseas Development Institute 151
Oxfam 150
Oxford Conference on Life and Work 139
Oxnam, Bishop Bromley 169
Oxton (Notts.) 15, 16–17, 18
Oxton (Cheshire) 28

Pacifism 93, 166
Palenque 61
Palestine 123, 127
Palmer family 203
Palmerston, Lord 210
Panama, republic of 88, 106
Panamericanism 88
Paraguay, republic of 26, 67, 73, 78–79
Paraguay, R. 31, 73–75
Parentintins, *see* Cauahib Indians
Parima, Sierra 30

INDEX

Parkstone 21, 23, 25
Parrott, Sir Cecil 125
Parsons, Sir Maurice 158, 226
Pastoral Measure 218
Patagonia 78
Patijn, C. L. 169
Paton, David 141
Paton, William 99, 137, 139–41
Paulo Afonso, Falls of 19, 69–70
Paul, Leslie 214
Payne, Ernest 174
Peace Aims Group 139-40
Peace Pledge 93
Pearl Harbor 127
Peers, Prof. Allison 84, 133
Pearson, Lester 197
Peking Union Medical College 90
Penn, William 16
Pentecostalists 85–87
Pereirism 56
Permanent Mandates Commission 166
Perón, Juan 90
Peterson, Sir Maurice 117
Perowne, Stewart 127
Peru 43, 47–50, 57–64, 67, 79–80, 89, 96, 112
Philip, André 169
Phillips, W. R. 20
Piauí, state of 69
Pilgrim's Progress 22
Piriapolis 49
Pitt 182
Pizarro, Francisco 63
Plate, R. 49
Plato 97
Platt, J. W. 113
Political Warfare Executive 113
Political Warfare (Japan) Committee 114
Pomayacu, R. 58
Poole 21, 23
Pope, the 170, 177–8
Port Harcourt 20, 155
Portugal 28, 37, 135
Portuguese 28, 126
Posadas 73

Potosí 58
Prayer Book (Alternative and other Services Measure) 213, 217
Prayer Book, revision of 213, 217
Prensa, La 49
Price, Cecil Lillingston 19, 23
Price, Joan (Gladys) Lillingston 19
Prieto, Indalecio 94
Puente Arce 66
Puente Ruinas 60
Puno 58
Purús, R. 30, 32

Quakers 16, 46, 189
Quecha 48, 60, 62, 66
Queen Anne's Bounty 217
Queretaro 68
Quindio Pass 61
Quito 64–65
Quixote, Don 233

Race problem 151, 185
Radcliffe, Cyril (Lord Radcliffe) 117–18, 123–4
Raza Cósmica, La 80
Read, Margaret 151
Reader Harris, Diana 158
Recife 82
Redundant churches 218
Reed, Bruce 226
Rees, Elfan 167, 182
Regent's Park 227
Reith, John (Lord Reith) 114–15
Religion and Churches 98–100, 229–238; family tradition 15–25; Quakers 16; vicarage life 15–21; religious education 18, 21; missions overseas 19–20; theological tastes 27, 52–53, 96–100; conversion 25–26; missionary vocation 26–27; pioneering 27–51; Roman Catholic contacts 84–85, 177–8; spiritual life and prayer 201–38; Bible, the 96–97; anticlericalism 16; 'Messianism' 70–72; Cicero, Father 70–71; superstition 72–73, 96–97; Jesuit Missions

74–76; social ethics 52–53; Christian unity 98–99, 163–94. *See also* Church of England, Ecumenical Movement, Church Assembly, Church Missionary Society, Commission of the Churches on International Affairs.
Religious liberty, *see* Human rights
Rembrandt 173
Repton 209
Rio de Janeiro 49–50, 68, 77, 87
Rio Grande 29, 54, 79
Rio Grande (Bolivia) 66
Rio Grande do Sul, State of 73–76
Rivera, José Eustasio 39
River Plate House 133
Robinson, Captain 23
Rochester, Bishop of (Dr. Chavasse) 222
Roman, Father 31
Roman Catholic Church 83–85; relations with the World Council of Churches 177–8; *Pacem in Terris* 189; CELAM 84, 188; Cicero, Father 70–71; Mexican Revolution 67–68, 80
Roosevelt, F. D. 88
Roosevelt, Theodore 88
Routh, Dennis A. 120
Rowan, Sir Leslie 151
Royal College of Defence Studies 195–6
Royal Foundation of St. Katharine 226–8
Royal Institute of International Affairs 94, 103, 151, 194
Royal Institute of Public Administration 133
Rubber 29, 38–41
Russell, Bertrand (Lord Russell) 97

Saar 91
St. Augustine 97, 180
St. Katharine's Dock 226–7
St. Mary's College 224
St. Paul's College 224

Salazar 93
Salter, Lord 195–6
San Juan de la Cruz 84
San Ignacio 74
San Pedro Sula 62
Santa Cruz de la Sierra 53, 75, 77
Santa Domingo, *see* Dominican Republic
Santa Rosa de Copán 62, 112
Santa Rosa de Lima 112
Santa Teresa de Jesus 84
Santarem 38
Santiago, R. 48, 85
Santos Dumont Airport 77
Santos, Manoel Gomes dos 34, 44
São Francisco, R. 69
São Luis 30
São Miguel 75
São Paulo 68–69, 73, 77, 85
São Paulo, state of 68
Sauba ants 32
Sayre, Francis B. 169
Scheuner, Ulrich 169
Schleswig-Holstein question 210
Scothorn, Robert 16
Scott, Sir John 208, 212
Seará, *see* Ceará, State of
Secca (droughts) 68–73
Sedbergh 122–3
Selborne, second Earl of 203
Selborne, Lord 203
Seleme 65–66
Seringueiro 39–40
Sete Missões 74–76
Seville 28, 79
Shakespeare, William (quoted) 141, 161, 164, 221
Shaftesbury 100
Shelley 236
Silsoe, Lord 211
Sinclair, Miss 140
Singapore 38, 127, 131, 154
Sintra 28
Sirionó Indians 53
Slavery 149
Slocum 44

Smith, Rae 119–21
Social Contract 97
Social Responsibility, Board of 207
Socrates 175
Solimões, R. 29, 34
Somoza, Anastasio 89
Southey 75
South Lodge school 20
Spain 28, 37, 135, 187, 231
Spain, Evangelical Church in 187–8
Spanish Civil War 90, 93
Spencer Johnson 25
Spengler 231
Spruce, Richard 36, 38
Stalingrad 129–30
Standing Committee of the Church Assembly 207
Stark, Freya 128–9
State Department, 164–5
Stepney 227
Stevens, Sir Roger 108
Stock, Eugene 146
Stockholm 125
Studd, C. T., and Mrs. 21, 27, 52
Student Christian Movement 139, 182
Sucre 58, 65
Sudan 187
Sudene Corporation 69
Survey Application Trust 54, 90–93, 225
Survival 197
Switzerland 19, 103, 182
Sydney Smith 128
Synodical Government Commission 215
Synod, General 148, 203, 207, 211, 214–17. *See also* Church Assembly
Syrians 79, 127

Tabasco, state of 68
Tacitus 122
Taca Airline 112
Talbot Rice, M. G. 158, 231
Tambaram Conference 101, 138, 140, 201
Tapajos, R. 32, 39, 45–46

Tavistock Institute of Human Relations 226
Taylor, J. V. 142, 144–6, 152
Tegucigalpa 62, 113
Teheran 129
Temple, William 136–7, 140–41, 201, 209
Templewood, Lord 110–11
Tennyson 22, 147
The Hague 197–8
Thesiger, Sybil 203
Thomas, M. M. 174, 193
Thompson, Admiral 118
Thompson, Messrs. J. Walter 119–21
't Hooft, Visser 151, 173–4, 193–4
Thucydides 97
Thurtle, Ernest 121
Tillich, Paul 165
Tipperary, Co. 16
Titanic 21
Titicaca, Lake 30, 58
Tocantins, R. 32
Tompkins, Oliver (Bishop of Bristol) 163
Torre, Haya de la 57
Torres, Camilo 83
Towards the Conversion of England 222
Toynbee, Arnold 140, 169, 231
Traherne 232
Transandine Road 64
Travel 26–76, 112–13, 129–30; in Amazonia 30–51; through gorges 47–49; lower Bolivia 53; the Andes 57–67; Peru 47–51, 57–64; Mexico 67–68; Ecuador 64–65; north-east Brazil 68–73; Argentina 73–75; south Brazil 73–76; in the U.S.S.R. 129–30; in Africa 152–6; in Australia 154; in New Zealand 154; for the C.M.S. 154–7; for the Churches' Commission on International Affairs 167–8; in war-time 112–13, 127–30; 'death' on travel 49–51
Trevelyan 231
Treviso 129

Trinity College, Dublin 17
Trujillo, Generalissimo 89
Tubbs, S. Kingsley 146, 157
Turkey 126-7
Twain, Mark 49-50
Tweedie, Owen 127
Tyerman, Donald 196

Uaupés, R. 47
Ucayali, R. 30, 60
Uganda 150, 152, 155
Ulster 16, 187
Unamuno, Miguel de 94
UNESCO 185
Union Castle Fleet 23
Union Corporation 122
Union Theological Seminary 165
United Bible Societies 202
United Nations 132, 149, 179-80, 182, 185-91
U.N. Department of Information 185
U.N. Peace Observer Commission 188
Universal Declaration of Human Rights 186-7
Uppsala, Archbishop of 16
Uppsala Assembly 170, 173, 176-7
Uppsala, University of 15
Urubamba, R. 47, 60-61
Uruguay, republic of 49, 56-57, 73, 79, 84, 106
U.S.A. 87-90, 118-21, 129, 132, 149, 163-5, 174, 190-1
U.S.S.R. 119, 129-30, 132, 149, 168, 190-1
U.S.S.R., churches of 169, 176, 179
Uxmal 61-62

Valverde 63
Valladolid 28
Vandenberg, Senator 163
Van Asbeck, Baron F. 166
Van Dusen, H. P. 164-6
Vargas, Getulio 56
Vasari 97
Vasconcelos, José 80

Vatican 84, 174
Vatican Council II 177, 188
Vaizey, George de Horne 20
Venezuela 30, 56-57, 64, 80, 82, 89
Veronese 100
Via del Norte 58-59
Victoria and Albert Museum 127
Vidler, Alec R. 234
Villahermosa 68
Violeiros 72
Von Ranke 97, 177

Walton, Sydney 142
Warren, M. A. C. 136, 142-5, 158, 201
Warwick, W. C. 111
Wasbrough, H. J. 228
Webb, Clement 235
Webb, Maurice 169
Weizmann 123
Welles, Sumner 164
Wells, Bombardier 20
Wesley, John 97
Westcott, Bishop 234
Westonbirt School 27
Whitlam, F. 169
Wickham, Sir Henry A. 38
Wigglesworth, Chancellor 203
Wigram, D. R. 158
Wilberforce, William 100, 149
Wilde, Oscar 100
Williams, E. 114
Williams, Francis (Lord Francis-Williams) 117-18, 123
Williams, R. R. (Bishop of Leicester) 126
Williams, Sir Robert 137
Windsor, Dean of 161
Windsor, Duke of 122
Wolfers 195
Wordsworth 22, 55, 175, 232
World Alliance for Promoting International Friendship through the Churches 166
World Christian Handbook 92
World Church Studies Trust 93

World Council of Churches 15, 51, 99, 100, 138, 139, 145, 163; Assemblies of 151, 169–73; debating practice 170–2; General Secretary 173–4; officers 173–4; Central Committee 170–2; Executive Committee 170; relations with Roman Catholic Church 177–8; laity 175–6; Church and Society 175; criticism 193–4
World Dominion 92
World Dominion Press, *see* Survey Application Trust
World War I 16, 18, 114, 139, 237
World War II 28, 36, 54, 73, 92, 103–133, 139, 163, 174, 194, 237
Worldwide Evangelisation Crusade 21, 27, 52
Wynne Wilson 21

Xingú, R. 30, 32, 36, 40, 44, 46–47

Yavita 31
Yemen 128
Yerex 112–13
Y.M.C.A. 49, 139, 224
York, Archbishop of (Dr. D. Coggan) 202, 209
York, Convocation of 210
Young, G. M. U. 228
Yucatan 61–62, 78
Yungas 62
Yurimaguas 58
Y.W.C.A. 23

Zapotecs 61